D0520883

RESTAURANT MANAGEMENT

A Comprehensive Guide to Successfully
Owning and Running a Restaurant

JOHN JAMES & DAN BALDWIN

Adams Media Corporation
Avon, Massachusetts

A Streetwise® Publication.
Streetwise® is a registered trademark of F+W Publications, Inc.

Published by Adams Media, an F+W Publications Company
57 Littlefield Street, Avon, MA 02322 U.S.A.
www.adamsmedia.com

ISBN: 1-58062-781-1

Printed in the United States of America.

J I H G F E D C B

Library of Congress Cataloging-in-Publication Data
James, John (John Randall)
Streetwise restaurant management / John James and Dan Baldwin.
p.   cm.
ISBN 1-58062-781-1
1. Restaurant management. I. Baldwin, Dan. II. Title.
TX911.3.M27 J33 2003
647.95'068—dc21
2002153897

This publication is designed to provide accurate and authoritative information with regard to the subject matter covered. It is sold with the understanding that the publisher is not engaged in rendering legal, accounting, or other professional advice. If legal advice or other expert assistance is required, the services of a competent professional person should be sought.
— From a *Declaration of Principles* jointly adopted by a Committee of the American Bar Association and a Committee of Publishers and Associations

This publication is intended to provide current and prospective business owners with useful information that may assist them in preparing for and obtaining business capital loans and investment funding. This information is general in nature and is not intended to provide specific advice for any individual or business entity. While the information contained herein should be helpful to the reader, appropriate financial, accounting, tax, or legal advice should always be sought from a competent professional engaged for any specific situation regarding your enterprise.

Many of the designations used by manufacturers and sellers to distinguish their products are claimed as trademarks. Where those designations appear in this book and Adams Media was aware of a trademark claim, the designations have been printed in initial capital letters.

Cover illustration by Eric Mueller.

This book is available at quantity discounts for bulk purchases. For information, call 1-800-872-5627.

Contents

Contents

Acknowledgments

This book would not exist without the knowledge, inspiration, and occasional tough love of numerous friends, mentors, family members, and associates. Special recognition is due Eula M. James, who was present at "Introduction" but did not get to read "The End," and to Laura Baldwin and Mary Baldwin. Carol Gordy contributed an enormous amount of research, and her insights have proven invaluable. A special thanks is due Kathy Welton of A.K.A. Associates; she brought this whole thing together.

Author's Note

Since birth, my father is the only person who has called me John, my friends have always called me Randy. Hence the name John R. "Randy" James.

Introduction

Owning and managing a successful restaurant may be beyond some people's wildest dreams. Harlan Sanders lost his restaurant when the highway moved. With little more than a few ingredients, a pressure cooker, and his dream, he took to the road, worked hard, and built a fast-food empire. Today we call him Colonel Sanders. More recently a young man named Randy James found opportunity in the trust of a mentor named Bill Atherton and turned a small restaurant job into a successful career owning and operating restaurants and clubs from Oklahoma to Florida.

If your dream is centered on a restaurant or even a chain of restaurants, this book can get you started on the road to a wonderful reality. The opportunities in the restaurant industry are only as limited as your vision. Ray Kroc was a traveling salesman when he met Dave and Mac McDonald, the owners of a small but popular drive-in featuring hamburgers. Today, McDonald's is the largest food-service organization in the world.

On the other end of the spectrum, a chef named Wolfgang Puck created a fine dining establishment called Spago that became internationally famous. Today, Puck owns a number of top-rated restaurants, writes cookbooks, has his own line of signature food products, and has a television cooking show reaching a national audience.

The person who said, "Plan ahead: It wasn't raining when Noah built the ark," probably wasn't talking about the restaurant business, but the advice is still appropriate. Before you begin planning ahead, it's wise to consider whether you *should* plan ahead. Clearly if this is your chosen profession, you will want to make plans. The most important question is, "Is this really a course you want to follow?" This book presents a number of topics and questions you should consider long and hard before taking any steps toward owning or managing a restaurant. The food and beverage industry is an exciting, challenging, and immensely rewarding career, but it's not an industry to enter casually or without in-depth thinking and a good bit of soul-searching. So here are a few questions to help start some thinking:

- Should you own your own or franchise?
- Can you develop and implement a business plan?
- What's your marketing plan?
- What's your mission statement?
- Which is better: single proprietorship, partnership, or limited liability corporation?
- How will you arrange financing?
- Where is the best location and how can you acquire it?
- Can you develop a realistic budget and live within it?
- What are the applicable laws, rules, and regulations governing your operation?
- Are there sufficient suppliers and can they deliver on time and on budget?
- Can you recruit the various types of talent you will need?
- Do you know how to train people?
- Can you keep your staff motivated?
- What is your experience with inventory control?
- Do you know accounting procedures?
- Are you capable of managing different types of people and personalities?
- Do you have a support group, such as an attorney, CPA, bookkeeping service, insurance consultants, and marketing professionals?
- What equipment will you need?
- Where are the support groups I'll need?

This is just a sample of the questions you'll have to answer yourself or find the people and organizations that can provide them. But don't let this list overwhelm you. This book answers all those questions—and more!

> **Chapter 1**

Asking the Hard Questions

Part One

Part Two

Part Three

Part Four

Part Five

Part Six

Do You Have the Necessary Knowledge, Skills, and Experience?

Restaurant management is a terrific career. Ownership is a great vehicle for personal success and even considerable wealth. Certainly it's a great way to make a good living, but this isn't a business for the inexperienced. Profit margins are thin. Rapid change in trends is common. People must be managed without being driven. Government regulations can be intimidating. All of that, and more, is just part of the job, but it is important that you be able to handle that job day in and day out. Do you have the necessary talents to pull it off?

Take some time out for serious self-evaluation. What areas of the restaurant business find your experience, education, and skills lacking? Make a list of the type of information you need and find out where you can get it. Check your local colleges and universities for courses on management, marketing, advertising and public relations, the law, accounting, business procedures, the Internet, and any other area where you may be weak or not up-to-date. Read through this book, then check your list again. You may find you need to add a couple things and, hopefully, you can cut a few out as well!

Can You Live the Lifestyle of a Restaurateur?

Before you say "piece of cake," seriously consider the commitment a restaurateur makes to his or her business. It's rarely an eight-to-five job, certainly not during the early years. Emotionally, it's a roller coaster for the owner and the owner's family. Although the business can be very good, the strain can be hard for many to endure. Quality time with the family may sometimes be defined as washing dishes all night when some of the kitchen staff skips work to catch the Head Banging Chipmunks in concert. More than considering the effects on your lifestyle, you should discuss the matter in depth with all concerned.

Family Demands Must Be Balanced

The demands of restaurant management on a family can be extreme. Invest as much family and community time as you can while planning out your restaurant. At the same time, prepare your family for the time you will be investing in the business after the grand opening. You can also look for ways to involve your family in the business.

Any venture requires sacrifice, and that's especially true during the preparation and start-up phase. Everyone expects to work long, hard hours to get a new business rolling. The problems can start creeping in when you're still working those long, hard hours years after the grand opening. This can drain the emotional vitality out of a family or it can turn loved ones into "that guy who looks a lot like Daddy used to look." Don't delude yourself. The restaurant business demands a lot of time. Your family, civic clubs, recreational time, and personal life may suffer at the expense of the business.

In balance, for people who love the business, there's nothing better. And you can achieve balance among your business, family, health, spiritual, community, and recreational lives. As the owner of a restaurant, you just may have to work a little harder to get there. Besides, even a busy owner-manager can find ways to work different aspects of his or her other lives into or around the business.

> The restaurant business demands a lot of time. Your family, civic clubs, recreational time, and personal life may suffer at the expense of the business.

You May Get Lonely

It's lonely at the shop. Although the owner may be surrounded by family, friends, good associates, loyal customers, and a wonderful staff, ultimately someone has to make the major decisions. Leadership requires responsibility, and that can be tough. Consider your ability to make and live with tough decisions. What's it like to fire a longtime loyal employee because the economy has tanked? There are hundreds, thousands of tough decisions an owner or manager has to make, and they never stop coming. This is a career for people who thrive on challenge and responsibility.

Your personal income can take a real hit. Starting any new business requires enough money to operate until the business makes a sufficient profit to stand on its own. One of the greatest mistakes people beginning a restaurant make is to go in undercapitalized. Make sure you have enough in the bank to keep going through the lean months…or years. You may have to use your savings to keep things operating or keep the family expenses up with a spouse's second income.

You'll Have to Meet and Greet Your Customers

A manager or owner must be a personable individual who enjoys meeting and greeting people. If you aren't a "people person," you must either develop it or select your staff to compensate for your lack of ability in this area. Personality is as important as portions in building customer loyalty.

Everyone likes to feel welcome and that their patronage is important. Many people will choose one establishment over another simply because that's where they find a friendly smile and a "glad to see you."

We know of many instances where an individual or a family will allow others in a restaurant line to go ahead of them just so they can be served by a specific waitress or waiter. That's called loyalty, and it should be returned. Strong relationships build long-term business and a lot of personal satisfaction. And never underestimate the power of "thank you" and "we appreciate your business."

What's Your Vision?

Is your vision to have a small place where a core group of loyal customers gather for fellowship as well as for the food? Do you want to earn enough to take care of your family? Is your goal to build something to pass along to your children and maybe even your grandchildren? Perhaps your goals are loftier than that. Do you want to own and manage the finest upscale restaurant in your community? Your area? Your state? Are your goals headed more toward building a business empire through franchising? Perhaps you're even considering the possibility of creating such a powerful concept that you can begin your own franchise operation. Is it possible that your idea could be the next McDonald's or KFC?

All things are possible in the restaurant business. Colonel Sanders lost his one restaurant when the highway moved and he had to make a living out of his car selling pressure cookers. Ray Kroc, founder of McDonald's, started with a single hamburger stand he bought from someone else. The family-run restaurant not too far from your home or place of business has been operating successfully and serving happy customers for years, perhaps decades or even generations. Whatever you want to do in this business, you can do. The key is picking the right direction and following your heart (but using your head).

Do You Have a Concept or a Menu That Stands Out? *Yes!*

You want individuals, families, and groups of people to come to your restaurant. To ensure that, you have to have a good reason for those folks to hop in the car, drive across town, and wait in line for "their" table. People may try out a new restaurant for any number of good reasons:

- It's a new restaurant.
- You're the nearest place at mealtime.
- Someone called a meeting or family get-together there.
- He or she likes to experiment with new types of food.
- Someone just liked the looks of the place.
- They walked in by mistake and are too embarrassed to walk out.

Whatever the reason is okay, but the important thing is to get these folks back as regular customers. Basically, you do that two ways: your concept and/or your menu.

Consider Your Restaurant's Concept

Randy often says, "Success isn't rocket science. All you need to do is be unique, work hard, and serve people what they want." The "unique" part is your concept of the type of restaurant you want to own or manage. An ethnic concept might be your cup of (oriental) tea. Or you might want an old-fashioned "greasy spoon," where the neighbors congregate for the gossip as much as for the food. Some people would prefer high-end restaurants with fine china and linen tablecloths. Perhaps you'd like an ultra-modern glass-and-brass dining establishment. Or a down-home steak house with sawdust on the floor and clipped businessmen's ties nailed to the roof. Your concept is a vision of your restaurant. Is it one that will draw customers again and again?

Restaurant Highlights 1999–2000

Americans love dining out. According to the National Restaurant Association (NRA), food service locations in the United States exceeded 595,000 units in 1994. The fastest-growing segment of the industry is the theme restaurant. The year 2000 was the industry's ninth consecutive year of sales growth. According to the NRA, 48 percent of adults state that restaurants are an important part of their lives; 39 percent say restaurants permit them to be more productive; 53 percent place convenience as a priority; 88 percent say dining out is fun; and about 10 percent have surfed the Net to review a restaurant's menu.

Restaurant sales are projected to hit the $577-billion mark in more than 1 million restaurants by the year 2010. This will represent about 53 percent of the consumer's expense for food. Dining out is an American tradition that appears to be growing.

It's never too early to start visualizing how your restaurant will be laid out and how you want it to look. An Italian restaurant can be a bare-bones arrangement of used tables and chairs, old Italian festival posters on the walls, and a menu that's no more varied than "thick crust or thin." It can be a small, cozy family institution with red and white checkered tablecloths, candles held in used wine bottles, and an owner who loves to sing "Figaro." An Italian restaurant can also be built on the upscale model, featuring linen tablecloths, the town's best chef, exclusive wines, and a dessert tray that reinvents the meaning of calorie. Which fits your vision?

Start seeing that vision come into reality. Begin thinking about the layout of your tables and kitchen and how you'll manage the traffic flow. Put yourself in your customer's eyes and take a mental look around. Do you like what you see? If not, start working on ways to make changes. A little creative visualization early on can turn a potentially harsh reality down the road into a pleasant one.

> Put yourself in your customer's eyes and take a mental look around. Do you like what you see?

Think about Your Menu

It's not too early to begin ____ng the type of food and beverages you'll be serving. The am____ ns that require answers will probably surprise you. ____ ____pening an Italian restaurant, will you want ____ ____mers want traditional pizza or gou____ ____clude calzones? Pizza means a ____ gas-powered unit or a brick ____ine means a wine list, wine ____'l have to find sources and s____ ____vell before opening day. D____ ____omestic brands, feature Itali____ ____r draft beer? If so, that mean____ ____reezer for beer mugs. You s____ ____more questions, all needin____

A m____ ____gain, ethnic restaurants from Indonesia____ ____Mexican, or Southern to sushi are extremely ____ ____t the country. Keep in mind that all types aren't popula____ ____cations. We doubt if there are many sushi bars in

Alabama or Wyoming. The Lucky Dog carts in New Orleans do a great business, but you don't see many of them in Chinatown or outside the gated communities of Scottsdale. That gets back to another part of Randy's quote. Place your vision in a location where people want to share it.

What type of menu do you want to prepare? What type can you prepare? Can you and are you willing to change your menu to meet the changing desires of a fickle public? A certain clientele will always want "meat 'n taters" while another will insist on strictly continental. And there are gradations and combinations of all types in between. Your menu is a critical element of your success and deserves the utmost attention. What do you have to offer? Will the public buy it—repeatedly?

*less bread
more soup
more salad
maybe bowls*

Your concept and/or your menu will dictate many decisions affecting the success of your business. For example: They make a statement that will attract or repel potential customers. "All right! This burg finally has a place to eat sushi." Or, "Raw fish! Sorry, darlin'. You put some batter on that thing, deep-fry it, and then maybe I'll eat it."

Each will, to a point, dictate your location. If your menu contains words such as *brie, truffles,* or *coq au vin,* you probably will not want to locate next to the junkyard or the hog-rendering plant at the edge of town. Each will influence the direction of your marketing plan. Generally, there's just no use in buying, preparing, advertising, or publicizing grits and hog jowls with collards and cornbread to a gated community with million-dollar homes owned by people who make Frasier Crane seem rather dowdy. To a great extent your concept and menu will determine the design, look, and atmosphere of your restaurant. Flaming torches, carved Tiki gods, and waiters in colorful Hawaiian shirts will only confuse the patrons of Vito's Portabella, Pizza & Pasta.

*define your
style*

Your concept and menu will affect your selection of personnel. Regardless of skill, experience, and personal charm, you will not find fat, bald men with moustaches carrying trays at Hooters. Servers at Mom's Greasy Spoon may only need four skills: a good memory, a pleasant personality, the strength to carry heavy plates, and an ability to laugh at the same joke several hundred times a year. The server at a continental restaurant in an upscale community will have to be fully trained in the skill and art of serving food.

Your concept and/or your menu are the building blocks of your success. You have many options. Just make sure that your foundation is solid before you start building.

A Bit of Perspective on Profitability

You may have heard about slim profits and the difficulty in maintaining a profitable operation in this business. That can happen, but there are always two sides to a story. The U.S. economy dipped into a slump prior to and during 2001, yet this industry outperformed the overall economy that year. For example, eating/drinking establishment sales increased 4.4 percent on a year-to-date basis. The sales gain for the overall economy was 3.4 percent. During that same period, employment increased 1.4 percent compared to the 0.6 percent gain in the overall economy.

Restaurants aren't recession-proof, but as a rule they are affected less than the rest of the economy. During the past thirty years, the national economy posted only five years of negative growth. According to a report from ✑*www.restaurants.org*, within that same period, the restaurant industry posted only three years of negative growth, and those losses weren't larger than 0.2 percent.

Do You Have a Mentor?

One of the best steps you can take as you think about running a restaurant is to find a mentor. Team up with someone who is successful in the business—someone who loves being a manager of a restaurant—and learn directly from his or her personal experience. That's one of the fastest ways to learn the ins and outs of a complex and ever-changing business.

More C's please - Charley Corey Konrad.

Look for Successful Role Models

Finding a good mentor is not as difficult as many think. Lots of top people are delighted to help someone on the way up. They're flattered at the respect and attention and they feel a sense of accomplishment and pride when the people they help out achieve success. Look around for successful restaurateurs and make an approach, either via an introduction by a third party or by just introducing yourself in person. Many business leaders aggressively seek out talented people to mentor. Don't be discouraged if you get turned down a time or two. Just keep researching and making contact, and your mentor will show up.

Remember that Mentoring Is a Two-Way Street

Mentoring is a two-way relationship, one that can last a lifetime. Always be on the lookout for ways to return the favor. Too often young people on their way up get a good start and then forget about those who helped them get that start. It's unfortunate and shows a lack of gratitude and basic human decency. On a practical level, it's also bad business.

Here's one last word on the subject—avoid negative "mentors." Every business has a number of people more than willing to tell some young person how rotten things can be. "You don't want to be in this business, kid. It'll break your heart." Such "expert" advice isn't worth the hot air it takes to blow it. Unsuccessful people in any business just love to share their misery. It seems as though they seek to justify their own failure by doing their best to see others fail, too. Your mentor should be someone who is successful, enthusiastic, and in love with the job.

It's important to remember the help you received from your mentor once you build your own success story. That's the time to start doing a little mentoring of your own.

Every Restaurateur Leads a Team

You must know how to recruit top talent, and that's no easy task. More than that, you have to know how to manage and motivate that talent. Personnel turnover is inevitable. Finding talented replacements and blending them into an existing organization is a skill in itself. For example, sometimes newcomers are welcomed with open arms by the staff. Other times they're greeted with cold shoulders or even hostility. "How dare the boss replace good old Bert with *her!*" Personnel problems have a way of finding their way directly to your bottom line.

The food and beverage business, more than many others, is a people business. As a base of loyal customers and as loyal employees, they are the lifeblood of your success.

Chapter 2

Making Basic Decisions and Conducting Research

Part One

Part Two

Part Three

Part Four

Part Five

Part Six

Deciding Which Type of Restaurant You Want to Operate

Okay, so you have a powerful idea, therefore your time has come. You want to own and/or manage your own restaurant. The challenge is to turn that ephemeral dream into a solid and profitable reality. We've covered some of the initial steps in Chapter 1. Now is the time to make a major decision. Should you own your own place or invest in a franchise operation? Only you can make that decision. Whichever route you choose, realize that it is a long-term decision, one with many serious benefits and consequences. It's not something to be taken lightly. Invest the time and money for consultation with your attorney, accountant, financial advisor, and business friends you trust.

Before making the decision, let's take a brief look at the types of restaurants from which you can choose.

> Invest the time and money for consultation with your attorney, accountant, and financial advisor.
>
> JOY

A Café or Grill

These are the small, blue-plate special outfits often found in rural communities and around industrial and commercial areas. They are frequently called "greasy spoons," which is for the most part a title of fondness. Patrons are blue-collar workers, office workers, and salespeople on the road, people who want a lot of good, basic fare at fair prices. Tablecloths, if present, are usually oilskin. Plates are thick, white, and heavy. The napkins are paper and are dispensed at the table from a metal canister next to the squirt bottles of ketchup and mustard. Menus must be basic, limited, and full of popular dishes. The owners realize that because profit margins are slim, they must get people in, serve them quickly, and move them out so other patrons can take their places. Wait staff can be surprisingly professional, and their personalities often draw more repeat business than the menu. Cafés and grills are generally single operations and are not franchised.

Fast Food

These are for the most part regional and national franchise operations: McDonald's, Burger King, Wendy's, and a host of others. Food items are ordered in bulk and delivered by company-owned trucks or from rented fleets. Many menu items are stored in the freezer and are not prepared until ordered. The goal is to provide meals and snacks as quickly as possible to as many people as possible. The menu in a franchise operation in Boca Raton will be identical to the menu in Bakersfield, Boise, and Baton Rouge. In a sense, the market for a local franchise can be considered national, although only in the sense of tourists or businesspeople passing through.

Labor costs must be kept in control. Cooking skills are at a minimum and generally consist of taking French fries out of the fryer before they turn into toothpicks. Service skills are also at a minimum, because the servers generally just take items handed from the cooking area, put them in a sack, take the customer's money (hopefully with a smile), and move on to the next person in line. Patrons in a sense serve as waiter and waitress. Paper napkins, straws, and plastic utensils are distributed from an area separate from or placed on the counter. Plates, if needed, will be plastic. The average cost of a meal will usually be lower than at a café or grill. Catering to America's need to drive and to get back on the road, many franchise operations feature drive-through windows.

A Family Restaurant

These are usually larger and more upscale versions of the café or grill and are dependent upon local traffic and repeat business. Some national chain operations also fit into this category. Olive Garden or Chili's aren't really fast-food joints. As more and more families have two wage earners, these operations have grown in popularity. Not only do mom and pop have less time to shop for and prepare meals, they have a bit more disposable income and can afford to eat out more often. Many menus feature special sections featuring children's meals at reduced prices as an inducement to the family trade.

You will find all types of family restaurants, from general purpose operations offering a little bit of everything to ethnic dining specializing in a single type of cuisine. The menus will be more varied than at a grill or fast-food restaurant and may feature luncheon specials or specials of the day. Alcoholic beverages are served in many family-style restaurants. Cloth tablecloths may or may not be in place. Napkins may be cloth or paper.

Restaurants Can Do Well in a Recession

Despite a recent trend in which families reduced the amount of expenses out of the home, the restaurant business has pretty much remained stable, according to a survey by *Restaurants and Institutions* magazine published in 2002. More than one-fourth of survey recipients reported they had eaten out more in 2001 than in 2000. Just over two-thirds of the recipients stated they planned to visit restaurants at the same frequency of the previous year. Mitchell J. Speiser, restaurant analyst for Lehman Brothers, Inc., said, "Americans are just going to continue to eat out, whether in good times or bad."

The experience has become part of everyday life. The nation's healthy appetite for restaurant dining points to a healthy business environment for the industry for some time.

Waiters and waitresses are friendly, fast, and well-trained. Mealtimes will be considerably longer than time spent in a fast-food franchise or a café. Because there are so many family restaurants in so many categories competing for the same customers, the owner faces a real challenge in making his or her place something special that will draw repeat customers. Often this special something is the personality of the owner or manager. Family restaurants are single operations but are also being franchised.

Fine Dining

Gourmet or upscale dining facilities rely heavily on high-quality food, the skills of a professional chef, and an elegant atmosphere that attracts and holds customers. Dining requires considerably more time, and the prices are the highest of the categories presented here. The cost of a meal can run from high to sums a lot of people would consider outrageous. In addition to superior meals, the restaurant may also feature cocktails, a list of unique appetizers, top-quality wines, specialty desserts, gourmet coffees, and even tableside entertainment. Management's goal is to turn a meal into a dining experience that the patrons will want to repeat.

Many fine-dining establishments can be found in upscale hotels and resorts. Often the chef is the real star and may attract a sizeable number of "fans." This is something for the owner to consider, because you often occupy the position of a talent scout. A great chef is a great draw—unless he or she moves on. Then the "fans" may play follow the "leaver." Retaining customers when a top chef leaves is a key responsibility of the fine-dining restaurant owner. Your customers deserve the excellent service they've come to expect.

Obviously there are too many variables in these types of establishments to list, and some can be difficult to categorize. Is it a midsize restaurant or just a very large café? Is Big Bubbah's Bar-B-Que 'N Brew a blue-collar roadhouse or a quirky upscale theme restaurant catering to young, upwardly mobile business types? What matters is which type attracts you. What kind of restaurant do you really want to own or manage? Once you've made that decision, you have to discover whether there's anybody who'll show up at your grand opening and if there's a chance you can make any money managing your dream.

Staying on Top of Changes in Your Market

In a very practical sense, you have to be a bit of a psychic to run a successful business. Trends are always changing. That's not to say you should change your concept or menu every time a new trend comes along. Crowds are notoriously fickle, and by the time you make such a radical change, they could have moved on to the latest hot fashion. By the time you install that expensive video projection system for your "Meal and a Movie" night, the crowd could be moving down the street to a competitor featuring "Dinner and a Dance."

A good manager always stays on top of trends, but that doesn't mean you have to follow them. It's just common sense to know what's going on and to make an educated guess as to where things are going. Are there any population shifts in your community that might shift your patrons with it? Will the current economy hurt or help your planned expansion? Who are the local movers and shakers, and do you want to attract or avoid them? What is the outlook for a qualified labor supply over the next three years? What happens if a supplier goes out of business? You can still visit your friendly neighborhood psychic. Of course, you'll still have to interpret her "I see *red* in your future." Does that mean you need a new coat of paint? Is she referring to tomato sauce and a need to change to an Italian menu? Or does she see the red ink of financial loss after you've opened up "The Communist Antipasto" down the street from the local FBI?

Four Ps That Determine Your Restaurant's Success

Consider the following four Ps that determine the overall success of your operations:

- **People:** To be precise, your people are the ones who deliver the product to the patrons who provide the profit.
- **Product:** That's the fare. Regardless of your location, your décor, your personable wait staff, and your own dazzling personality, the reason people show up at your door is to eat.
- **Patrons:** Patrons are those nice folks who gladly hand over their money every week to taste your fare.
- **Profit:** Without a profit you won't be in business very long. Profit is the ultimate goal. That's the way you stay a restaurateur.

Change Encourages Repeat Business

Friday's has an impressive ability to keep their store sales on the increase. Besides a fun atmosphere and good food, what's their secret? Simple. They change their menu often. It has been estimated that as many as 20 to 25 percent of restaurant patrons don't return as often as the owners would like because their menu is stale. After watching Friday's success, Randy started changing his menu four times a year (each season). He keeps 75 to 80 percent of his existing menu, the top sellers, and then adds some new items. He also has daily or nightly specials and tracks how well they sell. The most popular dishes are added to the regular menu. By constantly updating your menu, your customers will react with their repeat patronage.

Play "What If"

The best advice we can give for seeing the future is to play the game called "What if." Just imagine all the scenarios possible, ask that simple question, and come up with sound answers. Play the game and you'll be amazed to discover your own psychic power.

"What if" is a great way to exercise your mind and to anticipate opportunities and obstacles. The rules are simple. Think about any situation (past, present, future, real, or imagined) and ask yourself "What if?" Then answer with your best dream, worst nightmare, or most recent thought. What if we opened on the other side of town? What if we opened six months later/earlier? What if the mill closes down? What if my supplier of _____ fails to show up? What if my chef quits? What if a patron gets hurt on my property? What if a thief pulls a gun during the dinner hour? What if the senior citizens tour bus pulls up unexpectedly? What if we changed the menu? What if we didn't offer takeout? What if we opened banquet facilities? The game can go on forever or for at least as long as you're in business. It's particularly helpful during the development and prior to the start-up phase. There's no win or lose, only insight. Play it and play it often. You'll be surprised at the number of hardships you avoid and the number of hidden opportunities you discover.

Drive By Your Competition

Once you start in earnest, word will get out on the streets that a new restaurant is in the making. Certainly by the time you apply for permits from the city, your competitors will know that you're planning a move into their territory. Count on the fact that they'll be driving by to check out how your operations are progressing. There's nothing wrong with doing a little driving of your own.

Eat at Joes. Or Luigi's, the Kung Pao Palace, or whoever is your competitor. Get a taste of their food and beverage menu. Look at their décor and surroundings. Notice what works and what doesn't appear to be working well at all. Make notes on things you could change or do better to make your operations smoother and to better serve your clientele. Also, conduct a little head-hunting. If you find a great waitress, bartender, or whomever, file the name away and consider making him or her an offer of employment when you need that personnel.

visit & compare

Collect and Study Information

Create your own reference book, a collection of plans, projections, concepts, notes, helpful articles and printed matter, forms, case histories, wild and crazy thoughts, and anything else you believe has potential value.

You can keep these in a yellow legal pad, the familiar three-ring binder, or in your computer. When using computer files, be sure to make a hard copy of everything. Computers crash. Software goes bad. You don't want to lose six months or a year of valuable information. Some items that might make your list (and surely you will add more) could include:

- Restaurant industry news
- Restaurant, price, and labor trends
- Local restaurant reviews
- Trade association news
- Business and operational forms
- Case histories (failures and successes) and your analysis of them
- People and subjects to explore or who may be of assistance
- Good and bad ideas
- Information on suppliers
- Legal cases involving restaurants, lounges, and the food and beverage industry

Do Your Own Thinking

It is important that anyone beginning a restaurant conduct extensive research from as many sources as possible. It's just as important that you evaluate the information you receive and come to your own conclusions. Often, the experts don't get it quite right.

Restaurant Business magazine, one of the industry's national trade journals, ran an article in July 2001 noting some of its hits and misses. Here are a few of the misses. Back in 1903, the magazine predicted that the soda fountain would surpass the saloon in popularity. Apparently the editors believed that the public would reject bourbon and booze for banana splits. When was the last time you even saw a soda fountain? In the early '60s, they advanced the notion that "taco dogs," wieners served in taco shells with taco-style fillings, would sweep the nation. This craze would be followed swiftly by the adoption of "taco cones," tacos served in shells shaped like ice cream cones. Conveyor belts would permit faster more efficient customer service when installed in most restaurants, or so they said in 1958. And in 1909 the magazine noted that women would never successfully compete against men in the nation's restaurant job pool. Currently, about half of all restaurant workers are women. These notes aren't meant as a slap against a respected magazine. They got a lot of hits as well as misses. Rather, they're to point out an important fact: Regardless of the reliability of your sources, ultimately the responsibility for decision-making and for living with those consequences rests on your own shoulders.

Keeping Prices Low and Quality High

Prices rise. The cost of food, supplies, and labor are always going up, and at some time you will have to adjust your menu to keep things in balance. Be sure to read your market carefully. People expect prices to rise now and then, but you don't want to give your patrons a case of culture shock.

Watch Your Competitors

Keep an eye on your competitors. You don't want to be too far out of line. If your read of the market tells you that you shouldn't raise prices at the moment, there are alternatives. For example, you can alter your menu by eliminating items that the are most costly for you to prepare. Think about doing a partial menu overhaul. An updated menu can have two advantages. One, new items can spur new interest. Two, you can select menu items with lower costs, which can mean higher profit. If you can't raise your prices you can at least lower some of your expenses.

Never Compromise Your Standards

Never, never, never compromise your standards. Always keep the quality of your food and your food service high. If costs are too high, alter your menu as suggested above. Cutting quality has a way of backfiring. A pizza restaurant that shall remain nameless once decided to advertise a two-for-one offer. That's usually good marketing. In this case, however, the manager decided to "save money" by spreading the toppings for one pizza on two. People soon realized that they were paying for two pizzas but were really getting something far less. Business dropped off and the company lost a lot of formerly loyal customers.

Staff reductions are often necessary adjustments to market forces. If you have to cut back, you have to cut back, but don't reduce your labor costs to the point of reducing the quality of your service. You can cut back on staff hours by letting people off as business for the day decreases. Reduce the cost of your indirect labor, such as bussers, bar backs, dishwashers, prep cooks, or hostesses. Do you really need that busser, or can the wait staff or management pitch in and clean off a few tables? During slow hours, you can let your bartender off early and allow management to handle the shift.

Don't allow your choice of equipment to compromise your quality. Regardless of how much you saved on the "bargain," if equipment is slowing production or causing customer complaints, get rid of it. You can easily replace equipment. Replacing a lost reputation is significantly more challenging.

Think Carefully about Coupons

Sometimes a two-for-one offer is good marketing. It's not a tactic for every situation. Coupons or special offers must be in line with the image of your restaurant. If your theme or image will not support these type of promotions, you're better off in the long run to avoid them. People have a tendency to equate lower prices with lower quality.

Chapter 3

Conducting a Feasibility Study for Your Restaurant Idea

Part One

Part Two

Part Three

Part Four

Part Five

Part Six

Analyzing Your Restaurant Idea

In the film *Midway,* about the World War II battle in the Pacific, a character played by Charlton Heston discusses the quality of naval intelligence. The intelligence officer, played by Hal Holbrook, explains that his staff estimates are based on a bit of information here, a dab of intelligence there, and a lot of creative thinking. "You're guessing!" shouts Heston. Holbrook gives him a wry smile and says, "We like to call it *analysis.*" That pretty well describes a feasibility study. You gather as much information possible about your proposed business and then make an intelligent guess and/or analysis of the situation.

Understanding the Elements of a Feasibility Study

A feasibility study should consist of a review of at least the following elements:

- Geography
- Population
- The local economy
- The competition
- Local business and industry
- Tourism and conventions
- Local real estate

Geography

Where are you going to put your restaurant? You have to determine the boundaries of your trade area, the geographical limits of the people your restaurant can serve. More than 2 million people make their home in the Phoenix metro area. That's a tremendous market. But if your Tacos 'N Taters shop is located in the east valley, chances are slim to none that folks over in the west valley are going to drive an hour just to sit down to a plate of your world-famous guacamole spuds. The distance is too far, the inconvenience is too great, and there's lots of guacamole in between.

What, then, is the logical geographic trade area for your type of restaurant? You'll need to evaluate such things as accessibility to interstates and major traffic arteries. Can people quickly and easily get to your parking lot? Is there enough space for a parking lot, or will you have to provide valet parking? Check out the public transit routes, too. Talk to people at the chamber of commerce and in local governments. Find out what plans are being considered or are in the works for your target area. The proposed widening of the street in front of your proposed business could mean easier access for your customers, not to mention increased walk-in trade. Of course, there's that little problem of the year and a half of construction during which access to your property will be severely restricted. Can you manage the loss in profits during construction? Should you wait to begin till after the street is widened or should you look elsewhere? This is the type of geographical data that can make or break a business.

> What is the logical geographic trade area for your type of restaurant?

Population

Once you've taken a good look at where, it's time to get an idea of who. It is important that you develop an accurate and in-depth analysis of your potential customer base. Head down to the local library and take a look at the U.S. Census data. The research librarian can point you in the right direction and even help you locate other facts about the community. You can also access census information from the Bureau of Census in the Department of Commerce. Local resources will include the chamber of commerce, city planning departments, zoning departments, building inspectors, real estate associations, and the local restaurant association. Speak with the city councilman for that area and don't neglect the information gold mine of retired mayors and councilmen, who may speak more freely since they're not up for re-election.

Make sure to evaluate the economic history of the desired area(s). Is this community or neighborhood in transition? And from what to what? Does it show a steady rise in a population with enough income to support your proposed restaurant? Determine the age group(s) living there and where the trend is heading. Will your population base still be around in ten years? In other words, can you grow with the community or will the community's growth stunt yours? Here's a list of other essential information.

- Number of home owners
- Number of renters (homes and apartments)
- Number of dwellings
- Type of dwellings (single-family, apartment complexes, etc.)
- Existing zoning
- Proposed zoning
- Education level of area residents
- Employment classifications of area
- Marital status of people in the area
- Average household income
- Ethnic make-up of the area
- Proposed shifts in population density
- Age breakdown of area residents
- Type of businesses moving in or out

You can find any number of professional companies that conduct this type of research. Many more companies say they do, but have very little experience. We recommend that you interview a number of professional research organizations. Be sure they really know how to conduct market research before you hire them. Ask for references and call those references. A full-service advertising agency, marketing firm, or public relations company may create award-winning brochures and radio spots, but that doesn't mean they know beans about population density or city zoning policies. Find someone or some company with a proven track record in this specific area.

Additionally, you should conduct your own research by investing some time in the community or neighborhood. Drive around. Stop at some of the businesses. Have a beer at the local tavern or a cup of coffee at the Busy Bee Café. Talk to the waiters and waitresses, the postman, the neighborhood policeman, and anyone else who can give you some insight. Depend on your research firm for raw data and analysis, but don't neglect the importance of your own experience, insight, and gut instinct.

The Economy

A candidate's successful bid for president of the United States was helped in no small measure by an advisor who posted a sign in a prominent position, "It's The Economy, Stupid!" The local economy in your chosen area is just as important. You probably don't want to move an upscale restaurant into a neighborhood on a downward economic spiral. You could be mortgaging your business future to a bottom line that will ultimately bottom out. An honest evaluation of the economic health of the community is in order.

You've surely heard that the success formula for business, especially restaurants, is "location, location, location." There's more to success than that, but it's certainly an essential and perhaps overriding consideration. Make a mistake in choosing your location, and you will have to live with that mistake for a long, long time. Keep in mind that even if the business doesn't make it, you may still be responsible for the lease or purchase of that property. Does the location fit the restaurant you want to establish within it? Can the residents of the area afford to dine there, and is it likely that they will want to?

The Competition

Who has gotten in there ahead of you? This information is critical. If your type of restaurant will be the only one like it in the community, that could be great. But find out why. A German, Mexican, or Cajun restaurant might not be a good fit for a community that is rapidly being dominated by Chinese or Romanian or Moroccan immigrants. Then again, that might be just the niche the market needs to be filled. You, or your research firm, have to get in there and find out. Here's another factor to consider: Just

Profile the Economic Health of the Community

While you're down at city hall checking on zoning and population characteristics, visit the economic development offices and the city planners. Ask the people working there where the area has been, where it is, and where they believe it could be going. Check the zoning office to determine the nature of uses in the area: residential, commercial, industrial, or a mix of elements.

Standing Together May Be Better than Standing Alone

Don't be afraid of competition if you firmly believe you can be competitive and maintain profitability. Also, many cities have an area or several areas called "restaurant row" in which any number of operations are run side-by-side. Often the "row" is located near a major tourist attraction or an entertainment draw. For example, you'll often see a major shopping center ringed by all kinds of dining facilities. The same can be said for gambling casinos, sports arenas, and motion picture complexes. Whether you want a place on the "row" or a stand-alone, you must determine whether there is a sufficient market base to support your facility and that the base will be stable long enough to make your efforts worthwhile.

because there isn't a competitively themed restaurant in the neighborhood now doesn't mean there isn't one on the drawing boards. Head back to city hall and see what kind of restaurant building permits are being issued.

If direct competitors are located in your target area, you can:

- Change your concept
- Consider moving to another area
- Decide to get in there and slug it out

Local Business and Industry

Evaluate the nature of the businesses and industry in the area. Does the work force represent a viable market? Can you attract them to your restaurant? Do you want to attract them or are you after another market? Local business makes for good business, especially if the population likes to get away from the job during the lunch hour. Additionally, your facility might be structured to provide breakfast, lunch, or evening meeting facilities for the businesses in the area. Local business clubs are often on the prowl for a regular meeting place with good food and friendly service. Also, consider the benefits of catering lunches, meetings, and seminars for businesses in the area. Visits to the chamber of commerce and several of the local business and service clubs can provide a wealth of information. You can also pick up valuable networking contacts, potential customers, and get a taste of what the competition is serving for lunch.

Tourism and Conventions

Restaurants are always a major draw for the local tourism industry. Just look at how they are promoted in the convention and tourist bureau brochures, the city guides, phone books, and promotional handouts. Make a personal visit to the convention and tourist bureau to get a handle on the situation. What type of establishment or cuisine is the traveling public seeking? What do salespersons, managers, and executives enjoy when in town for business? What types of restaurants have drawn tourists in the past and what types have failed? Be sure to investigate the local fairs and festivals. During these times, tourists and locals tend to invest a lot of their dining funds down at the carnival. Instead of accepting your losses during those times, investigate the feasibility of joining in by opening a food booth. That's a great way to make a few dollars and expose a lot of people to your restaurant and its fare.

Local Real Estate Market

The shape of the real estate market is a key indicator for your feasibility study. If housing starts are slow and if foreclosures are numerous, the population may be in a recession and without the discretionary funds for dining out. If the dollars are turning in the housing and rental markets, then people clearly have money and are willing to spend it. Your challenge, then, is to get them to spend it down at your place.

You'll also need to get accurate financial data on lease and purchase costs for your building. Visit local real estate offices and commercial developers, people who have a handle on the local scene. Look for opportunities. Make contacts. And get a good picture of trends and changes occurring or expected to occur.

Include a SWOT Analysis in Your Study

Make a list of your Strengths, Weaknesses, Opportunities, and Threats—that's called a SWOT analysis. Examine internal factors: your personal experience and knowledge base regarding the kitchen, dining areas, marketing, finance, your ability to lead, management skills, technological skills, and general knowledge of your market. Think about your contacts for suppliers, employees, and in the business community in general. Be honest with yourself about your financial base or the lack of it. Consider what you can bring to the table personally.

What constitutes your local environment, including economic, legal, political, technological, social, and cultural factors? Look closely at the competition and the demand or potential demand for your proposed operation.

Conduct a thorough analysis of the neighborhood demographics, traffic patterns, access to your property, neighboring noncompetitive business, surrounding housing, current marketing trends, eating patterns locally and nationally, family make-up in the area, and the potential employee pool. Most important, determine whether there's a real need for your restaurant in your selected area.

Searching for Information

The more you know about the business, the better you'll be able to assess whether it is the right opportunity for you and your goals in life. Fortunately, there is a wealth of information readily available. Sources of basic information about all phases of the industry are all around you.

The main thing to remember is that you have a *lot* of information and resources literally at your fingertips, a phone call, or a short drive away. So log on, dial out, shift gears, and get moving!

The Internet

The Internet is an obvious first step. Log on to *www.restaurant.org,* the Web site of the National Restaurant Association, for all kinds of information about all phases of the business. Tap into other subjects related to the business for additional information, such as restaurant, lounge, brew, food service, and so on for a surprising number of sources. One word of caution—not every site on the Internet has the backing of a national organization such as the National Restaurant Association. Consider the source and verify important data from other sources.

Library

Your local library is another good early step. It probably carries one or more restaurant publications or may be able to get you copies from a larger or main branch. If you can think of a subject related to this industry, there's probably a magazine, a tabloid, or a newsletter devoted to it. These can be rather generic publications such as *Restaurant Business* magazine, *Restaurant News, Restaurant and Institutions* magazine, and *U.S. Foodservice News,* or they can be quite specific, such as the trade journals *Tea and Coffee, Frozen Food Age,* and even *Meat and Poultry.* Many of these and other publications will have Web sites.

Local and Regional Trade Associations

Local and regional trade associations may also provide a wealth of information. For example, Randy is a member of the Louisiana Restaurant Association. Check out your local phone book, the Internet, or a local restaurant owner for information. Chances are there's a public information desk in the organization. Ask about upcoming trade shows. Attending one of these functions will give you exposure to the real world of owning and managing a restaurant. You'll get to meet owners, managers, and suppliers of all kinds of equipment, products, and services. In addition to gaining valuable information, you can start building a network of professional associates.

> Attending trade functions will give you exposure to the real world of owning and managing a restaurant.

Local Chamber of Commerce

Your local chamber of commerce will have a new business development center or at least a business information department or section. They'll most likely have a number of relevant publications, studies, brochures, and other types of basic information. They can also put you in touch with reliable restaurateurs in your area who can act as mentors or at least provide some real-world experience. Consider meeting with their representatives of SCORE, the Service Corps of Retired Executives. This is a group of experienced, business-savvy individuals who volunteer their time and expertise to help people just like you get a good start in business.

Small Business Administration

Contact the Small Business Administration (SBA). This is a government agency dedicated to promoting the interests of small business. The agency runs the SCORE program, usually through the local chamber. They also run Small Business Development Centers (SBDCs), usually through a local university, which can provide advice and counsel that can be particularly valuable during your development stages. The SBA is listed in the white pages

Americans Love Dining Out

According to *Restaurant Spending*, a publication of the National Restaurant Association, the average American household spent $2,116 on dining outside of the home during 1999. That works out to about $846 per person. About 37 percent of the nation's dining-out dollar was spent by households with an average income of $70,000 or more. This is significant because that group represents only 19 percent of the nation's households. When families reach the $30,000 per year pretax income level, as a group they tend to invest more in dining out.

Age is also a factor. A person's peak earning years are generally between age 35 and 54, and households headed by individuals in that age bracket tend to dine out more than other groups.

of your phone book. The administration also has a Web site, *www.sbaonline.sba.gov.*

Local Colleges

Speaking of higher education, contact your local university, college, community college, or business school to see if they offer any relevant courses that are open to the public.

Regardless of what state you're in (we don't mean "panic" or "frenzy," but as in "of the Union."), you have at your disposal a department of economic development. That's what you're trying to do, isn't it, develop the economy? So give the office a call. They can provide direct information about the industry and probably provide you with a number of other sources, organizations, and individuals to contact.

Critically Evaluating Your Market

Of course, you've always wanted to open that intimate, candle-lit restaurant featuring an exquisite menu of European cuisine, but will your market support your vision? Before opening any business, you have to place your emotions in a small box, put them away, and carefully evaluate your chances of success. "What type of restaurants are in my market?" "Is there a need for my vision in my market?" "Are there competitors in my market?" "What do I have that will give me an edge on that competition?" "Where should I locate and can I locate there?" "Where is the local economy headed?" "Will I need a base of regulars, or can I make it with walk-in traffic?"

These are important questions that must be answered unemotionally and in the harsh glare of honest evaluation. To do otherwise is to set up a situation in which your dream can become your worst nightmare. Each market is different, and we can't evaluate it for you, so you need to do so critically.

Chapter 4

Organizing Your Restaurant: Going Alone or Partnering Up

Sole Proprietorship: Going It Alone

A sole proprietorship means that you're in business by and for yourself. You are the company—without you, the company would no longer exist. You're the only one who makes decisions about your restaurant, and after you pay for expenses and taxes, the profits are yours to keep.

Every type of business has its own risks and rewards, and a sole proprietorship is no exception.

Understanding the Rewards of a Sole Proprietorship

It's been said that the first step in a business plan for a sole proprietorship in the restaurant business should read, "Win Tri-State Lottery." Winning a fortune, inheriting Uncle Joe's stock portfolio, or discovering the Lost Dutchman Gold Mine would certainly give you a leg up and some real security in this business, but it's not really necessary.

You Can Call Your Own Shots

If the "KISS" rule (Keep It Simple, Stupid!) appeals to your management style, then owning your own restaurant is the way to go. It's the simplest, easiest option to manage and monitor. You, the owner, are in charge, responsible only to yourself and the bank, savings and loan, financial institution, or brother-in-law who provided the loan to get you started. You earn all the praise and take home the lion's share of the profits. Of course, if things head south, you have to accept the blame, try to find some way to dig yourself out of a financial black hole, and come up with an explanation that will satisfy your brother-in-law and keep peace in the family. That's the challenge. Can you go it alone?

Quick Decision-Making

You can move fast. There's no upper management, regional director, or finance committee looking over your shoulder. If you have an exciting idea and want to give it a try, you can jump right in immediately. For example, if you want to add a menu item or change the entire thing over the weekend, you can start typing on the computer, make phone calls to suppliers, and have a meeting with the chef about your new recipe book. You can move with the same speed to revamp your advertising, remodel your décor, remove a nonperforming employee, or revise your business plan in the event of changes in the market.

As the sole owner you can take immediate advantage of new opportunities. If the city's street improvement project will effectively shut down your business, you can, if you want, decide to shut down your operations, move to a better location, or take appropriate steps to redirect traffic to your parking lot. This happened to one of Randy's colleagues many years ago. The city invested more than a year in road repairs, which eliminated the main access to the man's restaurant. Virtually overnight, brightly colored, easy-to-read signs with retina-burn red arrows appeared for many blocks around his restaurant. Each sign pointed to another sign which eventually led to the "back door" of the parking lot. Customers followed the signs, the restaurant stayed in business while others failed, and once construction was completed, the place thrived.

Minimal Paperwork

Legal documents can be kept at a minimum. Generally, there are few legal measures required to set up a sole proprietorship, other than the standard business license for your community. You'll be required to maintain tax and other records just like everyone else, but going it alone means you don't have to deal with complex partnership agreements, making official reports to partners, and listening to "advice" from those partners. Your legal fees for initiating and maintaining your business can be kept at a minimum.

My Customers Want Something Different

From time to time, your customers may want something different: different menus, different décor, different hours, different amenities, and so on. If you're involved in a franchise, there is little that you can do when customers want change—the corporation will probably leave little room for flexibility on the local level. An independent operator has more options, so you can change quickly and respond to changes in the market.

Be wary, however, of making change just for the sake of change. And remember, too, that the complainers in life often are rather vocal. The silent majority is just as often, well, silent. Responding to the boisterous few may alienate the quiet but happy group of loyal customers.

Your Profits Are Yours to Keep

The money you make is the money you keep. Naturally, profits have to be folded back into the business to keep the operation going, but after those expenses are covered, your money remains your money. It's considered personal income. Once paid for, your property and your equipment become assets. You can use them, sell them, rent them out, leave them alone, or send them to the trash heap at your discretion. Your flexibility is practically total because you answer to no one other than your own good sense, and of course the tastes and desires of your customers. Sole proprietorships may experience certain tax benefits, too. For example, as noted, your profits and assets are considered personal income. Should you incur a business loss, that loss may be used to decrease the amount of your personal income tax.

The Downside of a Sole Proprietorship

There are two sides to every story, and one of them is always a downside. That rule applies to sole proprietorships, too.

Unlimited Liability

Just as your profits are personal income, your business debts are considered personal debts. They don't belong to the partners or the corporation because there is no partnership or corporation. Everything rests on your shoulders. You have unlimited liability for debts and obligations incurred by your business. The cost of that new stove, repairs to the roof, food and beverage, advertising, toothpicks, you name it, are all yours—personally. If you can't meet your obligations to a creditor, he or she can come after your personal assets to satisfy that debt. Try to explain that to your spouse as a creditor hauls off Junior's piano to cover your bill for Tater Tots.

Tax liabilities may also present problems. Corporations may earn a number of tax breaks, but these aren't applicable to sole proprietorships. As your restaurant prospers and your income increases, this may become a more significant consideration. The ongoing advice of a good accountant is essential to see that you and your facility stay out of hot water.

Fewer Financial Resources

Going it alone means flexibility in decision making. If you want to expand or build a sister restaurant in another part of town, you can decide to do so. Here's the "but." Arranging adequate financing to back those decisions may be a problem. Banks and financial institutions are often quite shy about lending money to sole proprietorships. Corporations and partnerships generally get better treatment. That's just the name of the game, and you'd best just accept it and play by their rules. If your plans are acceptable to the lending institution, you'll probably get the loan, but you'll be held personally responsible for it. In addition, you'll most likely be required to put up personal assets nearly equal to the amount of the loan to secure it.

You're in Your Own Pressure Cooker

Taking on the world of business alone is not for everyone. It takes a lot of courage, which Hemingway defined as "grace under pressure." As a sole proprietor you will have more than your share of pressure cooking. You will have more than your share of opportunity to show the strength of your backbone, too. Owning your own restaurant offers tremendous challenges and equally tremendous rewards. In the restaurant industry, it's not really enough to love the business, to have a desire for your own restaurant, or even to be driven to success—the real determining factor is your *passion* to excel. When the pressure's on, you might remember the words of the poet Ovid, who said, "Courage conquers all things." If going it alone is your cup of tea, then go forth and conquer!

Partners Can Extend Your Capabilities

A partnership is nothing more than an agreement between two or more individuals to create and manage a business.

Become a Numbers Person

You'll need a good accountant to help keep your restaurant financially sound. Find that person or that company early so he, she, or they can take care of your financials while you're scrambling up that learning curve. An accountant can also provide a lot of information and education along the way. Don't hesitate to ask, "Uh, what does that mean?" When you get the answer, be sure that you understand it.

Take a class. Look to your local community colleges, business colleges, and business groups. Even with a good accountant on your team, you need to master this subject. You have to know where those numbers come from, what they really mean, and how to change them to better numbers through better management.

It's more complex than a sole proprietorship, but not quite as complicated as putting together your own corporation. If you don't want to go it alone, but don't want to enter the "corporate rat race" either, this in-between step might be just the option. Just remember, in-between doesn't mean halfway.

While the start-up isn't quite as fast as with a sole proprietorship, you can crack the whip and get things moving rather rapidly. Restrictions on forming a partnership aren't nearly as complex or cumbersome as they are for creating a corporation. You and your partners can open the chuck wagon any time you want. It's a good idea, and one this book highly recommends, to write a comprehensive partnership agreement. The services of a good attorney are essential. Make certain that you and your partner(s) are in full agreement on all aspects of the business. Assume nothing. Leave nothing unsaid. The one matter you think is unimportant might create a rift or even destroy the business later on.

> Make certain that you and your partner(s) are in full agreement on all aspects of the business. Assume nothing.

"I thought we agreed to split the profits fifty-fifty right away."

"Well, I thought we agreed to plow our profits back into the business."

"Oh, yeah?"

"Yeah!"

Then the maturity continues with a bunch of name calling, insults, and words better left unsaid. You endure long, unpleasant silences. Squabbles break out for no apparent reason. Loyal customers, who don't enjoy the tension, tend to drift away. In an amazingly short period of time, your business is stranded like a wagon on the lone prairie with the sounds of drums and war whoops from your creditors charging over the hills.

Create a Road Map for the Partnership Journey

Your partnership agreement can easily determine the success or failure of your venture. It is essential that you work closely with an attorney to draw up this document. To ensure fairness, and perhaps to alleviate inevitable suspicions, work with an attorney with no ties to either party. A brother-in-law or a cousin may provide excellence service at more than reasonable rates, but the nagging possibility of favoritism will inevitably enter the mix at some point. The more time and thought you put into this agreement up front, the less trial, trouble, and tribulation you will suffer down the road.

Lack of preparation usually ends in disaster. We suspect the failure of most partnership restaurants is due more to the lack of a good agreement than to market forces.

Here are a number of topics you'll need to address. Keep in mind that every situation is different, and you'll have to structure your agreement according to the skills, abilities, and needs of the individuals at hand. Your attorney will be able to guide you as to the specific details and structure according to your needs.

Partner Rights, Responsibilities, and Limits

Will the partners have any say in the day-to-day running of the operation, or will they be "hands off" partners?

Is their input solely financial, or will they be expected to provide advice and counsel? Will they be accessible to restaurant management?

Are they silent partners? When can any given partner have access to the books, and by what process?

Contributions from Each Partner

Who provides what and on what basis? Are the partners expected to provide cash infusions without contributing to management duties?

Partners' Liabilities

Spell out any liabilities clearly so that everyone is on the same page going into the agreement.

Voting Procedures and a Process for Resolving Disputes

Set up a formal structure to follow whenever a vote on any matter needs to be taken. Have this in place up front so there's no debate when you need to take a vote.

Do you go by a vote of the majority or call in an outside arbitrator?

Buying and Selling Shares

How should a partner go about buying shares from another partner? Should all the partners be informed when shares are about to be offered for sale?

Also, before selling shares, does a partner have to first offer them to the partnership or members of the partnership?

Conditions and Process for Termination of the Partnership

Again, clearly spell out the procedure so that there are no surprises if dissolution becomes necessary or desirable.

The partners who enter into a relationship thinking "whatever happens, we can work it out as friends" are entering very dangerous territory. This is understandable. Most partners have entirely different viewpoints to the business. Generally, there is a working partner, who actually manages the restaurant, and a "silent" partner, who fronts the money or a substantial portion of it. The working partner is down there sweating in the kitchen, smiling in the dining area, and swearing at the fates who have denied him a delivery of beefsteaks in time for the Friday night All-U-Can-Scarf special.

The financial partner sees little or none of this. All he or she knows is that the profits aren't coming in quite as fast or in quite the quantity expected. Other problems can arise. For example, because the silent partner isn't really involved in the day-to-day operations, he or she can easily lose interest in the business and can be drawn into other ventures. These other areas could draw off energy, capital, and moral support when it's needed down at the restaurant. On the other side of the coin is the silent partner who won't shut up. He decides that as a partner, he should roll up the old sleeves and get in there and help "run" the business. This can quickly lead to major conflicts and a strain in the relationship or even disruption of the partnership.

The Advantages of a Partnership

A powerful advantage of a partnership is your ability to combine resources. Obviously, there are financial benefits, but you can also benefit from a wider range of experience in management, restaurant skills, dealing with governments and regulations, marketing and advertising, and other areas. A great chef or cook may be a lousy businessperson, yet aligned with someone with a solid business background, he and the partner could create a successful restaurant. Each partner contributes his or her best skills to make the total operation a better, more successful one.

As with a sole proprietorship, all the profits flow directly to the owners instead of a corporate entity. You'll agree on the split up front and include that in the partnership agreement. Not all profit distributions are fifty-fifty. You'll have to negotiate the figure based upon an evaluation of what each partner contributes. Valuable contributions aren't all cash either. For example, a well-known and respected chef has a name value, and in terms of marketing and attracting customers, that value can be considered a real asset worth a specific sum or percentage of profits. Also, if you do experience losses, they may be applied against your personal income to reduce the amount you have to pay.

> Not all profit distributions are fifty-fifty. Negotiate the figure based upon an evaluation of what each partner contributes.

Potential Disadvantages of a Partnership

The trail to success can be a bumpy one. You'll encounter a number of disadvantages to a partnership agreement. All of these can be compensated, handled successfully, or at least endured. But you have to be prepared for them.

One of the more obvious conditions relates to debts and taxes. Just as your profits head directly to your bank account, so do your debts and liabilities. There's no firewall between you and your creditors or government agencies. Each partner has unlimited liability, and that means creditors can seek satisfaction for their debts by attaching your personal finances and assets. "Ah, Junior, about those piano lessons…"

Taxes are inevitable regardless of what form your business takes. Each partner will be taxed at his or her appropriate rate. Also, just as with a sole proprietorship, you are ineligible for certain tax breaks available to corporations. Again, that's just part of the game.

"Too many cooks spoil the broth." Or the tacos, lasagna, kung pao chicken, or the burger and fries. Personality conflicts are inevitable, and this is a matter each partner must consider carefully. Many wonderful friendships and solid business relationships have been destroyed by a poorly considered business partnership. When your attorney sets up the partnership agreement, include a buy/sell clause that explicitly defines how partners can terminate their participation in the agreement, and a clause that protects the rights of the other partners. A solid relationship on the golf course or around the dinner table doesn't necessarily carry over to a business relationship, especially when times get tough, as they always do.

A good way to assess your ability to handle these conflicts is to play the game of "What if." What if he decides to hit me up for more money? What if she wants to change my menu? What if I want out? What if he/she starts hitting on the wait staff? What if we get audited? The game is based on a basic rule of human behavior: Whatever *can* go wrong *will* go wrong. How will you and your partners' relationships hold up under that kind of strain? This is a matter worth more consideration than you probably realize. See that you invest that time before making any partnership agreement.

Do as We Say, Not as We Did

When picking a partner, "it is best to be different but the same." This difference refers to selecting someone with a different set of skills, base of knowledge, or experience as a partner. Everyone has holes in his or her resume. Use partnering to fill those gaps and make your organization stronger.

Before signing on the dotted line of a partnership agreement, get to know your partner, his or her personality, and especially the views on conducting business. Ask questions. Play "What if" scenarios together or do whatever it takes to ensure that your strategic thinking is similar. You don't have to think exactly alike, but you at least need to be in the same arena.

Chapter 5

Organizing as a Corporation or Buying a Franchise

Part One

Part Two

Part Three

Part Four

Part Five

Part Six

PART ONE   DECIDING WHETHER—AND HOW—YOU WANT TO RUN A RESTAURANT

■ CHAPTER 1 Asking the Hard Questions ■ CHAPTER 2 Making Basic Decisions and Conducting Research ■ CHAPTER 3 Conducting a Feasibility Study for Your Restaurant Idea ■ CHAPTER 4 Organizing Your Restaurant: Going Alone or Partnering Up ■ CHAPTER 5 Organizing as a Corporation or Buying a Franchise

Taking the Corporate Route

This is by far the most complicated route, but it has its attractions, and a lot of business pioneers have followed that road. A corporation is a group of individuals who organize under a legal form that grants them as a body the rights, powers, privileges, and liabilities of an individual quite distinct from the individuals who make up that body. It is a separate body and exists separately from its shareholders. A corporation has the right to buy, sell, and inherit.

Advantages of Establishing a Corporation

Here's a look at some of the major advantages of corporations over sole proprietorships and partnership (see Chapter 4).

Limits on Liability

One of the most attractive advantages of a corporate structure is the limit on your personal liability. None of the individuals constituting the corporation can be held liable for the acts, debts, or obligations of that corporation over and above the amount those individuals owed or paid for the purchase of shares in the corporation. That's a firewall. Of course, all bets are off if one or more of the individuals signs a personal guarantee to accept responsibility for the corporation's acts or its debts and obligations.

Tax and Other Financial Benefits

Corporations benefit from a number of tax breaks and benefits unavailable to partnerships and sole proprietorships. Putting that "Inc." behind your name may also put you in a good position to offer a greater variety of fringe benefits packages to employees and officers of the corporation. Check with your tax accountant or your attorney for details and for the rules and restrictions in your state.

Easier Financing

Financing from banks and lending institutions is generally much easier for a corporation. Of course, the amount of financing and the conditions will depend upon your situation, creditworthiness, and the reputation of you and your partners. Investors often feel much more secure with a corporation because of the limited liability aspects. They like the idea that creditors aren't able to touch their personal finances. As a corporation, your restaurant may even get lower loan rates than businesses owned by individuals or partners.

Continuation of Your Restaurant after Retirement or Death

The stability of the business is significantly enhanced by the use of a corporate business entity. When the owner of a sole proprietorship retires or passes on, often the business dies at the same time. Partnerships face a similar situation. This is especially true when one partner is the working partner or when each of the partners contributes a specific and necessary set of skills that can't be replaced by the others. A corporation, on the other hand, is a separate entity from its shareholders. It continues regardless of the passing of any or all of its members. Another advantage is that shares can be purchased or transferred without interrupting the day-to-day management operations.

> A corporation is a separate entity from its shareholders. It continues regardless of the passing of any or all of its members.

Disadvantages of a Corporation

There is, of course, a downside to forming a corporation. This section fills you in.

Legal Complexities

Corporate entities are complex. Legal documents must be negotiated, drawn up, signed, and adhered to. Laws and regulations governing corporations can be changed, sometimes radically, at the whim of the regulators or legislatures. Constant monitoring is necessary. All of this effort requires the costly work of accountants, lawyers, and financial advisors. The process can be time-consuming, and while you're busy negotiating, signing, and writing checks, the fickle marketplace is moving on.

The government's tax and regulatory entities keep a close eye on corporations. As a separate legal entity, the organization owes state and federal income taxes. Corporate earnings and dividends paid to the investors are taxed on an individual basis. This amounts to double taxation: once at the corporate level and again at the personal level. You can't deduct business losses from your personal accounts because they belong to another "individual." Losses and tax credits must stay within the corporation and can't be passed along to the shareholders.

Difficult to Dissolve

Because a corporation is a separate "person" under the law, dissolution is much more difficult, time-consuming, and costly. A sole owner can say, "To heck with it," close his or her doors, and walk away. Partners can look at each other, shake hands or make obscene gestures, and do the same thing. The task is a little more daunting in the corporate world. You'll have to make sure that all the obligations of this separate entity are fully met or at least satisfied. Additionally, numerous documents will have to be filed with the appropriate government bodies. The process can be quite a chore, especially when the shareholders have physically, financially, and emotionally "let go" and want to move on to the next project.

Getting to Know Your Customers

Even if you decide to head up a corporation to protect your restaurant, your role as the manager and/or owner doesn't change. You still have to get out on the floor and talk to your customers. The best way to find out what they like, don't like, and would like to see is simply to ask them. A good technique is to conduct a written survey. You can include the form with the customer's bill. Be sure to offer something, such as a free appetizer on their next visit, in return for their efforts. You can also test changes in your menu by offering them first as specials. Again, ask the folks for comments on the changes.

Understanding What a Franchise Is

Back in 1929 a restaurateur by the name of Harlan Sanders began trying to create the world's best fried chicken. He invested ten years of his life in search of that recipe. The journey of Colonel Sanders and his recipe from a single frying pan to the near-universal KFC franchise is quite a story and worth a book in itself. In essence, the single most important factor in the unqualified success of the colonel, his recipe, and now the organization that still bears his likeness can be found in the single word "franchise." Lots of people can make great fried chicken. Bringing that chicken to the world required the discipline, vision, and resources of an organization—a franchise.

Franchising is buying an existing restaurant concept and getting as your return a percentage, and only a percentage, of the profits. You may run your operation or even a number of operations, but you're never a sole proprietor. You will answer to the organization and its layers of bureaucracy. When you purchase a franchise, you are buying three key elements:

- The name
- The concept
- The management system

Those items are the heart of any franchise operation and the cornerstone of its success.

The Upside of Owning a Franchise

Owners of franchise restaurants are automatically granted certain benefits. Among the most significant are: existing experience, assistance with training, bulk purchasing savings, advertising and promotional support, and an existing network. Experience is valuable, and with a franchise operation, others

Subchapter S and Limited Liability Corporations

Double taxation may be avoided if you form a subchapter S corporation. This is a means by which the federal government provides some tax relief to corporations meeting certain size and stock ownership standards. Some states offer similar benefits. The S corporation can be taxed as if it were a partnership while retaining the benefits of a corporation.

Another option to explore is the limited liability corporation, called an LLC. An LLC provides the same limited liability and tax benefits as a partnership. So, even if you decide to take the corporate option, there are still options within options. Which course is the best one for you is a matter only you can decide, ideally after considerable research, concentrated thought, and consultation with your attorney, accountant, and financial advisor.

have gone over the rough parts of the road ahead of you. The company has a well-considered, carefully researched, and real-world tested way of doing business. Compared to single operators, you start out well ahead in the race to success. Because of this experience, the franchise knows what works and what doesn't, and that includes training. You'll probably receive very specific training instructions and perhaps even direct assistance in training and educating your employees. By definition there are other units in the operation and that combined buying power can earn significant savings on food, beverage, and supplies. You may be able to apply the same principle to your advertising efforts. Certainly the franchise will have an existing advertising program. They'll most likely provide you with very specific guidelines and even production materials such as prepared print advertising "slicks" and artwork and radio and television scripts. You could even receive some cooperative advertising funds. One of your greatest franchise resources is the existing network of other franchise operators who can provide practical experience, advice, and counsel through your early days and, equally important, throughout the lifespan of your franchise operation.

The Downside of Owning a Franchise

It's a law of nature that every up is followed by a down. Some potential downside considerations are the franchise fee, lack of personal identity, the potentially costly assumption of automatic success, competition within the franchise, and long-distance relationships.

Creative Types, Beware!

Franchising may be the preferred route for an entrepreneur, but it's not the best choice for someone who wants to make his or her unique statement in the world of food and beverage. A good franchise is no guarantee of success, but there are advantages. New franchises on the whole have a much higher success rate when compared to the average independent operator opening that first café or family restaurant.

Franchise fees, which you pay to join the organization, can be substantial. You may have to continue some types of payments throughout the life of the agreement. If you've always wanted "your" place, you can't "have it your way" with a franchise. The company knows what works and what doesn't and will require strict adherence to all policies and procedures. Your identity is the company's identity.

Many people buy into a franchise with a false sense of security, assuming automatic success. "It's a McDonald's. How can I fail!" The answer is that there are uncounted ways to fail, even with a well-known and respected franchise. There's just no guarantee of success. You could find yourself in competition with one or more franchise owners within the same trade area. This is great for the company, but it does nothing for your profit picture or that of the other owners. Lastly, you'll be answering to a business structure that's most likely located hundreds or thousands of miles away. Often, distance multiplies the time required for problem solving, getting important information, or for regular contact.

None of these issues necessarily has to be a deal-breaker in your decision whether or not to franchise, but they are important points, and you need to consider them. And remember, just as every up is followed by a down, so must every down be followed by an up.

Deciding Whether to Buy a Franchise

If your dream is to own and operate your own place, franchising probably isn't for you. But if you're out to build a business or business empire in the restaurant business and you aren't committed to a particular concept, franchising could be your best choice. The key in making your decision is to know what you really want to accomplish in the restaurant business. If your dream is to mingle in the dining area among smiling customers enjoying your unique fare, then shouting "burger, fries, and a shake" from behind a counter

A Franchise Is Two Businesses

If you go the franchise route, it is essential that you remember you will be running two related but distinct businesses at the same time. You can't achieve success without attending to the very different needs of each. For example, the restaurant requires you to cater to the eating and drinking needs of a large customer base. The franchise requires you to report to and follow the dictates of a relatively small number of businessmen and businesswomen who are always looking at the bottom line of the entire organization. You're one cog in a very large machine.

won't make you very happy for very long. Take a moment right now and visualize your future in this business. What do you see? Whichever choice floats across your mental screen and touches your heart, that's the direction to follow.

Fast-food operations such as McDonald's or Burger King dominate the franchise world. Their draw to the buying public is consistency. You know you'll get exactly the same burger, fries, and a shake at the tip of Florida as you will in Alaska and all points in between. That's the key reason you have so little flexibility in franchise operations. The company knows what works. They continually research, develop, and test new products to keep up with public tastes. They have very little, often no patience for individual expression. People don't step into Taco Bell for a taste of the local rata-touille or beer-battered frog legs.

Regulations are strict. They have to be. The organization knows that the customer expects specific food and beverage items, services, and amenities at each facility regardless of its location. Anything different throws them off and may actually *turn* them off.

One positive aspect of the franchise is that the owner/manager doesn't really have to have a lot of restaurant experience to become a success. Think about it. The menu is already established. Food and beverage orders are pre-determined. Customers are already responding to regional and national advertising. A management system is already in place. We're not implying that any dolt can buy a franchise and succeed. Quite the contrary, the job is demanding and requires skills in business, sales, marketing, accounting, legal

Change: It's Inevitable

Change in the restaurant business is inevitable. It will come and it will have an impact on your business, whether you run a franchise or market your own restaurant concept. As a restaurant manager, it is your job to manage that change. You can go with the flow, resist change, or adapt in small increments. What is most important is that you move in the direction of your customers' long-term best interests.

considerations, employee training, health and safety issues, and in managing people. And they have to be willing to work very hard.

When investigating the possibility of purchasing a franchise, be sure to involve your attorney and your accountant. If you have a financial advisor, put him or her into the mix, too. A franchise agreement is a major, long-term commitment. The franchise fee can be quite high. Make sure this is the route you want to go. Conduct in-depth research. Listen to the advice and counsel of experts. And make sure you have picked the right cat to copy.

Essential Points to Consider When Researching a Franchise

Here's a list of important considerations when looking down the road toward a franchise business.

Financing

What is the amount of your investment? How will the financing be arranged? What financing options are available? What is the duration of the franchise agreement? Can you arrange your own bank or investor financing, or will you be required to finance through the franchise?

Contract Termination

It is important to know all the conditions for termination of the agreement and all the steps in the process. Are there any death or disability clauses? Can your children inherit the franchise? What are the conditions or limits on reselling your operation?

Trade Zone

You must get a clear definition of your trade zone. Is it an exclusive area, or will you be competing with other members of the same franchise? Are the boundaries clearly defined or rather loose? Having another franchise operation in the same zone isn't necessarily bad, provided the market will support them. How does the franchise justify two competing stores in the same neighborhood? Are there plans for additional franchises in or near your trade zone, and if so, what is the notification procedure? Look at the annual reports and information on the Internet to determine the stability of the franchise. Look in the news media and trade magazines for additional information.

Expansion Opportunities

Inquire about the franchise's plans for expansion. Do you think the organization might be about to overextend itself? What are the trends in the industry? Do they favor the type of operation you are considering, or is the market dwindling? Find out whether the organization is adding or dropping stores. Compare the number of restaurants ten years ago to those in operation today. How many future openings are proposed?

Public Awareness of Franchise, Name, and Theme

Public awareness and perception of the franchise, its name, and its theme are critical. How do people feel about the franchise? Have there been any major public relations problems recently (tainted meat, for example, or customer injuries)? Consider how long the franchise has been in operation and how consumer perceptions may have changed over time. If restaurants have failed, find out why.

Location

Location is also a crucial matter. Will the franchise provide site selection, or will you be allowed to select your own? How much input will you have on choosing the site? How much assistance will the company actually provide? What are the site standards?

Marketing

Pay attention to the amount of advertising, public relations, and marketing support the franchise provides. Can you do some of your own, or must you go through a corporate procedure first? Can you do any marketing

Public awareness and perception of the franchise, its name, and its theme are critical.

on your own? What are your financial commitments to advertising pro-grams? How much support do you receive and in what form (reimburse-ments, direct dollars, advertising buys from the company, preprinted materials, etc.)? Does the company offer sales incentives?

Financial Obligations

What other financial obligations accompany the franchise agreement? How much product, if any, must be purchased from the franchise? What are the equipment specifications? Are you eligible for financial aid from the franchise?

Also, look into the training programs and support offered by the fran-chise. How many are available and how often? Who has the responsibility for the costs of training programs and materials?

Chapter 6

Developing a Mission Statement, Business Plan, and Initial Budget

Part One

Part Two

Part Three

Part Four

Part Five

Part Six

Going on a Mission

A mission statement is a short description, twenty-five words or less, of what you want your business to be. Do not confuse a legitimate mission statement with those long paragraphs of unintelligible corporate jargon found in many corporate brochures, advertising materials, and annual reports, such as, "We enhance stockholder value through strategic business initiatives by empowered employees working in new team paradigms that foster, enhance, and reward techniques to accomplish a broad spectrum of results toward the bottom line." We guarantee the customers don't have a clue what that means, and neither do the employees who are supposed to be carrying out that alleged message.

A real mission statement is short, simple, and easy to understand by everyone in the group. That applies to the smallest café or to the nation's largest franchise. Every employee, manager, and stockholder should be able to grasp its entire meaning upon first reading so that they can do their part to execute it.

Looking at a Sample Mission Statement

Here's a mission statement and mission highlights statement used in one of Randy's presentations. Nothing, other than the name of the celebrity for which the facility was to be named, has been changed. "FSB" refers to the name of a famous sports celebrity.

Your Mission Statement Is Crucial to Your Success

Invest a lot of time in deciding precisely what you want to accomplish with your restaurant. Be specific. Think ahead. Avoid flowery words, inexact phrases, and meaningless buzzwords. "I want to own and operate the most profitable hot dog stand at Center and Main Streets" is just fine. Give it some time. Give it some thought. Write it down, live by it, and move on to the next step—developing your business plan.

FSB'S—A THREE-COURSE EXTRAVAGANZA
One part food, one part recreation,
and one part branded merchandise.

FSB is an icon with universal appeal. We want to make the name also synonymous with great food and good times. Nowadays, people want more from their time and money. FSB's will satisfy those needs and provide a competitive edge over other restaurant or entertainment venues.

Mission Highlights The company mission is to create a Disney-like atmosphere appealing to all ages with sports, food, and games as the common denominator—a premier gathering place for sports figures and enthusiasts alike. The company mission is to:

- Provide a high-class sports environment where adults can play and family members can interact with each other.
- Highlight the career of FSB along with other sports heroes. Create a "Wall of Fame" depicting local and national sports figures.
- Be the ultimate event center for all sports activities in the Ark-La-Tex geographic area.
- Provide an area to sell logoed and sports-oriented merchandise.
- Serve great food to ensure repeat business locally and a "must see" atmosphere to attract tourists.
- Position FSB's as the leader in sports viewing and social interaction—the place to see and be seen.
- To grow at a rate of one new location per year.
- To give incentive to original investors for future similar ventures in other locales.

Everyone in the company could easily understand the corporate mission and how their roles contributed to the successful achievement of the company's goals.

Putting Your Mission Statement into Action

Many years ago, Avis Rent-A-Car executives invested six months in developing the company's mission statement. It read, "We want to become the fastest-growing company with the highest profit margin in the business of renting and leasing vehicles without drivers." In business terms, that's positively eloquent. That single sentence clearly defines the business of the company, renting vehicles, and its chief objective, the highest profit margin. An unseen beauty in that statement is that it eliminates spin-off businesses and side ventures from the road map, thus keeping the company focused on its real goals.

As the owner/manager, it is your responsibility to see that the mission statement is carried out every day, in every way, by everybody in the organization.

> As the owner/ manager, it is your responsibility to see that the mission statement is carried out every day.

Using Your Business Plan as a Working Tool

The film *Jerry McGuire* featured a scene in which the Tom Cruise character, a sports agent, was trying to convince a client of his commitment. The client, Cuba Gooding Jr., would not believe him until Jerry kept shouting "Show me the money!" The scene was so popular that the phrase entered the language, and you hear it all the time for all kinds of reasons. Some of those reasons apply to the restaurant business. A business plan is essential to your success because it's a way to shout "show me the money" in two areas:

The plan proves the value of your concept so you can get your financing. The bank or the investors show you the money. There is a corollary. If the plan indicates a very small chance for success, you can regroup and revise your plans rather than going to the bank and have them play "show you the door."

The plan guides your business to success. You get to show the money to the bank, your investors, and your own pocketbook.

Reviewing the Four Elements of a Business Plan

A business plan can be divided into the following financial elements:

- Feasibility study
- Initial budget
- Investors package
- Financials

This is Business Basics 101, and you can find numerous examples of business plans in any number of good books. *Streetwise Small Business Start-Up* is a good place to begin. They will all follow this basic format. A visit to your local library or favorite bookstore is in order. Here we'll just briefly cover the basics and introduce you to that format. Some of this you can do on your own, but it is highly recommended that you consult with your accountant and financial advisors throughout to get help with the more complex matters. Certainly you should get an "all clear" from your accountant on the final version before taking a step further.

Feasibility Study

Chapter 3 helps you conduct a feasibility study, and while you conduct one to help you determine whether your restaurant idea is a good one, you also include it in your business plan.

The Initial Budget

You'll create a budget each year you're in business, of course, but your first will probably be the most critical. Everything will be built or will crash in upon that foundation. It should list all the costs for starting up your restaurant, which are generally broken down in to real (or hard) costs and intangible (or soft) costs, both of which are discussed later in this chapter. *Real costs* refers to building materials and equipment, such as two-by-fours and nails, stoves and refrigerators, tables and chairs, and even knives, spoons, and forks, and so on. *Intangible costs* refers to services such as business consultants, food and beverage advisors, interior designers, marketing professionals, or training personnel, and various fees you'll encounter.

The Investors Package

Again, if you've just hit the Powerball, you probably won't be looking for investors or a loan from the bank. If last night's television viewing didn't have you jumping up and shouting "I won! I won!" then you'll need to develop a financial package to show the money folks. Whether dealing with

Consultants and Advisors

Restaurant managers and owners need all kinds of advice, and it is best to get the best advice possible. Your lawyer and accountant should be chosen at least partly on the basis of previous experience in the restaurant business. That's not so important for many of the other consultants, but experience is a big plus. Ask for references. Discuss the fee structure with every consultant and make sure you understand all possible additional or hidden charges that might pop up. Don't be shy about asking tough questions. "Saving" money by avoiding some consultants may cost you a lot more than the consultation. For example, you could bypass your attorney at some point only to discover later that you lack a certain permit. The biggest event of your grand opening could be the great shutdown.

a bank's loan committee or a group of investors, they will all want to know two things:

- How much money you need
- How they will get their money back

They'll want to know how much money you (and your partners) are willing to put up. If you're not willing to invest your own funds, you might have a rough time convincing someone else to hand over theirs. Keep in mind that your experience, proven track record, resources (a highly recognized chef, for example), your standing in the community, and other factors can count for something, too. Some kind of collateral will be required to secure the loan. You may be required to place your house or some other valuable asset, such as the old family farm, as a personal guarantee of the loan.

Financials

Financials is another term for financial statements, which are covered in depth in Chapter 7.

Estimating Your Intangible (Soft) Costs

Intangible costs are listed first because they include a lot of consultants, and you'll be consulting with a lot of people before you write the first check for rent, paint the first wall, or make your printing order for your first menus. In addition to consulting fees, these costs cover permits, cash on hand, and the pre-opening costs of insurance, advertising, and labor. Let's take a very brief look at these expenses. Again, this is just an overview of the items involved. Your actual evaluations, estimates, and expense sheets will be more detailed.

Insurance

You'll need very good insurance very early on. Accidents don't always happen in a busy kitchen or in a room full of happy customers. The restaurant, you, and any partners will need protection in the event of an accident, injury, theft, or property destruction during construction.

Marketing, Advertising, and PR

Another expense is marketing, advertising, and public relations. You have to let your future customers know about your offering, the theme, style of food, and that you'll be opening soon. Even if you do a lot of the copywriting and designing yourself, you can still run up a substantial promotional budget. Lots of computer programs allow you to design your own advertising materials. Make sure you, or someone working for you, has the skill to make those materials professional in content and appearance. Don't forget the cost of advertising media even if the media is just the neighbor's kid handing out fliers in the mall or shopping center. Budget every item.

Labor

Labor costs begin well before you hire the first employee. You have to invest in the newspaper advertising to attract them, the application forms, your time interviewing prospective employees, and the time and expense of training your staff.

Other costs include building permits, vending permits, liquor licenses, and other fees or taxes applicable to your specific location. Be scrupulous about covering these expenses. A fee not paid or a permit not obtained could result in closing down part or all of your operations until the matter is cleared up.

Cash on Hand

Cash on hand means precisely what it says, a set amount of money you have available during the workday to make sure you keep working all day. Generally, this is the money you'll need to make change for your customers or to cover the cost of additional food and beverage when the tour bus unexpectedly pulls up in your parking lot. It's always a good idea to have some ready cash to handle an emergency. Cash on hand is an often-neglected budget item.

Determining Your Tangible (Real) Costs

Your Restaurant's Space

Real costs are those associated with the day-to-day running of your business.

By far the most expensive item on the list is your restaurant space, which can be a stand-alone facility or an area within or adjacent to another structure, such as a shopping mall, hotel, or resort. One of your first major decisions is between renting space or buying your own.

Buying a space obviously gives the owner the benefits and pride of ownership. More important, you have considerably more control over the property compared to leasing. Purchasing requires a considerable amount of money. The buyer must have deep pockets or access to large sums of money. Many loan committees shy away from restaurants, but if your plan is sound, you should, with persistence, be able to find an organization willing to back your vision. Don't be discouraged and don't give up.

The cost of even a small building can be considerable. Any lending institution will probably want you to make a deposit of at least 20 percent of the purchase price, so you have to come to an understanding of your own definition of *considerable*. Even if you get the loan, you may not be any better off in the long run. A key consideration is the amount of money available for operating capital. If all of the loan is applied to land and the building, can you earn enough capital during your start-up period to stay in business? What if, as is common, building a loyal clientele takes longer than you anticipate? People may not automatically line up outside your door the first day you open. Many folks take a "wait and see" attitude toward a new restaurant before sitting down to open a menu. Once in business, you must have enough operating capital to stay in business until you break even and move from red ink into the black.

A long-term lease is favored by many restaurateurs, especially those who are just starting out. The rule of thumb recommends a basic five-year lease with options for additional five-year periods whenever the lease expires. Leasing property is a sound way to reduce your initial and long-term expenses compared to buying property.

A lease doesn't require the large down payment or the long-term commitment to paying back the loan that you face with buying a building. Keep in mind that *long-term*, like *considerable*, is relative. Should your business fail in your first year and you still have four years on a five-year lease, those four years of payments for an empty building can seem like an eternity. Of course, you can always seek out another business to sublease the property, but there are no guarantees that you'll find that business.

Equipment

What and how much equipment you need depends of course on the nature of your proposed restaurant and menu. The equipment list for Hector's Hot Dogs would be about as minimal as you can get. Things are more complex at the food court, on restaurant row, or over at Ralph's Steaks for Big Crowds Bar and Grill. If you're starting from scratch, your costs will be substantial. If you're renovating an existing restaurant, you may be able to use most or all of what is already in place. In that case, take extra care to ensure that the old equipment is functional and that it can really meet your needs. You won't save anything by keeping equipment that cannot meet the demands you and your customers or the city inspectors will place on it.

Here's an important tip about used equipment. Your customers really don't care and probably never think about whether you're using new or used equipment—*unless they can see it*. If your design incorporates a kitchen open or partly open to the public, make sure your equipment looks new even if it isn't.

Construction Costs

Whether you're building a new facility, renovating an existing one (lease or purchase), or moving into a leased space, you will need at least some construction.

Unless you have considerable on-the-job experience in construction and the time to supervise a complex and specialized process, you should consider hiring a general contractor to handle your construction chores. A contractor will certainly cost more than a do-it-yourself approach, but he or she will more than likely make up that difference in efficiency, quality of construction, experience in the business, and possibly in lower costs for materials and supplies.

Your attorney should review any construction contracts. The contract should have a firm completion date. It should state that the work will be done to your satisfaction and that it will meet all applicable codes and requirements.

Pricing a Kitchen

The average cost to equip a kitchen at restaurants such as Applebee's, Chili's, Outback Steakhouse, etc. is approximately $125,000 to $150,000 as of the date we're writing this book. If you shop around for quality used equipment, you can save thousands and could even cut your equipment costs in half.

Excellent sources for information, pricing, and sources for new and used restaurant equipment are found in many of the food and beverage industry trade journals. Read up, ask around, and get referrals on your major purchases. If you're looking for all-new equipment, call the headquarters of the manufacturer and get the address of your nearest distributor. Arrange for a sales call and demonstrations.

Evaluate every piece of equipment carefully as to your real need. Purchasing or leasing equipment is another important decision. Only you can decide what works best for your concept, and you will have to live with that decision. If you believe that you will have a steady cash flow and good profits, purchasing is a good route. If you are concerned about cash flow and possible limited capital, leasing may be a wiser course. There are many leasing companies that can provide individual equipment items and even complete packages. Some companies can even provide cash registers and POS (point of sale) systems. Smaller, less costly items such as stoves or refrigerators may save you money up front. However, when you're finally operating, the slowdown in production, longer waiting times, and the inevitable customer dissatisfaction may devour those "savings" and more.

You'll need to order small wares, such as china, glassware, flatware, tables, chairs, bar stools, and other supplies. How much of what? (We'll discuss that in detail later.) You should be in pretty good shape if you order one and a half to two times the amount of silverware as you have seats. Obviously, you'll need to order food and beverage. What many first-timers forget, however, is to order enough food and beverage for the shake-down period to train the staff. A week's worth should meet the training needs of most operations.

Chapter 7

Understanding Financial Statements

Part One

Part Two

Part Three

Part Four

Part Five

Part Six

PART TWO FINANCING, TIMING, AND DESIGNING YOUR NEW RESTAURANT

■ CHAPTER 6 Developing a Mission Statement, Business Plan, and Initial Budget ■ CHAPTER 7 Understanding Financial Statements ■ CHAPTER 8 Establishing a Time Line for Your Opening ■ CHAPTER 9 Determining a Location ■ CHAPTER 10 Designing Your Space

Reviewing the Various Financial Statements

Financials are the various forms or spread sheets that present financial "pictures" of your operations. The three that are most standard are:

- Income statement
- Balance sheet
- Cash-flow analysis

All three are discussed in this chapter.

The Income Statement

Sometimes called a "P&L" (profit and loss statement), the income statement is considered the most important financial document a restaurant owner or manager will draft. It details income and expenses, which tells you whether you're making a profit, holding your own, or losing ground.

Talk to people. Look up the restaurant association Web site. Visit your mentor. Do whatever is necessary to get the most accurate figures possible. Combine all of these figures to get your estimated weekly cost of labor. Multiply by the number of weeks you'll be open to arrive at the estimate for the entire year. Use percentages in your Microsoft Excel worksheet. When you adjust your income, the variable portion of your labor will automatically adjust.

The income statement contains the following sections.

Income

The income section of the income statement requires you to estimate income (or revenue). Estimating revenue requires that you come up with a figure representing your "average check." That's easy for a restaurant that's been in business a while.

If you have yet to open, it's a bit more complex. Basically you multiply your average check figure by the number of patrons you plan to serve. This matter can get a bit complex, and it is recommended that you run the numbers with your accountant or someone with a lot of financial experience in the restaurant business.

Food and Beverage Costs

Also known as the "cost of goods sold" section of your income statement. It follows the income section. Get an idea of the average cost of your menu. Cost out as much of the menu as you can. List all ingredients. Determine how much of each ingredient you'll need to create one portion. Determine the cost of that portion. Document all this—you'll need it later. Get together with your food and beverage suppliers—they can help you do this. Price your menu at the level that you think your target market will be willing to pay. The cost of a portion divided into the price for that item is your cost percentage.

Some cost percentages will be high. Some will be low. You need to estimate what you feel the sum of all these highs and lows will be. Are you preparing Mexican food, for which there are a lot of lows, or seafood, for which there are a lot of highs? Your expense for ketchup in a sports bar featuring burgers and fries will be significantly more than that of an upscale French restaurant. Review and determine what you think your food costs will be. About 32 percent is a reasonable figure.

Bar costs are easier to estimate. Break it down into liquor, bottle domestic beer, bottle import beer, draft beer, bottle wine, and glass wine (listed as house wine). If you give your vendors an idea of what you will be charging and what you'll be carrying, they can probably give you a pretty close estimate of your cost percentage.

> Price your menu at the level that you think your target market will be willing to pay.

Labor Costs

You will have both fixed (salaried) and variable (hourly) labor costs. It's fairly easy to compute a rough estimate of your yearly cost of labor. Here's how you do it. You'll start by creating a weekly figure. First, you already know the number of people working on a salary and the amount of those salaries. Write those down. Next, note down the number of hourly wage jobs in your restaurant. Estimate the number of hours each will work and multiply times the hourly rate you'll pay. Factor in different hourly rates you know you'll be paying for the same jobs. For example, Bartender Midge might be an old hand at the business and can bring her own loyal clientele, a substantial boost to lounge revenue. Bartender Joe might be just starting out and could be earning a much lower figure. The same can be said for your chefs, waitresses, and other help.

Add salaried figures with the hourly figures to get a fairly accurate weekly estimate. Will you be open fifty-two weeks a year, or will you be closed for vacation, the off-season, during the snowed-in winter months, the annual hurricane, or for some other reason? Factor that in. Now add in the employee benefits you are required to pay, such as social security (7.65 percent as of 2002), state unemployment tax (varies from state to state and depends on your experience rating), federal unemployment tax (.008), and workers' compensation insurance (restaurant associations will sometimes have great deals on workers' comp; check on it). You may also want to provide your employees with benefits on your own, so add those costs in also.

You need to be able to estimate the number of wait staff, bussers, and kitchen help you will need according to the number of tables you have and the type of service you offer (fast food, casual, high class, etc.).

Fixed Expenses

Fixed expenses are pretty much set. They may vary a little (and when they do, they're called semivariable), but will normally be set. Most general and administrative costs are fixed.

Marketing Expenses

Marketing expenses aimed at the factory workers within a half-mile of your sports bar could consist of little more than small ads in a community newspaper, weekly special fliers, and a hand-lettered menu in the window. This will be quite different from the French restaurant that has to compete in the city's expensive four-color magazines. Production costs of your advertising materials can vary widely, too. Creating a four-color ad is an involved and expensive process. A lot of restaurant owners produce their fliers with a desktop publishing program on their office computer.

These are probably your easiest costs to figure because they are, obviously, fixed. They include:

- Property taxes
- Lease payments
- Mortgage payments
- Municipal expenses (garbage collection fees, greenbelt fees, etc.)
- Depreciation
- Amortization
- Equipment rental/purchase
- Start-up costs

Taxes and Other Items

Figure your income tax by estimating your restaurant's yearly revenue. Subtract all your expenses from the other categories. Apply your income tax rate to this figure to estimate the amount of tax you will owe.

Other items include such things as interest expense, depreciation, and amortization. This is a wide-open category depending upon many factors such as location, target audience, amenities, and so on. Whatever style of restaurant, its location, and market, you will have "other items" on your expense form. Don't neglect this category, because the total could be substantial.

Profit

Profit is income minus expenses. The easiest way to get started is to use a spreadsheet program such as Microsoft Excel. If you don't know it—learn it. You can't live without it. First, remember that cost of goods sold, labor, and variable costs will all be based on percentages. You will live and breathe percentage.

This is the "magic number" that everyone is most interested in determining. Subtract all expenses, including income tax, from your revenue to figure your (hoped-for) profit. If the figure looks sound, then you can feel relatively comfortable in proceeding with your plans. "Relatively" is an important word, because much of your calculation will have been based on estimates. If the figure alarms you, go back through your estimates and figures to see if there is a way to reduce expenses without taking the heart and soul out of your plans. This phase is why the restaurant term "cutting down to the bone" has so caught on with the public. This is also where your Excel worksheet is extremely valuable. If set up correctly, you should be able to play the "What if" game. "If I reduce this, what will happen to my profit line?"

Break-Even Analysis

A break-even analysis is a bit tricky to estimate because there are so many variables involved, but it is an essential part of your plan, and you must make the effort to slug your way through it. The purpose is to determine if you can make enough money to cover your expenses.

You'll use two types of expenses: fixed and variable. Your estimate will inevitably be rough because of a couple of hard realities. First, it has to assume that your business will remain stable. This may be true, but economies have their ups and downs, which have tremendous effects on local businesses. Second, it depends upon fixed expenses remaining fixed, and that's not always the case. Food prices go up. Taxes get raised. A healthy economy may require increased wages to hold onto good employees. That street construction blocking your parking lot may require doubling or tripling your advertising budget just to let customers know you're still in business. Success and an increasing customer base also means an increase in food, beverage, and other supplies.

For these reasons, you should work out your break-even analysis with your accountant or a financial advisor who understands the restaurant business. This is such an important calculation, it should be done only with the help of experienced professionals. To get an idea of your break-even, first estimate your sales—take your total mixed expenses. Then add your cost of goods sold percentage plus labor cost percentage plus your variable cost percentage. Here's the formula for determining your break-even point.

Fixed costs ÷ 100 − (COG% + labor% + variable cost%)

Example: Fixed costs = $100.00

Variable costs = 10%

Labor costs = 10%

COG = 28%

$100.00 ÷ (100% − 48%) = $100.00 ÷ .52 = $192.31.
This is your break-even point: $192.31 in sales.

Sales = 192.31

Minus: COG Sold = 53.85 (28% of sales)

Labor Costs = 19.23 (10% of sales)

Variable Costs = 19.23 (10% of sales)

Fixed Costs = 100.00

Profit = 0

Balance Sheet

A balance sheet is like a piece of cake—a small slice that is representative of the whole thing. It gives you a picture of your financial status at any given moment and is a valuable working tool. You will find it extremely useful, as will your accountant, bookkeeper, banker, financial advisors, and investors. The process is simple, involving only listing items and using basic addition and subtraction. You will be comparing your assets, or what you own, against your liabilities, or what you owe to others. The difference between the two will provide your net worth, sometimes called "owner's equity." Keep in mind you're only looking at a small piece of the long-term picture. June's balance sheet might be considerably different from the January calculation.

A balance sheet gives you a picture of your financial status at any given moment and is a valuable working tool.

You may figure your balance sheet for today or use it to estimate projections into the next quarter or for the end of the year or even further into the future. You don't have to be obsessive about this and invest an hour every day in preparing a balance sheet. Some companies only do one a year. It's a valuable working tool and, as a small slice of the whole, can help make managing your operations the proverbial "piece of cake."

Cash-Flow Analysis

That's the idea, after all, for cash to flow, right? A cash-flow analysis will give you a good idea whether the current is swift, sluggish, or stagnant. In other words, the document will let you know if you can pay your current bills. How much cash (including credit card items) is coming in? How much cash is going out? Is there anything left over? This document is one of your most useful, helping you keep expenses in perspective and locate problems or potential problems in time to correct them.

Quick Asset Ratio

The quick asset ratio isn't really a part of the financial statements, but it is a very effective tool for analysis. It compares your current assets to your current liabilities. Current assets are considered liquid assets. That is, they can be sold (liquidated) within a given year. Your inventory and cash in the bank are examples. Short-term liabilities are your expenses that must be paid within the year, such as your accounts payable. The more favorable your current assets are to your current liabilities, the better you'll look to prospective investors or financial lending institutions and the more favorable their response to your financial needs is likely to be.

Financial Resources

Let's see, there's finding that Lost Dutchman's mine. There's winning the Powerball. And then there's the inheritance from good old Uncle Joe. Right? If you fit into one of the above categories, you can skip the rest of the chapter. If you're like most people in the restaurant business, you'll need to get at least some of your financing from other sources.

Home Equity Loans

First look close to home. In fact, look right at home. As you know, the longer you live in and make payments on your home, the more equity you build. Equity is simply the value of your home minus any liens against it. If your house is worth $100,000 and you owe only $50,000 on the mortgage, then your equity is $50,000.

Banks and local lending institutions are often quite open to making home equity loans. It's a win/win situation for the bank. If the business proposition succeeds, they get their money back. If the business fails, they get your house. You will be risking your own capital. Lending institutions are famous for being reluctant to loan money for opening a restaurant because of the failure rate. Don't try to slip by a "fast one" on the bank by stating another reason for the loan. That's called bank fraud, and the consequences can be extreme. State the real reason for the loan. There's no reason to hesitate. The bank isn't investing in anything. Even though the loan is processed through the lending institution, you'll be financing the business with your own money.

Loans from Friends and Family

If your equity isn't enough or if you're a renter with no equity at all, consider tapping into the resource of family and friends. Also consider acquaintances who might be willing to listen to a good proposal.

Make no mistake about it. Getting money from people you know on a personal basis can be a perilous adventure. Keep in mind that the real-world definition of adventure is "what happens when things go wrong." Cave-ins, fires, floods, open warfare, and running from Grizzly bears come to mind. The key is to treat this business as business. Approach the people exactly as you would approach a bank or savings and loan. Prepare your documents professionally and in detail. Put together a complete financial loan package. Practice your presentation. Try to anticipate all possible tough questions and be ready with confident answers, even if some of them are "I don't know" or "I'll find out." Don't depend on personal relationships to ease you over the tough spots. You shouldn't try that anyway. Your family and friends deserve the same consideration you'd give a bunch of strangers down at the bank.

Quick Tips on Making a Presentation

The market for your restaurant may be young, trendy people sporting spiked hair, and you may even be wise to adopt that style at work. Dress that way for a loan presentation and the only thing that will be spiked is your loan.

Speak English. And keep it simple. Don't try to "speak on their level" by using jargon and terms with which you aren't familiar.

Create excitement. Don't jump up and down, wave your arms, and raise your voice. Let them hear the confidence and the joy in your voice.

Stick to the basics. "This is how much I need. Here's how I'd like to pay it back. . ." Back up your statements with solid documentation. Be yourself.

Never give up. Learn from your experiences and move on.

Put Everything in Writing

Even if urged for a "hand-shake" agreement, insist on correct paperwork. Involve your lawyer and your accountant. Suggest that the others have their lawyers and accountants look over the documents, too. A few months down the road you don't want to be playing a game of financial "he said/she said."

Be sure that your loan agreements and contracts are specific as to everyone's rights. Be just as specific as to the limits on your investors. People who put money into a project often want to get involved to "protect my investment." Many a restaurant has been protected to death by the involvement of investors who know little or nothing about the business. Let everyone know that you'll be making regular reports and that all investors will receive their proper documentation on time.

Loans from Banks and Lending Institutions

Banks are often reluctant to get involved in financing restaurants. Don't give up. Banks do make restaurant loans. You just have to find the right one. The loan committee will be looking at a lot of factors of varying importance, but two are overriding concerns:

- Can you pay the principal?
- Can you pay the interest?

If they are not comfortable with the answers to those questions, you'll be saying "thanks for your time" and moving on.

Some of the other factors they'll scrutinize include:

- What you can put up as collateral to secure the loan
- Your personal commitment to the project (full-time/part-time)
- Your financial commitment to the project, including the amount of your own money that you're investing
- The value of your intangibles, such as the chef's reputation and following
- Your relationship to those intangibles, such as a long-term contract with that chef
- Your expertise in the restaurant business
- Your business expertise in general
- Your partners or investors
- Your ties to the local community
- Your profit potential
- Your ability to weather the changes of the economy
- Their personal impressions of your as a person, including your confidence and honesty

The criteria for making a loan can vary considerably from bank to bank. A loan committee at one institution may be open and friendly while the committee across the street may make applicants jump through all kinds of hoops. The best policy is to hope for the best, but be prepared for the worst experience. As with approaching family and friends, have all of your documents complete, detailed, up-to-date, and looking professional. Know the answers to the hard questions and be prepared to answer them confidently.

Don't let someone's aloofness, disinterest, or even hostility throw you. Some people are like that, but others practice role-playing just to see how the loan applicant acts under pressure. Keep your cool and maintain a professional demeanor regardless of someone's apparent attitude.

Small Business Administration Loans

The Small Business Administration (SBA) is an agency of the federal government. Its purpose is to encourage small business by offering low-interest loans to qualifying applicants. Technically, the SBA doesn't make loans directly.

Two of the most popular SBA programs are the 7(a) and the 504 Certified Development Company (CDC) loan program. Funds from a 7(a) loan can be invested for practically any sound business reason. Loans are available at market rates for periods of seven to eight years. A 504 CDC loan can only be used for major fixed assets, such as property or major equipment. The loans are offered long-term and at fixed rates. The SBA made nearly 44,000 7(a) loans totalling $10.5 billion during fiscal year 2000, according to *Restaurant USA*. The 504 CDC program made more than 4,500 loans for a total of $1.8 billion during the same period. The agency guarantees up to 90 percent of a bank loan to a small business. Their programs are targeted to businessmen and businesswomen who cannot get reasonable financing through traditional banking or lending institutions.

You can contact the SBA directly for information. Your local lending institutions are very familiar with agency programs and policies and can help you explore that option.

Big Money Is Available for Big Dreams

Traditionally, lending institutions have been less than enthusiastic about making loans to restaurants, especially large loans for major expenditures. That trend is not absolute. The $190-million deal by Metromedia Restaurant Group to refinance its S&A Corp. is an example.

S&A operates the Bennigan's and Steak and Ale chains and plans to expand both. Additionally, the corporation will create new prototype restaurants, revitalize their public images, and expand the franchise program.

So big money is available to finance big concepts. That doesn't mean it will be easy. The financial community looks at each approach with care and caution. Owners will have to have earned outstanding credit, a favorable debt-to-income ratio, financial stability, a good sales/operational costs ratio, a marketable concept, and a proven track record, according to *Restaurant Hospitality*.

Chapter 8

Establishing a Time Line for Your Opening

Part One

Part Two

Part Three

Part Four

Part Five

Part Six

Committing Six Months to One Year to Development

Six months seems a bit short, but it has been done. We recommend a time line that begins one year before your grand opening. You've already received specific guidelines on many of your earliest activities. Visiting with the local restaurant association or the chamber of commerce are two examples. Conducting a feasibility study, developing your business plan, and approaching lending institutions are other considerations you'll want to handle early on. We won't repeat that information here. Instead, we'll touch on a few other considerations that may not seem quite as important but that you shouldn't neglect.

Creating a Time Line or Critical Path

Don't commit everything to memory. A lot of information needs to take solid form. Time lines are a perfect example. A time line is something like a calendar of events targeted at getting you to your grand opening without forgetting some essential element—like paving the parking lot, getting your permits approved, or ordering pizza sauce. Here are four different time lines actually used in some of Randy's operations: a new restaurant opening check list, a 120-day opening flow chart, a one-week opening plan, a bar opening plan. Feel free to use and adapt these to meet your own time line needs.

Reviewing What It Takes to Open Your Restaurant

Six Months Prior to Opening

First, choose business advisors, including an accountant, attorney, banker, and insurance agent.

Then, prepare your restaurant business plan.

- Decide which type to open (pizzeria, continental, family, etc.)
- Consider several potential locations
- Begin to think about staffing
- Start talent search for management
- Develop menu ideas
- Create a summary of your operations
- Complete a market analysis of customers and competition, marketing, pricing, etc.
- Run your financial statements
- Project your total funds needed

Present your completed business plan to lending resources.

You also need to determine the type of business organization you intend to operate—sole proprietorship, partnership, corporation—and choose your business trade name. Before settling on a business name, verify that the name is available at the city clerk/business licensed office. Contact your Secretary of State if you're creating a corporation.

Four Months Prior to Opening

Four months prior to opening, select your location, contact the health department for building requirements, contact the planning/building codes department for building requirements, and contact the fire marshal's office for building requirements. The fire marshal will look at occupancy loads and requirements for exhaust hoods and sprinkler systems.

If you need to make improvements, you may also need to contact an architect to draw floor plans for building improvements. After you've decided what improvements need to be made, get three estimates. If you're leasing, negotiate favorable lease terms.

You'll also want to start looking for the right people for your business, especially a general manager.

Three Months Prior to Opening

Three months prior to opening, you have some specific tasks before you such as the following.

> Before settling on a business name, verify that the name is available at the city clerk/ business licensed office.

- Sign your lease
- Open your bank accounts, including a commercial account and payroll account
- Order checks and deposit slips and ask for drop bags and night drop keys
- Apply for merchant account/Visa/MasterCard
- Contact utility companies: electric, gas, water, telephone (and cable, if applicable)
- Buy phones and install telephone system
- Acquire building permits
- Begin construction on improvements, if needed

You'll also want to begin brainstorming menu and food ideas: Determining your product to be sold, food costs so that you can price the menus, and a style; writing menu copy; selecting artwork; laying out the menu and making corrections; and proofreading the menu.

You'll also begin determining what smallwares you'll need, especially those that aren't standard items to order.

Hire a general manager and allow him or her to review plans and progress of all areas. Also, begin targeting an opening date and decide on an accounting and cost system.

Two Months Prior to Opening

Two months before your opening, you'll begin to contact restaurant equipment dealers and order restaurant equipment:

- Food prep and cooking equipment
- Cooler/freezer
- Booths, tables, and chairs
- Restaurant smallwares

Begin selecting the rest of your employees and begin training. At this point, you'll want to hone in on your exact opening date, begin planning for your opening advertisement, review your cash register system options, think about customer flow in the restaurant, and alert the heath department of your opening date.

Six Weeks Prior to Opening

Six weeks prior to opening, you'll want to review the layout of the menu, revise it as needed, and determine the quantity to be printed.

You'll also need to confirm which suppliers and vendors you'll be using and open your supplier/vendor accounts, if necessary.

Finally, check the progress on your equipment and add any smallwares you may still need. Also, plan preview parties and invite local media members.

One Month Prior to Opening

One more before the big day, apply for all required tax numbers, including a federal employer ID number (Internal Revenue Service form SS-4), state employer ID number (Department of Employment Security), and state and local sales tax license (Department of Revenue).

You'll also want to apply for all additional business licenses and permits you may need, including a city/county business license, beverage license, and health permit. Now is also a good time to contact your state restaurant association and apply for membership.

Work with your insurance agent to begin coverage for workers' compensation, general liability, product liability, fire and theft, and group health insurance.

If your uniforms, aprons, or caps will require imprinting, order these now. This is also the time to print your menus.

Work with your crew to create written procedures on nonstandard food/specification sheets and brainstorm menu abbreviations and ticket writing. Determine how tickets will flow from the wait staff to the chefs.

Check the status and ship dates of all remaining equipment (know location/status of everything!) and resolve remaining unknowns.

Comment Cards and Mystery Shoppers

Use comment cards, but read them objectively. Your "complaint" could actually be the result of a fight with a spouse, the boss, or a coworker. The complainer is just taking it out on you. When you get a negative comment card, do whatever you can to turn that negative into a positive. Call up the individual. Express your concern and do your best to make that person happy. Complimentary meals are very inexpensive compared to negative word of mouth.

You can also hire a mystery shopper to check out your food and your service (see Chapter 16 for more on mystery shoppers). This is an excellent way to discover problems. It's also a great way to discover things that are going right. Often this research will reveal loyal, hardworking employees in need of some recognition.

Team Meetings

A smart owner will conduct a weekly meeting with his or her management staff. This is an opportunity for an operation analysis. Use a mini-income statement that includes:

- Sales
- Costs of goods sold
- Labor costs

Cover all these areas in detail, pointing out successes and failures (for more on income statements, see Chapter 7). Suggest solutions to problems and ask for solutions, comments, and ideas from your managers. It's your show. Run it as you see fit, but it's a good idea to seek input from the people who are out there "on the lines" every day.

Meet with the rest of the staff at least once a month. Discuss all the issues you have, pro and con. Ask for comments and suggestions on any problem areas.

Begin selecting and training any remaining staff opening. Determine (tentatively) who will work the opening day. Do phantom hourly labor schedules and write an employee policies/procedures book. Determine who will be doing what training during the pre-opening sessions

Three Weeks Prior to Opening

By now, you should contact food vendors and discuss inventory requirements for produce, dairy, coffee, and soft drinks. Contact a linen company and hire an exterminator. Order china and flatware, contact a dish machine company, and order your cash registers. Buy office supplies and set up the office.

Continue advertising and interviewing for staff as needed. Place a "Now Hiring" sign in the window.

Order your imprinted materials, such as menus, guest checks, napkins, paper cups, and takeout items, letterhead, envelopes, business cards, and fliers.

Two Weeks Prior to Opening

Now is the time to begin your pre-opening advertising. Finalize your hiring for new staff and schedule training dates. Place your initial food order for training, seeing that the restaurant is completely set up before new staff training begins.

Ensure that all equipment is in place, hooked up, and operational. Operate the equipment as much as possible to break it in. Get final building inspections, health approval, and permits.

Order all smallwares and glass for tabletops. Unpack and wash all your smallwares and ensure that they aren't damaged or broken.

Make sure your food arrives and is tracked as inventory. Finalize your recipes and review all restaurant specifications and procedures.

Managers and openers need to agree on duties and chain of command. Conduct pre-opening training, keeping an eye out for possible leaders and supervisors.

Planning Your Opening: The Week Before

As opening day approaches, some restaurateurs come to think that the apocalypse can't be far behind. Unexpected disasters may come in from left field. Even the simplest of matters can turn into problems of unbelievable proportions. Again, having your schedule or time line in a convenient place can help you avoid, solve, or knock those problems way back out there in left field where they belong. Let's look at a time line/check list for the Sunday-to-Sunday prior to opening day.

Notice that not only does the time line include training sessions, but also allows time to correct any problems discovered during the training and shake-out phase just before opening.

Sunday

Menu/Food/Smallwares:
___Equipment operational
___Dispensing systems installed and operational
___All fixtures and décor finished
___Music system in and working
___Waitress/service areas complete
___Phone system installed and working
___Rail system installed
___Plumbing, HVAC, and electrical complete
___Smallwares checked in, washed, and stocked
___*All* food in—local and specialty
___*All* specifications and procedures finalized and posted
___Menus and guest checks in unit
___Cash register set up and in unit

People/Training/Miscellaneous:

___Commitment to opening date

___Openers arrive, meet w/management and check off items on this date

___Crew hired and training and bake-off schedules posted

___Management and openers agree on duties and chain of command

___Review plans for training and bake-off

___Management ready to train service employees

___Ticket/cash flow finalized

___Kitchen storage set up

___Miscellaneous operations supplies checked in

___Bank procedures and credit card sales set

___Advertising—commit to opening ads and programs

___Building inspections passed

___Licenses secured and posted

___Health codes met

___In-store office materials in place

___Prioritize items as critical to opening

___7 P.M.—Employee orientation meeting

___Introduction of management and openers

___Policies and procedures set in writing

___Paydays and break policies established

___Uniforms and dress code established

___Parking situation settled

___Training and bake-off schedules

___Kitchen training begins (10 A.M. day and 6 P.M. night)

___Organize materials/area for training

___Tour restaurant

___Utensils/equipment identification and use signs posted

___Dry storage/walk-in/freezer functioning

___Menu/abbreviations/ticket reading and flow

___Questions and answers with staff

Monday

___Organize materials/areas for training
___Have storage organized
___Know where *everything* is
___Countdown list (review everything left to be done)
___Management creates work schedules for opening week
___Review kitchen countdown and do your own

Tuesday

___Prepare for training
___Countdown list
___Review systems with coordinator
___Review sections
___Plan set-up of stations and salad bar
___Management
___Review kitchen training progress
___Review countdown list and complete it
___Plan for bake-off
___Review staffing systems
___Instruct employees
___Review menu/abbreviations/ticket writing and flow
___Smallwares and service items identification and use
___Customer service
___Questions and answers

Wednesday

___Prepare for training sessions
___Plan for bake-off preparation
___Service training
___Prepare for training sessions
___Plan for table set-up
___Countdown list

Create A Scheduling Grid

A great visual tool for controlling allocation of labor resources and labor costs is a scheduling grid. Draw a grid (a regular series of equal-sized boxes) on a sheet of paper with one block for each one-half hour open and one row for each employee. Color in the blocks of time you will assign to each person, using a different color for each type of job. This will give you a good picture at a glance of who is doing what. Never hesitate to adjust your scheduling grid. Keep an eye on the floor. If traffic drops off for an appreciable period of time, let one or more employees take the day or evening off. There's no reason to pay for employees who are not working. Your employees must clock out properly. Always have management initial their time cards.

___Management (service training)

___Do countdown lists

___Prepare for hostess/cashier training

___Instruct cook staff in food preparation procedures

___Test and review

___Table numbers/section/call lights mapped out

___Waitress stations/beverage making stations set up

___Salad bar set-up/opening duties/closing duties

Thursday

___Prepare for training

___All needed products and items in

___Systems reviewed and final check

___Bake-off personal placements

___Preparation for bake-off finalized and done

___Prepare for training

___List all needed items

___Systems reviewed and final

___Countdown list

___Bake-off plan set

___Products to be served at bake-off selected

___Food order completed

Friday

___Structured training bake-offs, noon to 2 P.M.

___Dinner 7 to 9 P.M.

Saturday

___Decide what to do about what went wrong during the bake-off

___Restaurant clean

___VIP cocktail party

Sunday

___More training if needed

___Positions set for opening

___All kitchen and service preparation completed

Bar Opening Plan

Here is an example of the plan for the bar operations the week prior to opening.

Sunday: Beverage dispenser installed and working, draft beer system installed and working, sinks operational, bar coolers operational, glassware in store, consumables in store (especially bar mixes), fruit either in store or ordered, cash registers installed.

Monday: Bar mix recipe instructions written and posted, glassware and bar smallwares identification instructions established, glassware and bar small-wares cleaning and storage instructions established, nonperishable bar consumables issued and stored.

Tuesday: Basic drink recipes written up for highballs, rocks, and simple cocktails; fruit cutting instruction and practice; basic prices structured; service concept discussed.

Wednesday: More basic drink recipes written for cocktails, exotics, cream specials. Cash control instructions.

Thursday: Bar mixes made, most fruit cut, call orders discussed, coordination and cooperation between bartenders and waitresses discussed, check-out procedures discussed, charge card procedures discussed, bar and C/W tests completed, glassware and bar issues washed and stored.

Friday: Bar fully operational; bar stocked and staffed by 11 A.M.; lunch bake-off from noon to 2 P.M.; bar cleaned, restocked, and operational by 6 P.M.; practice check-out procedures reviewed..

Saturday: Bake-off reviewed; procedures and service improved; bar cleaned, stocked, staffed, and operational by 7 P.M.; VIP party; bar properly cleaned and restocked at closing.

Sunday: Additional training (if necessary); bar completely clean, stocked, and organized.

Determining When You Need Capital Injections

How much money do you need and when do you need it? Only you can answer these questions with accuracy. The preceding time lines should be of considerable help in determining when certain expenses will have to be met. Knowing that, you can backtrack days, weeks, or months to determine when you will need to acquire that money. Use these time lines as a guide, but adapt them to meet your needs, the needs of your market, and the needs of your lending institution.

Visit your banker early to find out the average length of time required to grant a loan application. Money is like inventory. It does you no good back there in the pantry or the freezer. It only has value when put to work. You don't want too much inventory too early, which would put you in the position of paying interest on capital you aren't using. Still, like inventory, when you need it, you need it right away. Scheduling capital injections properly is a valuable timing skill. Industry often adopts an inventory process called J-I-T, or Just In Time, delivery of raw product, materials, and supplies. The idea is to get the needed material as close to the actual time it is needed as possible and not a day later or a day sooner. Money is an essential raw material in business. J-I-T is a good policy for restaurant operations, too. Just make sure to make the "in time" part of the equation.

Sequencing Critical Commitments

Just as in determining the timing of your capital injections, the sequencing of critical commitments from your suppliers is determined in part by your needs, the needs of the restaurant, the needs of your financial lenders and materials suppliers, and the dictates of your market. Again, the time lines presented in this chapter will help in scheduling all of your tasks. Do not, however, depend solely on them. Examine and study each item carefully. Analyze its place in the overall sequence of events and determine if any adjustments need to be made for your specific situation. Then adjust accordingly.

Once you make a change in one area, go through the entire time line again to see if or how that change will affect other items. For example, suppose you come upon a great deal on kitchen equipment earlier than you'd planned on making that purchase. If in the long run the purchase will save you considerable capital and make your operations more efficient, you might have to move up your timetable on acquiring financing from your lender. The savings may make the early expense well worthwhile, but it could also bring up other issues such as earlier payments on interest, storage costs during construction, or additional insurance to cover the equipment while in storage. Everything affects everything else. Use your time lines to help follow the cause and effect ramifications of each decision.

Monitoring Customer Acceptance

A key element of monitoring customer acceptance is the use of your own two eyes. If there are no customers, then you're not being accepted. To discover whether the problem is a temporary aberration or a long-term trend, examine your sales. If they decrease over time, you have a problem on your hands.

Talk to your customers. Investigate firsthand to see if any problems are causing a drop in patronage. A good technique to get objective answers is to approach customers outside of your building as they are leaving. Be very specific: Did you enjoy the quality of your meal? How were you treated by your waiter or waitress? Did you enjoy your experience here? Did you enjoy the pinto beans or would you prefer to have black beans? Would you like a choice?

Chapter 9

Determining a Location

Part One

Part Two

Part Three

Part Four

Part Five

Part Six

Site Selection Is a Balancing Act

A good location is important for most businesses. It's an essential factor for success in the restaurant business. Some of your most profitable time invested in research will be in finding the best possible location. Neglect or treat this aspect lightly, and in a surprisingly short amount of time after you open, the neighbors will be saying, "I wonder what happened to that little restaurant on the corner?"

Selecting a location puts you center stage in a balancing act. You have to balance many factors. Price isn't the only concern, and it may not even be the most important consideration. Key factors are:

- Price
- Traffic
- Visibility
- Accessibility
- Lease/purchase terms
- Duration of lease
- Size/expansion options
- Image of the neighborhood
- Safety and security
- Potential evolution of the neighborhood

All of the factors have to be weighed against each other. For example, a walk-up restaurant may seem unique, and the price of a second-floor space may be attractive. On the other hand, there's a reason second-floor restaurants are unique. Traditionally, they draw less traffic. A great leasing rate on a great property in a terrible neighborhood probably won't be such a great deal in the long run. An intimate "linen tablecloth" restaurant featuring continental cuisine will have a tough time moving curly fried *pomme de terre* in an industrial area that shuts down at the end of the day. A lot of traffic is of little value if it cannot exit and find its way to your parking lot or if no one can see your sign or storefront. Location is a matter to investigate and research from the beginning of your efforts, because without a good location, you won't have much of a beginning.

Key Questions on Location

You'll need to find the answers to all kinds of questions about your proposed locations. Many of them will be site-specific, but this list should give you a good start and point you in the right direction for additional topics. Consider the following as a list of basics. Add your own list of questions to address topics specific to your situation:

- What are the advantages of a stand-alone versus locating in a restaurant row?
- Who else, other than realtors, can be consulted on location matters?
- How much will we depend on walk-in traffic and how much on a loyal, local clientele?
- Which realtors/brokers have restaurant experience?
- Does the selected location match the image and client base of my restaurant?
- What support can be obtained from local business organizations and trade groups?
- Where and how serious is the competition?
- Are there construction/remodeling permits issued for other restaurants in the chosen area?
- What are the logical reasons for competitors to have chosen their locations?
- What is the cost of the trade-off I'm making (image versus low rent, etc.)?
- How much will it cost to overcome that trade-off?
- Is that cost affordable?
- Can the customers get there easily?
- Are there other attractions nearby that will draw traffic?
- Have I contacted all my consultants as needed (accountant, attorney, psychologist, psychic, etc.)?
- What have I forgotten to check out?

Moving a Little Bit of the Country to Town

A lot of urban diners enjoy home cooking and will become loyal patrons of the establishment that can provide it. If this concept appeals to you, here are a few guidelines to making the dining a real "down home" experience.

Find a location that has a "country" feel. There are places even in the largest cities that provide this.

Make an effort to show every customer personal attention so that they feel welcome and unrushed. Instill this attitude in all your employees.

Be kid-friendly. Family values are a hallmark of the "down home" lifestyle, and people will want to dine out with kids, grandkids, and friends.

Most important, make sure your cooking, the quality of food, and its presentation measure up to your customers' expectations. You can't give less than your best just because they're "city folk."

You Can Find Big Profits in Small Cities

Some of Randy's earliest experiences in the restaurant business were with the Pizza Hut organization. He learned valuable lessons about sites, site planning, and site selection during his tenure.

First, consider that Pizza Hut is the largest pizza chain on Earth, operating 12,000 restaurants, delivery-takeout units, and kiosks, such as you'd find in malls or convenience stores.

Randy notes that when he worked for the company, the units located in small towns and with the smallest population base had the highest volume of sales. The reason, according to Pizza Hut's Web site, is basic to selecting a location—no competition.

Urban versus Suburban Locations

A major consideration is the choice between locating in an urban center or somewhere out in the suburbs. You'll find plenty of advantages and disadvantages in each. How you balance those depends on your individual desires and goals.

In a City, Take Advantage of the Work Week

Downtown has a large population base from which to draw. However, even in cities that are up and running 24/7, that base declines rapidly after the close of the business day. That's not necessarily bad. A lot of working people will choose to eat their dinner downtown, so some of those dwindling numbers may stick around for a couple of drinks and a good meal. It's far more pleasurable than fighting traffic. They can unwind from the business day or continue to conduct business in a more relaxed atmosphere. If married, both spouses may be too tired at the end of the day to prepare meals, and they might view your restaurant as an urban oasis. Walk-in traffic can be considerable.

Customer Loyalty Is Essential in the Suburbs

Another element to factor in is that everybody in the suburbs drives. Unless you're in a mall or shopping center, you can't depend on walk-in traffic. There isn't any. It's all on wheels. That requires a greater allowance for parking and a location that provides an easy entrance and exit for automobiles and large family-packed SUVs. If you have a lounge or offer beer, wine, and liquor, consider your possible liability relative to DUI laws. Visibility and signage will have to be designed to attract the attention of people passing by at thirty-five to fifty miles per hour. "Good Eats!" may not be the most creative sign in the world, but it will be read far easier than a sign carrying your menu, the name of your world-famous chef, and a "ya'll come" quote from the owner. Your storefront will have to be inviting to someone listening to the radio, trying to control a couple of kids, and whose mind is on that jerk up ahead with the left turn signal on constant blink.

A suburban restaurant is captive to local trade and depends on a loyal customer base for survival. Make sure your restaurant or your theme will fit in, will match the demographics of the area, and will be a welcome addition to the community.

Many a neighborhood filled with sports bars and "greasy spoons" have shouted a collective "thank goodness" at the opening of a fine dining establishment. A lot of suburbanites work downtown or in other areas, so your work week traffic could be slow. Then again, everybody's home on the weekend, so weekend trade could be more than enough to make up the difference.

Providing Parking Spaces

Parking will be a problem. In many areas there's just no convenient parking at all. Will your customers be willing to park some distance and walk to your facility? Can they do that safely, or do they believe they can do that safely? You may have to consider the added expense and staffing of valet parking for your patrons. Of course, public transportation can eliminate some of those concerns, but the more upscale your image, the less likely are your patrons to catch the bus.

Mature Markets Require Design Flexibility

What happens when you have a design for a 10,000-square-foot restaurant but only 9,500 square feet of available space? You could move on and scout out another location, but that's getting to be more and more of a problem in mature markets. The goal is to find a really good location and then adapt the restaurant to the physical challenges present.

There are three key considerations in this situation. First is cost. Retrofitting an existing building is generally more expensive than moving into your ideal space or building from scratch according to the company plans. Second is work flow. You have to design your place of operation so that customers, waitpersons, bussers, and kitchen staff can work smoothly and efficiently. Third is signage. Make sure that people can readily identify your restaurant. This is particularly true for franchise operations.

If you want to park your restaurant downtown, you'll find that space is scarce and on a per-foot basis very expensive. You can check this fact of life out for yourself by comparing the prices in downtown restaurants. A burger and fries or a bowl of consommé will be pricier down at Main and Center than on the suburban Sunnyvale Lane. That's neither good nor bad. People expect to pay a bit more down among the high-rises. People living in and near downtown tend to dine out and to entertain guests at restaurants more than suburban dwellers, so your nighttime traffic doesn't have to disappear after the 5 P.M. rush.

A significant factor could be your plans or desire for expansion. Granted, space is expensive, but you also must consider whether that space will be available when you need or if it will even exist.

You'll find two key advantages in the suburbs: price and space. Costs per square foot are generally much lower for lease or purchase and there's plenty of room. If you want a lounge or banquet facilities or to expand that way in the future, you can be pretty sure there are plenty of locations that will meet your needs. The same goes for parking and storage space.

Just ask any restaurant operator how important parking is. Just as with a bad location, inadequate parking can cause a quick death to even the best of concepts. Most cities have specific parking regulations, which are found in their building codes. The Southern Building Code calls for one parking space for every one hundred square feet of total building space. Districts zoned B-4 in downtown areas usually prohibit off-street parking. That's one reason why downtown parking is tough to get and always at a premium rate. For instance, if you owned a 6,000-square-foot restaurant anywhere other than downtown, you'd be required to provide sixty or more parking spaces. Downtown, you'd not be allowed any spaces at all. Chances are, spaces are just not available.

Valet parking could be an option, though probably not for a burger joint or a pizza place. If your downtown location is an upscale operation, valet parking may be a necessity. Valet parking can be a valuable service for you and your patrons. It can also be a source of headaches. Make sure you contract with a reputable firm.

Working with Brokers

Real estate professionals come in all sizes, shapes, forms, races, and belief systems. As with every other industry in the world, you'll encounter true professionals, unbelievable incompetents, decent and hard-working agents, cheats and crooks, and a little bit of everything else. The key is to find the right agent or broker for you and the particular needs of your restaurant. That means research.

Choose Wisely

First, unless someone is knowledgeable in commercial real estate, do not automatically sign up your cousin in real estate. The same goes for your neighbor, someone at the Rotary Club, or any other family member or acquaintance who just happens to be in the business. The industry is full of part-timers, many of whom move in and out of the business with surprising rapidity. Few decisions are more important than the selection and lease or purchase of your location. Finding and negotiating that ideal spot is a job for someone who really knows the business, not someone who is merely dallying in real estate or even a professional who has no experience in the commercial end.

Ask around for the top commercial real estate firms in the area. You've already made contacts at the chamber of commerce and other business organization in your earlier research. (Haven't you?) Return and ask for several recommendations. Don't put the member of some organization on the spot by asking for a single recommendation. A number of firms are probably members, and you'd be putting someone in an awkward spot. A little more research will weed out any misdirection. Check out the company ads in the newspapers and city publications. Get a feel for their expertise. Call the Better Business Bureau to see if there are any red flags. The local restaurant association may also know of several firms specializing in restaurants or at least commercial real estate.

Visit the likely candidates. Don't just drop in and say, "Here I am. Help me." You'll wind up in the lap of whichever agent happens to have office duty that day. Tell the people you're researching firms and you'd like to speak to someone who knows commercial real estate and preferably someone with experience in restaurants. Visit all your likely candidates. Be sure to meet the agent or broker who will be working with you if you choose that firm.

Many factors will affect that decision:

- Company reputation
- Company experience
- Size
- Broker's experience and reputation

Discuss Details

Once you've selected your broker, do not allow him or her to dash out to the car to begin searching for the perfect spot. Insist on explaining your needs in detail. Cover the desired area, your market, needs for traffic access, sizes of the building, expansion plans, special considerations such as wiring or ventilation, and so on. Make sure your broker is out there looking for *your* building and not just another commission check.

Brokers know the market. A good one who understands your needs should be able to find several likely locations in a short period of time. Don't expect to move quickly if you allow the broker to carry the ball alone. Work with your broker and your broker will soon have you working on your grand opening.

> Make sure your broker is out there looking for *your* building and not just another commission check.

Lower Real Estate Fees

Real estate brokers earn their keep by earning commissions on the real estate they sell or lease. Commissions for commercial real estate are higher than for residential sales, sometimes as high as 10 percent. That's a pretty hefty figure, particularly on a large structure or even a small one with a high price. (The investment in a small "box" in pricey downtown might buy or rent an entire warehouse out in the hinterlands.) What's to keep the prospective restaurateur from negotiating down that high commission? Nothing. It happens all the time.

As a business owner, you'll be in a position to negotiate all kinds of costs and fees. Why wait till you open your doors? Go ahead and start negotiations while getting those doors. You may or may not meet with success (another reason to evaluate several real estate firms), but there's no harm in making the attempt. It's always good to have a backup firm to approach. From the broker's point of view, 9, 8, or even 7 percent of a good deal is a lot better than a 100 percent of no deal at all. And every one of those percentage points you knock off can save you hundreds, thousands, or even tens of thousands of dollars over the life of your business. If negotiations fail, well, you really haven't lost any ground. You're right where you started. So why not give it a whirl?

Go Discount

You can also research the services of dependable and respected discount brokers. You won't receive full service, but you will receive professional service. Many of the tasks a broker handles, you or someone from your staff or investment group can handle. Using a discount broker gets you the professional services you must have but allows you to reduce your costs in the process. Depending upon your real estate experience, time frame, and specific needs, this is a route worth investigating.

The bottom line remains the same, however. Your objective is twofold—getting the best possible price on the best possible property. A great price on a lousy location is no deal at all.

Evaluating a Building

Before purchasing or leasing a building to convert into your restaurant, look at it. *Look* means a lot more than glancing around during a walk-through. Get down to the details and look in, around, under, and over everything. What works, what can be worked with, and what has to be scrapped before you can move in?

Know Your Landlord

If you'll be leasing property, get to know the landlord. Then go out and see what his or her other tenants have to say. If the landlord is troublesome, you'll waste valuable time in arguments when you should be managing the store and making your customers happy.

Review Your Budget

Be honest with yourself about the budget. Sacrificing quality for short-term gain can cause a lot of long-term grief. Used equipment tends to break down, slowing down or eliminating prompt service to your customers and running up maintenance and repair bills. Do you really want to fool with that old stove (refrigerator, freezer, steam table, etc.)? Will you be better off in the long run buying quality materials and equipment?

Invest in Your Storefront

Invest in your storefront, especially if the place has been occupied by another restaurant. Change things around. Move the door. Repaint in a different color. Work closely with your designers and architects to give the place a new look without breaking your budget.

Above all else, be totally honest with yourself. Be practical and think every step through. You're building a dream, so do all you can to make sure it remains a beautiful one.

Signage Visibility

This is a no-brainer, but you'd be surprised at the number of otherwise intelligent restaurant owners who neglect this essential part of self-promotion. Customers have to be able to see the signs advertising your restaurant. If you're downtown, that might mean placing your name on your front wall and hanging a sign over the sidewalk to make sure pedestrians near and far can see it. You might also place other signage or even a menu at eye-level in your front window. Restaurants in the suburbs face different obstacles and must place signs where drivers occupied in various tasks (driving, watching other cars, listening to the radio, chewing gum, yelling at kids, etc.) at thirty-five to fifty-five miles per hour.

It seems that every city has a different set of signage ordinances. Some cities will not permit a sign more than six feet tall while others permit signs as high as sixty-five feet or higher. For some reason, college towns are generally the toughest. Be sure to check carefully with city hall before you begin construction. If you hire a sign company, the organization should be up-to-date on all appropriate ordinances.

If your location is off by itself, you will most likely need a sign that grabs the customer's attention. Keep it simple and easy to read, but be sure to include your phone number. In fact, your address and phone number should be on just about anything you print. Don't get so "creative" that your sign is difficult to read. Customers tend to keep on driving by. Work with a reputable sign company to get your name out there. After all, it's your money—and your image. A good sign should be working for you 24 hours a day, seven days a week, all year long.

One of the best ways to check out signage visibility is to put yourself in the place of your potential customer. Walk or drive by your facility and do so early on, even before beginning construction. Where are the best sight lines? Where are the visual obstacles? What might become an obstacle in the future? Will construction of another building, the placement of an outdoor advertising bulletin, or the growth of that pine tree blind your customers to your signs? Take a look and then take action to make sure your customers can take a look at you.

One of the best ways to check out signage visibility is to put yourself in the place of your potential customer.

Community Involvement

You want to be welcomed by the neighbors, and it's in your interest to prove early on that you are also a good neighbor. These people can be among your best customers or, if not handled properly, among your worst enemies. Your task is simple—make friends. Walk around the block or the neighborhood. Introduce yourself and your business to the people you meet. Every once in a while during construction, go back and say "hello" again. Hand out some of your fliers or brochures. Give out certificates or your business card or something similar offering a free dessert or free cup of coffee during your opening weeks.

Don't neglect the value of having a number of community "spokesmen" on your side. Make friends with the local policemen, the mail carrier, and the ubiquitous retired guy making his daily rounds. Get on their good sides and they'll be spreading the good word about that great new restaurant opening up down the street.

We've recommended conducting a lot of your research through the local chamber of commerce, restaurant association, tourism and convention bureau, and other business groups. As you progress through your construction/renovation schedule, it's a good idea to join these organizations and become an active member. This is a way to build and extend your business network. Every restaurant owner should be a member of such organizations and should insist that his or her managers do the same. It's good for the community and it's good for business.

Consider hiring a local advertising or public relations firm. Research them carefully and make sure you and the firm are a "good fit." They can help you with introductions to important individuals, organizations, and events. Make a genuine effort to show that you want to become and will become a valued member of the local community. The key to success is basic. If you want to be embraced by good neighbors, just be a good neighbor.

> Make a genuine effort to show that you want to become and will become a valued member of the local community.

Do You Know Your Budget?

By now you've drawn up your first budget, including what you can spend on your building. Rough it may be, but it is still a guideline and a working document. Keep working it. Refer to your working budget throughout the lifespan of your restaurant, but pay very close attention during your pre–start-up and opening periods. These are the times when a lot of those rough estimates could create a bumpy financial ride.

Keep Tabs on Your Tabulations

Continual monitoring of the budget is a must for one very serious reason: things change. There's always a need to fine-tune the operation. You don't have to be obsessive about this, just consistent. There's no need to put the spouse and kids to bed and then stay up till the wee hours of the morning fretting over the rising cost of toothpicks. Your budget isn't set in stone.

It's natural to experience changes. The point is to stay on top of things so problems can be short-circuited and opportunities seized. Just review and adjust the document periodically—and you're the one who decides what period is appropriate.

Things always change. The price of concrete just increased and there's a provision in your contract with the company building your parking lot that allows an increase in price to cover the increase in materials. All kinds of things can happen and not all of them have to be bad. The unavailable land you've wanted for future expansion could suddenly become available. The expense could certainly affect your budget, but the purchase could prove to be a wise investment as your business grows.

There's always a need for fine-tuning. Many of the reasons for fine-tuning are because life just doesn't stand still. But you're always looking for ways to shave costs here and there without sacrificing the quality of your operation. It's possible that you could come across some used kitchen equipment in excellent shape and for sale at bargain basement prices. That would affect your budget, too, and would require a bit of fine-tuning. The extra money could go toward the purchase of that extra land, for example, or it could be placed in the contingency fund for use in later fine-tuning.

Make a Monthly Variance Report

The objective is to keep tabs on your overall operations by keeping tabs on your budget. One of the best tools is called a variance report. It's a basic financial document that compares your projected expenditures against your real expenditures. Make these reports on a monthly basis. It's called a variance report because it's designed to weed out variances in your budget.

Let's say you're looking at the financials and you notice that the bill for your roofing expenses is a good bit less than budgeted. That's good, right? That could be. The roofing company may have gotten a terrific price break on materials and has passed along the savings to the customer. (It could happen!) Perhaps the weather cooperated and the anticipated tornadoes never arrived and the work was completed so far ahead of schedule, the company felt a need to come well in under budget. Or maybe they left out the tarpaper and roofing tacks. The point is, you have a variance in your budget and it is telling you that it's time to investigate a specific budget item.

It's comparable to waking up with a scratchy throat and a stopped-up nose. Your body (budget) is communicating that you'd better take care of certain items right away or you'll start a round of uncontrollable sneezing. At the risk of pushing the analogy, you could "blow" a significant portion of your budget if you don't take appropriate action.

Variance reports should be simple, easy, and quick to use. The report compares projections on variable expenses (sales commissions, for example) and fixed expenses (such as salaries, taxes, utilities, etc.) against the actual monthly costs to determine your net profit after taxes for the month. Speak with your accountant or scroll through your accounting software for a sample of this basic financial document.

Chapter 10

Designing Your Space

Part One

Part Two

Part Three

Part Four

Part Five

Part Six

Deciding Whether You Need an Architect

Before we get into the topic of interviewing, hiring, and working with architects and designers, there's an important question to address. Do you need the services of these professionals in the first place? Think carefully, because these folks will require a major investment in time, energy, and money. In some instances you will not have a choice. For example, if you're building from the ground up or planning on a major remodeling job, your city and state codes will require that you hire a licensed architect. Working with professionals need not be a chore; neither does it have to be a process in which you have to take a back seat to someone else. If you know exactly what you want and have good communication skills, your contractor can probably follow your designs. There's another dimension. If you aren't pressed for time and want to do some of the work yourself, you'll also have a lot of fun.

Interviewing and Selecting

Don't feel intimidated by the prospect of interviewing professionals. Architects and designers occupy valuable occupations, but they're still people you hire to do a job. You are the boss, and you should act like it. Lawyers, computer programmers, preachers, and other specialized occupations develop their own language. It's a necessary form of shorthand communication. That language can be threatening, frustrating, and obscure. Don't put up with it. Insist that the professionals with whom you work speak plain English. Ask for definitions. If you don't understand something, don't hesitate a second to ask for clarification. Establish the game rules up front so that you know what you're talking about instead of fumbling around in the dark. Lack of understanding does not work in your favor. This is especially true when your architect or designer thinks he or she is being understood. A simple nod of your head signifying "yes" when you really don't know what's going on can add a small fortune to your construction costs.

The philosophy of hiring designers and architects and the steps for interviewing and selecting them applies equally well to contractors. Different tasks are involved, but the principles remain the same. You should have a good rapport, get and research their references, have all fees and costs explained in detail up front, etc. The contractors you contact will probably want to be hired on a percentage basis. That is, they'll want anywhere from 10 to 30 percent over the cost of time and materials needed to complete the job to your satisfaction. Obviously, the more the job costs or the more prices rise, the higher the contractor's profit. This isn't the kind of incentive you want to employ. Instead, hire your contractor for a flat fee. Include in your contract any penalties for cost overruns, and be fair and open-minded about it. If the contractor makes a mistake and has to order extra plywood (or whatever), that should come out of his or her end of the deal. If you change your mind halfway through the project an decide to add a balcony/bar, then those extra costs should come out of your pocket.

Look Around

There are several ways to begin looking for architects and designers. Start by looking at buildings instead of people. Visit other restaurants, nightclubs, lounges, and related facilities. Always take your notepad (pen and paper or computerized) and write down your comments. Note everything that is important. If you don't like something, make a note. If you see something that really appeals to you, take a note.

Start a clip file. Take photographs of properties, signs, parking lots, etc. that strike you as good ideas for your restaurant or as options you'd never choose in a million years. Put your notes in this file. Clip articles, advertising materials, and other relevant data from newspapers and magazines. Later on, when the file starts getting a bit thick, you'll have compiled a great little idea file. You'll also have a lot of information to help your architects and designers bring your dream into reality.

If possible, take a trip to Las Vegas. Even if you don't gamble, don't take in shows, and don't like the desert, make the trip. The best minds in the world have built some of the best, most creative facilities in the world. These people really push the limits of architecture and promotion. The colors alone are worth the trip. Sure, what you see will be out of your price range (that's an understatement), but those hotels and casinos offer a world of ideas. You can implement some of them on a smaller scale in your facility. Again, take notes, take pictures, and take home lots of ideas.

Take photographs of properties, signs, parking lots, etc. that strike you as good ideas for your restaurant or as options you'd never choose in a million years.

Ask Around

When you come across a restaurant you really like, ask to visit with the owner or manager. Compliment him or her and direct the conversation toward the building. Most operators are like proud parents and will be more than willing to brag about their "baby." Some topics to cover are:

- Name of the architect/designer
- Name of the firm
- Location of the firm (local boys?)
- Completed on time?
- Completed on budget?
- Any problems encountered
- Any recommendations

It's important to get as much information as possible. For example, the building could look fabulous, but it could also be structurally unsound because the architect specified the wrong materials. The owner you're speaking with could be the person who bought it from an original owner who went under because the designer went over on the budget.

Check the yellow pages or the Internet for the names of individuals and firms in your area. Pick up the phone and start getting some information directly from the source. Don't neglect sources from other communities or even other states. Randy had a very satisfying experience working with a designer from Dallas, quite some distance from the site of the job. They had met at a trade show. Randy was impressed with the man's abilities but was initially worried about working long distance. The designer assured him there would be no distance-related problems. They worked together daily via the Internet, and Randy was able to communicate his needs and desires throughout the process. The project worked out very well and saved not only time, but money, too.

Check out your local contractors and builders and their trade organizations. You'll find lots of home builders, but concentrate your efforts on commercial contractors. Try to fine people and companies with experience in building restaurants and clubs. They will be far more up-to-date on building codes and regulations than someone who specializes in residential building.

They'll also have a better handle and more experience dealing with the materials you'll need to incorporate in your design.

Start Interviewing

When you've made a list of possible suppliers and have weeded out all but the most promising, meet with them one at a time. You'll have lots of questions. Here are a few to help you get started.

- What projects have you recently completed?
- Have you done any restaurants or clubs? Where?
- Can you deliver within my time frame?
- Do you understand my theme?
- Are your flexible enough to meet my design needs?
- What are your fees?
- Do you have any specific limitations?
- How will you handle problems that might come up, such as changes and special requests?
- Can you provide references?

Once you've selected your architect and/or designer, meet with them regularly. Have them create some preliminary drawings and examine them closely. If you like what you see, stay the course with this individual or firm. If you don't like what you see, express your concerns and see if you can work out your differences. Of course, you can walk away and find someone more suited to your needs if things don't work out. Be sure to pay the company for the time invested in creating those drawings.

If you decide against working with an architect, you'll still need a professional to make a set of drawings for you. Your city will require it. These drawings will address such issues as carpentry, plumbing, and electrical wiring. These are very important documents and will need to be (literally) up to spec.

The people you select will become part of the team that makes your dream come true. Make sure they "click" with you and that you are all on the same page. Listen carefully to their comments and suggestions. Evaluate what they say and make your decisions accordingly. Always remember, the dream is your dream. They can't create that dream if they can't see it.

> Have your architect create some preliminary drawings and examine them closely.

Two Types of Designers

Facilities designers specialize in key areas, such as serving areas, food prep areas, and kitchens. Functionality is a key aspect of a smoothly running operation, and a skilled facilities designer can help see that the kitchen staff isn't tripping over each other in the rush to serve your customers. Ask around for recommendations from your restaurant association and restaurant supply houses. You might also look up the Food-Service Consultants Society International.

Interior designers help you create the atmosphere of your restaurant. They provide the look and feel, the sight and sound, and even the touch that can add so much to a patron's enjoyment of the dining experience. They'll be listed in your yellow pages or on the Internet. Check out the American Society of Interior Designers.

Providing that inspiration and that vision is your job. Take it seriously.

Selection of Materials

This part of the job is very individualistic. The size, shape, and scope of your dream will determine the materials used to bring it into reality. City ordinances will specify minimum standards for construction, and those will requirements will be well-known to the professionals you hire to build your dream. Consult with them regularly and be sure to get full justification for any materials that exceed those requirements.

Your main challenge in selecting materials relates to your chosen décor. Here the choices are virtually unlimited but should be made in accordance with your theme and design. Large, exposed, rough wooden logs work quite well in rustic steak houses. The patrons of a petite French café would probably find them out of place. On the other hand, expensive decorative wallpaper found in a fine-dining establishment wouldn't exactly fit in with a place that has sawdust on the floor. The key is to choose materials that enhance the overall theme of your restaurant so as to enhance the customers' dining experience.

Work very closely with your architect, designer, and contractor when making these selections. Make up your own mind and call your own shots, but always listen to the experts first. You'll find that many items are essential, but good professionals are aware of many short cuts that are equally or nearly as good that might do the job just as well for a smaller investment. Always get the prices and a clear explanation of the difference in quality.

Selecting Your Equipment

You'll need lots of equipment, everything from cash registers and computers to sound systems and intercoms. But all of that is really peripheral to the real heart of your operation—your kitchen. That's where we'll focus our attention. After you've made your decisions about your menu and the basic layout of your restaurant, your next big task is to set up your kitchen to best serve your patrons, your staff, and your own business interests.

Visit Suppliers

Kitchen equipment suppliers can be among the most helpful of all your suppliers. They will be especially helpful if you've never designed a kitchen before. Take full advantage of their willingness to help you. In many areas these companies have paid staff specializing in kitchen layouts and equipment specifications. If that service isn't available in your area, get some professional help. Their services will be well worth the money. Good, reliable equipment is essential for a smoothly running and profitable restaurant.

If your budget permits, buy commercial-grade equipment. You'd be surprised how many restaurant owners try to slide by with equipment designed for residential use. Residential cooking and restaurant cooking may use the same ingredients, but they are worlds apart. Your kitchen is a work area, and an intense one at that. Your equipment will be in use practically from the moment you open until the moment you wave "so long" to your last customer of the evening. Residential equipment just can't hold up to that kind of use. You'll be buying replacements in no time at all. Worse than that, the residential equipment could "conk out" on you during a busy breakfast, lunch, or dinner. Disappointing your patrons is no way to build a loyal customer base.

You can certainly save a good bit of money by purchasing used equipment. Be sure to thoroughly examine each piece of used equipment you consider. Find out how old it is, and, if you can, find out where it was used. A food processor used at a 200-capacity restaurant will probably have seen more wear and tear than the one used down at Mom's Little Ol' Café. The only serious warning about buying used equipment is to avoid used icemakers. Buy a new model. The old ones just won't hold up, and you'll be in the market for a replacement in short order.

A kitchen should be divided into four areas: production/cooking area, preparation area, dishwashing area, and the storage area.

Production/Cooking Line

You must make sure that this area flows well. This part of your kitchen operation is the lifeline to the dining room. People show up at a restaurant to eat, and they don't want to invest a lot of time waiting around for the fare to arrive. They also expect their dishes to meet certain standards of appearance. A well-designed production/cooking line makes a significant contribution to meeting those expectations.

If things don't work well here, they won't and can't work anyplace else in your operation. This is an absolute fact of life in the restaurant business. This area is your assembly line. Like one of those clean, modern manufacturing plants, everything must come together at precisely the right moment. Keep the order in line from the start of the line to the finished plated item. Do all you can to see the physical steps your cooks must take to produce any given plate. If you have too much crisscrossing of cooks and orders, you have an inefficient kitchen on your hands. Your costs inevitably rise as your margin of profit inevitably falls.

You will need room for:

- Grills or cooking tops
- Fryers
- Steam tables
- Refrigerated make tables or refrigerators
- Freezers
- Prep tables or prep space

You'll also have to design space for your china or plates. It's best to keep them hot or at least warm, so you'll need space for that need. Also, you'll need food racks. And what about trash cans? Can at least two cooks work the line without running over each other? All of these factors have to be designed well in advance of construction. You don't want to run into any of the problems just mentioned. Eliminate them on paper before they become a headache in the back of the restaurant.

> People show up at a restaurant to eat, and they don't want to invest a lot of time waiting around for the fare to arrive.

Preparation Area

This is where the bulk of your food preparation will occur. You will need space for:

- Two- to three-compartment sink
- Prep tables
- Steam kettles
- Mixers
- Other equipment according to your menu needs

You'll need to locate this area near your refrigerators. You'll find the walk-in type of refrigerator the most convenient, most practical, and, over the long term, the most cost effective. Also, be sure to set up a space where your incoming inventory can be checked.

Dishwashing Area

This is the where your wait staff and bussers will drop off trash, dirty linens, and dirty dishes. Locate it away from the cooking line and as close to the kitchen entrance as possible. This area should take up about 4 to 6 percent of your total kitchen space. You'll need:

- Dirty dish area
- Dishwasher
- Clean dish table
- Storage space for clean dishes

Here's a great tip on saving money. There are companies that will sell you a dishwasher outright, but conduct a bit of research before making your decision. Some companies will provide you with a machine at no cost if you agree to buy their chemicals. You savings could be substantial. Check it out.

Storage Area

Storage space is very important, so don't skimp on your design. "Pencil it in" up front rather than attempt to squeeze things in later on. Dry goods, beverage items, paper goods, and cleaning supplies all require storage that is safe, clean, and convenient. Check with your local health department about specific requirements for your community. Remember to keep a close eye on the goods stored by the back door, because you will have employees who do.

Your kitchen will become a beehive of activity. How active depends upon the number of seats in your restaurant and/or the number of employees you have working at any given time. In this relatively small place you'll have orders coming in, wait staff buzzing in and out, bussers dropping off dirty dishes, bartenders coming over for ice and supplies, orders waiting to be picked up, and a good bit of other activity. This can be a place of great confusion and chaos or one of complete unison and harmony. Which description fits your restaurant will depend upon your design.

Careful selection and time invested on making the right choice up front on your kitchen equipment and layout will not only reap more profits, but it will allow you to enjoy a lot more sleep at night. Don't make your purchases based on price alone. That creates a false economy, and you'll pay for it later. Remember, you can cut your labor costs by selecting certain equipment over other types of equipment. Don't allow yourself to be intimidated into buying custom pieces that are an unnecessary expense. Don't buy equipment you really don't need, either. Think. Plan and shop around for the best value you can find.

Other Equipment Needs

After your kitchen, your bar will be the most equipment-heavy part of your operation. You can have a simple service bar where drink orders are filled according to orders from your wait staff. You can also have a stand up or stool-bar set-up. Of course, you can run both types at the same time, as many places do.

Among the equipment you'll need: refrigerators for bottled beer, soft drinks, and other beverages or mixers; lines and taps for draft beer service; storage area for keg beer; two compartment sinks; glass washers; storage for glasses and mugs; ice makers and ice storage space; television set(s) and/or a sound system for music; anything else you believe will enhance the experience of your customers.

In the front of the restaurant you'll need a POS system. The initials stand for "point of sale." This can be your most expensive equipment. They come in all sizes, shapes, and capabilities. Your system should at least record sales and print out a ticket for the customer. You'll find it handy to purchase a POS system that breaks down your sales into desired categories, such as "total food sales" or "total bar sales." The breakdowns can be as broad or as narrow as you deem necessary for your own tracking and inventory control.

Designing Traffic Patterns

One of the best ways to design and evaluate traffic patterns is to play the "What if" game again. Play it two ways: one as a customer and then again as an employee. Early on, even before you draw up your plans, use your full imagination to visualize the sights, sounds, smells, and textures of your soon-to-be restaurant. Continue playing the game throughout all phases of design and construction. As more and more visualization tools become available, such as your design plans, put them to work to further spark your imagination.

Play the game as different employees. As a member of the wait staff, can you move quickly and easily from kitchen to and through the dining area? Are there spaces that will impede the flow of traffic? As an imaginary busser, can you move clean and dirty dishes through the kitchen without stumbling over the cooks? As a chef, can you complete a meal from one place or will you have to continually move back and forth to put your ingredients into your dishes?

Play the game as a customer. Can you walk from the outside through the greeting area and into the dining area unimpeded? Does the greeting station block patrons or invite them in? Is your table too close to other tables in the area? Are you

Display Equipment

A popular trend among many restaurateurs is to display samples of their fare to boost sales. Extra room must be designed in, and you'll also need some specialized equipment.

Meals or dishes that are already prepared and must be proportioned to the customer's request can be showcased quite effectively in a case with a see-through front. Look for the type that feature glass fronts that swing out and up. They're easy to clean.

Hot foods require a display case that can maintain a constant temperature and humidity. The size you need to purchase depends on the size of your operations. If you're a small operation, you can get by with a countertop model. Cases that open from the front and back are very convenient. Patrons can reach in from the front while your staff can replace items from the rear.

afraid the clutter might cause an overloaded waiter to spill his tray on you? Do you have to step up or down any inconvenient and potentially dangerous steps? Are you too near the kitchen doors or the restrooms? Do you feel comfortable in this environment?

Using Space Efficiently

A good kitchen for a restaurant is not only efficient, it is user-friendly. Your kitchen staff has to be able to move about easily and quickly. If you've ever been in a poorly designed kitchen when a lot of patrons have shown up, you know the nightmares that can follow. People bump into each other. Food items get spilled. Plates are dropped and chaos seems to reign. Frequently, poor design is the fault of an owner who tried to shave a few dollars off his or her design costs. The hassles, spillage, and lost productivity are far costlier than those design dollars. A smoothly functioning kitchen is more a function of design than space. Make sure your people can move about economically without spilling the tomato sauce on the ice cream.

Labor is a major cost factor. When creating your designs, make sure you consider everything possible to avoid creating a space that is labor intensive. People don't like to work in spaces that are inefficient. This can be a serious consideration in a market where the labor supply is tight. *Never design a kitchen without first knowing what you will be preparing there.* Create your menu before you create your kitchen. Otherwise you will not only be creating an inefficient work area, you will also be increasing your labor costs. Other costs are affected, too. The longer a patron waits for his or her meal to arrive, the longer that table is tied up and is unavailable for new customers.

Allowing for Change

No one can read the future, but you can make some educated guesses. Use those guesses to design in allowances for change in the future. For example, if you might open a new door or widen an existing one, put in your plumbing, electrical, etc. so that you won't have to undo a lot of work and reroute it later on. If you're toying with the idea of someday adding a banquet room, go ahead and design it (budget permitting) so that you'll have the plans when needed and so you can avoid that undo/redo work when it's time to start hammering, nailing, plumbing, and wiring.

This is another area where the "What if" game can get your creative juices flowing. What if we put in a patio? What if we added a row of booths in the bar? What if we need more parking space? When you've finished playing, evaluate how serious you might be about someday instituting those changes. Then just make all the allowances you can so your work will go a lot easier and more efficiently when that day arrives. One of the best ways to allow for change is to allow your imagination to explore the future.

Safety and Sanitation Considerations

Proper safety and sanitation must be designed into your restaurant from the beginning. Again, city codes and regulations will have a minimum set of standards. The professionals you've hired should be up-to-speed on the latest requirements so that you're facility is in full compliance. You really do want to be in full compliance. Don't try to skirt an issue or slide by safety and sanitation rules. You'll get caught, and the expense of shutting down your restaurant to bring things up to standard can be devastating. Besides, you want a safe and sanitary work environment to further enhance the pleasure of your customers.

As with most things in business, rules and regulations vary from community to community. Here are a few rules that should pretty well apply across the board. Of course, you will check with your local government to make sure your restaurant complies fully with all applicable regulations.

"Typhoid Mary" was a real person early in the last century. She carried but was not made ill by the disease for which she earned her nickname. Unfortunately, a number of persons were exposed to the disease via Mary and died. She was eventually traced and then put in isolation. Mary worked

Design in Energy Savings

A commercial food-service outlet will generally use five to ten times as much energy as a comparable building in a different business.

Work closely with your designers and architects to have energy efficiency built into your operation. Here are a few suggestions to consider.

Your dishwashing area should be equipped with low-flow, prerinse spray nozzles.

Install or retrofit with energy-efficient lighting. Business continues into the dark hours, and the savings from energy efficient lighting mount up quickly.

Make sure that your thermostat has "unoccupied" and "night set back" features and be sure to use them.

See that you kitchen staff turns off the exhaust fans when the equipment below them is not in use. Monitor use of hot water so that it is used only when required. Turn off appliances when not in use.

at a restaurant. You don't want to repeat the experience. Restaurant owners, managers, and employees have a special responsibility to the public to be of good health.

You see those little signs posted in restaurant restrooms all over the country, "All employees must wash hands before returning to work." There's a good reason. Diseases are easily transmitted by hand from person to person, chef to food, waiter and waitress to customer. Not only must you design proper facilities for such sanitary measures, you must make sure and continue to make sure your employees follow the procedures.

Sneeze guards should be placed over exposed food areas, such as salad bars or dessert selections. This could easily already be a requirement in your community. It's still a good idea even if not required. Just like germs, word gets around, too, and you don't want people talking about how "folks sure do seem to get sick a lot after eating at Joe's."

Easy-to-miss steps up or down should be clearly marked. This is especially important for restaurants with that dim, romantic lighting.

All exits should be clearly marked and in accordance with the appropriate safety regulations. Safety lighting is probably mandatory. Design spaces for fire extinguishers where appropriate and see if a sprinkler system is mandated for the kitchen and the dining areas.

See that the unloading of fresh and frozen food can be accomplished quickly. Food spoilage can be a major source of lost income. Be sure you have created enough room for someone to actually inspect those food items, too. Frozen food can be a particular problem, so speed is of the essence. If it thaws out, you have a bunch of useless semi-cold garbage on your hands. You can't refreeze it and still maintain quality.

Your food preparation surfaces should be designed with ease of cleaning in mind. The same can be said for your refrigerators. Institute regular cleaning schedules and also teach your food prep and cooking staff to clean up as they perform their jobs.

> All exits should be clearly marked and in accordance with the appropriate safety regulations.

Chapter 11

Planning Your Menus

Part One

Part Two

Part Three

Part Four

Part Five

Part Six

PART THREE   THE NUTS AND BOLTS: MENUS, SUPPLIES, AND PERMITS
■ **CHAPTER 11 Planning Your Menus** ■ CHAPTER 12 Purchasing Supplies ■ CHAPTER 13 Securing Permits

Engineering Your Menu

Our title sounds a bit more like a major downtown construction project than a delightful meal, doesn't it? Well, building a menu is a major construction project. As you'll see in the next section, your menu is the foundation of your success. Despite all the extras you may offer, the reason people walk in your front door is to eat good food. In this chapter we'll explore menu options, how to improve your menu, how to supply it, and even how to write and design one that helps keep customers coming back to read, select, taste, and enjoy time and time again.

Menus: The Core of Your Business

The heart and soul of your business is your menu. It's also the key element of your image with the public. Your menu defines you in the public eye. The Western-themed menu with corral fencing, horseshoe, and branding iron artwork tells the patron even before he or she starts reading that they won't be ordering *Poulet Saute aux Truffes* or *Trout Meuniere*. However, the next time Dad says, "I'm in the mood for a good steak," guess where the family's heading?

Start with Concepts

What type of menu works best? That's a loaded question. The choice of a menu depends upon many factors. Among them are the types of menus already being read at your competitor's restaurants, the wants and needs of the market, cost factors, and your ability to offer certain menu items. Unless you have already selected your menu and have studied the market in depth, this means you have to conduct a good bit of research. Don't take a single shortcut during this process. Remember, you're building a foundation for your entire business, and it is a major construction project.

Look at the Media

The Internet is a major source of information for all types of research. You can find valuable information from restaurant organizations, suppliers to the restaurant industry, individual and chain restaurants, famous chefs and well-known cooking advisors, and other sources. Keep in mind that anyone can put just about anything on the Internet. Consider the source of any material you want to use. It's a good idea to restrict your search (or at least your belief) to legitimate sites, such as the National Restaurant Association or your state's association, well-known manufacturers and suppliers, and knowledgeable personalities.

The recent introduction of the Food Network is a wonderful source of ideas for food and beverage preparation, recipes, techniques, and presentations. Other cable and broadcast networks often feature food and beverage programming. Certainly, your local stations will have some programming devoted to cooking. These are often great electronic "swap files" for good ideas on local culture, tastes, likes, and dislikes.

> The Food Network is a wonderful source of ideas for food and beverage preparation, recipes, techniques, and presentations.

Many national publications are devoted to food and beverage preparation, cooking, and presentation. *Gourmet* magazine is a good example. Other national, regional, and local publications offer valuable information. Pay attention to trends, those that are hot, those that are fading fast, and those that might be on the horizon.

Your local newspaper might offer similar material. Of particular interest will be restaurant reviews. Here you can gather in a wealth of information about menus, décor, entertainment, and other important factors. Locally, you can also get a handle on what's popular and the level of professionalism that's expected by your patrons.

Visit food and beverage distributors. If you're in at least a midsize market, chances are you'll have a number of distributors within the city limits. If you're in a smaller market, make the trip to a larger one and knock on a few doors. These people are on top of what's happening in the restaurant business across a broad range of issues. They have to be. Some of the things you can learn from a good distributor are:

- Menu items that are selling well
- Hot items that are declining in demand
- Food and beverage pricing
- What their customers are ordering
- Shelf life and storage concerns
- Delivery schedules

- Opinions, thoughts, and speculation from experienced people in the business

Eat at restaurants near your target location. See for yourself what the local patrons are enjoying. Speak with the wait staff to see what's going on with local tastes. Local preferences can make or break a menu. For example, you can order a plate of enchiladas with red sauce in Wyoming, Colorado, New Mexico, Arizona, and Texas, but you will find entirely different rolled tortillas on your plate in each location. That's not to say that your menu has to follow the trend. Often just being a bit different is enough to attract customers, at least at first. The point is to know the local tastes before making that decision. Also, when talking with the wait staff, take notes on people you might want to hire for your own operation.

Collect Menus

Most owners or managers will be flattered at the attention and will gladly comply. Take the menus home and study them as if they are a textbook. Look at the items offered, the combinations, the pricing, but also examine the presentation. Can you easily read it? Would an older patron with poor vision be able to read it? Is it easy to navigate from one section to the other? Is it too heavy with artwork? What would you keep and what would you discard?

In all of your research, never lose sight of the fact that you don't have to reinvent the wheel. Just redesign successful operations that are already out there. Make what works work again, but with a unique style of your own.

The "Four Ps" of Marketing

If you aren't already familiar with the "Four Ps," then it's time for a little practical study. These are:

- Price
- Product
- Position
- Place

All four elements define your restaurant's success or lack of it. You must have a good handle on each one by the time you begin serious work on your menu. Know your market. What price range will your patrons willingly pay? On the high end, what places you in the "too ritzy for me" category? On the low end, what range places you in the "must be cheap place" slot?

Know what products or menu items you'll be selling. This knowledge will also help you in other areas. For example, very delicate food items may require special or additional storage or preparation equipment. And, of course, additional or more expensive items will have a bearing on the prices you charge.

Position refers to your image in the marketplace, and it's wrapped up in the other three items. Positioning is always in relation to your competition. Are you the "funky" restaurant catering to the college crowd or are you the family restaurant serving John Q. Public? Are you kid-friendly, or do you want to cater to an upscale audience that appreciates fine dining on linen tablecloths? Would you prefer to serve burgers and blue-plate specials year round, or respond to the ever-changing dictates of the tourist crowd? Whatever choice you make must be reflected in your menu.

Place, of course, is your location, and that's always a key factor in your success. Your location can often be used as a decorative item on your menu. For instance, a lot of Cajun and seafood restaurants down south are located on lakes, rivers, and bayous. Art elements are often drawn from their surroundings.

Tasting and Pricing

Let the games begin. Cook! You'll never know how good your menu is until you cook, present, and taste it. Here's where your early contacts with distributors can pay off even before you become a regular customer. Remember, most of

Menus Can Spell Success

Many a typical restaurant has achieved atypical success through its menu. Back before World War I, a Russian immigrant named Nathan Handweker wanted to sell more frankfurters. He realized that volume sales could be a key to his success—more sales meant lower prices. He set up a walk-up counter near Coney Island so that his customers could "grab a dog" on their way home. He called his hot dogs "Nathan's Famous."

Roy Allen out in California wanted to move more of a beverage called root tea. In a brilliant bit of name changing, he started calling the drink "root beer." The change not only gave the drink and the restaurant an identity, it allowed him to charge more for "beer." In 1919, he opened a unit called Allen's A&W Root Beer.

these companies really want to help you get started. Their support builds customer loyalty and helps out the bottom line. You win. They win. Ask for help, advice, and specific suggestions. Look for ways to provide the best possible quality while keeping your prices under control.

Taste a Variety of Items

Do not limit your taste-testing sessions to what you think your final menu will be. Experiment. Try a lot of different items and a lot of different combinations. No one can read the mind of the public, so don't even make the attempt. You'll probably be surprised at what people like and don't like. "I can't believe they didn't like my guacamole-radish dip!"

Select your product-testing people from segments of the market you want to attract to your restaurant. As much as you value their opinion, the members of the Hoity Toity Upscale Dining Club won't be of much real value in developing your burgers and brew menu. Have fun. Don't hold back. If an item doesn't work, then just scratch it off the list. You might even find a surprise hit or two. Take notes. Ask for opinions and suggestions on ways to improve the items. Ask about the presentation while you're at it. Would your patrons prefer larger and heavier plates? Would plastic or cloth placemats be better? Do you even need placemats? What type of décor would these people enjoy? Use the opportunity to research more than just the menu.

While conducting your testing sessions, think about the variety you can offer: tastes, textures, high-fat/low-fat options, heart-smart meals, different types of meat, accompanying menu items, desserts, liquor, and visual presentations. Take photographs of your completed plates before serving, and study them for visual effect. Be sure to write down all the recipes and any specialized techniques used during the process.

Even if you think you've arrived at the final version of your menu, keep on testing and refining. Double-check every item and every price until you are as sure as you can be that you have found the right formula. The extra time, energy, and expense invested before you open can pay off for years into the future.

Refine Your Pricing Structure

Again, visit your distributors. They can help you cost out your menu items, and therefore your entire menu. As an owner or manager, you have to strike a careful balance. The menu has to be structured so that the restaurant can make a good profit over time. Pricing also has to be affordable to a large enough customer base to ensure that those profits keep coming in over time.

Those are pretty vague guidelines, right? That's why you have to continue researching. Study the price structure on all of those menus you've collected. Continue eating at other restaurants and ask friendly but very specific questions of the wait staff. If an item seems to be priced a bit too high, ask, "Do you sell many of those at that price?" Follow up by asking what makes the expensive item so in demand. Ask questions about prices that appear too low. Your competitor may have found some low-cost secret ingredient, or he or she just might be cutting down on quality. Find out.

Selecting Menu Types

Creating a menu, the kind your patrons hold in their hands to read and drool over, is an important task. Even if you want a very informal or even rustic look, the menu must be professional. The simplest menu must meet a tough set of standards and expectations from your customers. Here are the major considerations you face.

Restaurant Prices Are Retail Prices

Don't cost out your menu at a set food cost level. That's just not a good idea. You're in retail. You'll need to offer some items as loss leaders to bring in customers. They'll be back and order other more profitable items if they're happy with the food and service. Always think in terms of the big picture, of the entire menu. You could take an acceptable loss on an entrée, but easily make up the difference in a mixed drink or dessert item ordered during that same meal.

Vendors Can Save You Fortunes

Never neglect the vast number of resources at your service, many of them at very low or even no cost. Randy's experience developing the menu for Iguana Joe's is a perfect example. Randy contacted a good vendor with a couple of paid chefs on staff who had experience in this area.

Randy's menu had to be unique, yet not so "off the beaten track" that it wouldn't attract customers. The chef created a menu that Randy called "just about perfect." Had he gone to a professional in menu development, Randy's costs could have easily run into the thousands of dollars.

The services provided by that vender didn't stop there. The company allowed their chef to monitor the opening of the restaurant and even participate in training the staff. Of course, Randy bought the bulk of his food and supplies from this company. That's the beauty of sound business relationships. Everybody wins because everybody helps everybody else.

Outsourcing or Do-It-Yourself?

The need for flexibility may be the deciding factor here. Will you be offering the same standard menu or menus over time, or will you be making a lot of changes? If you plan on making changes, how often? Once a year, twice a year, four times a year, monthly, during special seasons and holidays, or just on your whim? Determine how much time will be taken in the production of additional menus. Can you afford the effort?

Some restaurants can get by with a standard everyday menu by inserting a simple typed "Today's Special" menu whenever necessary. The investment in time is small and the cost practically negligible. More upscale restaurants charging higher prices usually can't get away with this and will require a more professional presentation, which costs more time and money. A good way to judge what's best is to ask what your customers will expect.

Cover Design Is Critical

First impressions last, and one of the first, most important impressions a new customer gets is from that menu in his or her hands. Often a quick glance at the cover is all someone needs to form a positive or negative impression. There are four major options in the production design of your menu. Let's look at the pros and cons of each.

Lamination: Plastic-coated menus stay clean because spilled food and drink can't soak into the paper. They're easy to wipe clean and can be reused immediately after such a spill. They're also durable. The disadvantage is that lamination is an expensive process. Also, because the menu is coated, you can't change it. Laminated menus aren't recommended for menus with high prices. The images of upscale food and plastic are in conflict.

Multifold Insert Menu Covers: These can be changed easily and often. You can reprint and insert the new menu in a short period of time and at a reasonable cost. These are durable, they last a long time, stay clean, and can be wiped off easily. On the downside, the initial printing cost is high, so you'll need to plan on using them for a long time to justify that cost. Also, they shouldn't be used for upscale restaurants.

Die Cut Menus: These can be very effective marketing tools. They're distinct, eye-catching, and memorable. An example would be a menu cut in the shape of a toaster for a restaurant specializing in breakfast service. You can really differentiate yourself from your competitors with such a specialized menu. Die cut menus are expensive. Unless you have a substantial budget, you'll need to stick with a standard list of items.

Hiring a Menu Design Specialist: This option is well worth the money if you're operating an upscale restaurant. For many such operations, a professional's touch is mandatory. The sky is the limit. Of course the term "sky" is defined by how much you are willing to spend on the project. Again, what will your patrons expect?

Select Readable Typefaces

Sometimes called "fonts," typefaces are available in hundreds of styles, some dating back hundreds of years. Many of those "ancient" faces are still among the best and most used. Your choices are for all practical purposes unlimited. Select your type carefully, because it will be a reflection of your entire operation.

Your typeface should match the theme of your restaurant. You can be "wild and crazy" with a kid's menu, mixing faces and sizes and breaking a lot of rules of good design to appeal to an unsophisticated audience. A family-style restaurant will require something a bit more formal, although the atmosphere created can be relaxed and friendly. Good design and proper treatment of artwork or art elements should balance the effect of the chosen type. A restaurant charging high

Boost Sales with Special Menus

Consider a special menu for special items to increase your sales and profit. Bar sales have a higher profit margin than food items, so elegant restaurants may have a wine menu in a leather casing. A funky restaurant may put a menu on a Popsicle stick or a menu die-cut to resemble a pretzel featuring the beer list inside. Nonalcoholic drinks designed for kids and nondrinking adults can also improve the bottom line. Set them in a special position on your menu.

Use your imagination and get creative. One bar uses an old-fashioned viewfinder to display its dessert menu. Another uses CD cases and another old 45 RPM records with the drink list as the "label." Specialty glasses, funny swizzle sticks, toys, etc. make the drinks, and your restaurant, something special to remember.

prices should use formal type and formal design. Script typefaces are often used to add a touch of class, but be very wary of using fancy fonts that are hard to read.

Remember, though, that people must be able to read your menu. Do not get caught up in a fit of "creativity" or a desire to win a design award at the next trade association convention. If your patrons can't read it, they can't order it. Consider the visual needs of your customers. For example, if you have a lot of elderly customers, you'll want to use simpler faces in larger type. Here are a few readability guidelines.

> People must be able to read your menu. Do not get caught up in a fit of "creativity."

Use at least twelve-point type. Fonts come in different sizes, referred to as point sizes. Twelve point is the size found on most typewritten pages. Ask, "Can my customers read this?"

Use contrast. Printing dark type over a dark color or complex design makes your menu harder to read, and that takes money right out of your pocket. Don't print light type over a light color, either.

Use lots of white space. A lot of "gray matter," too much type bunched together, makes it hard for the reader to find the item he or she wants. You're not getting more for your money by filling up every area of the menu with typography. A good use of white space is also helpful in your advertising.

Make your menu easy to navigate. Too many menus look as if the designer has just slapped down a bunch of type in random order. Guide your patron with large headlines, explanatory subheads, large graphics, and everything placed in a logical order.

Don't allow your graphics to outweigh your menu. Use them to support, not supplant. People are looking for "Bacon and Eggs....$5.95" and not for a brochure for the local art museum. Always remember the main attraction—the menu items.

Choose Appropriate Colors

Your favorite colors may or may not be appropriate. What counts most is what color or combination of colors enhance your menu and the food items on it. People react emotionally to colors, so make your selection based on what appeals to your customer base.

Green generally means good health. It's a color of life associated with growing things. Restaurants emphasizing healthy choices often use green.

Yellow is the color of the sun. It's a cheerful color often associated with breakfast. Yellow is a way to shout "rise and shine."

Red grabs your attention, as in "that's red hot." Red is a favorite color in Mexican establishments for that very reason. As this book is being written, the Chili's chain is using an animated red chili pepper in its television advertising. There's a very good reason.

Brown is an earth color. It's masculine and natural and is often used in health food and natural food restaurants.

Blue is cool and clear, like water. You'll often find a lot of blue used in seafood restaurant menus, signage, and advertising and promotion.

White is a symbol for purity and cleanliness and is applicable for virtually any restaurant.

Black is clean, elegant, formal, and prestigious. High-end restaurants often make good use of black in their menus.

Place Profitable Items Strategically

Even if you want your menu to look loose, design it that way. Place your most profitable items where the customer's eyes will latch onto them. On a single page the best position is slightly above the center line. If you're using a two-page menu, the best location is on the right side just above the center line.

Other tricks of the trade used to make items stand out is to put them in a slightly larger typeface, make the type bolder or in italics, box the item, put more white space around it, use arrows or artwork as pointers, or even set it at an angle on the page.

Promote Your Business with Your Menu

People sitting in your restaurant are a captive audience. What better time or place to promote that restaurant? Always include the following items in your menu: Prominently place the name, address, phone number, Web site address, and e-mail address so they can remember who you are, where you are, how to contact you, and how to come back for more. Display your hours of operation so they can arrive "not a minute too late" or end up waiting in the parking lot or, worse, driving down the road to become regular customers of a competitor.

Use your menu as an advertising vehicle to cross-promote other services. If you provide catering services, banquet facilities, birthday or anniversary specials, or merchandising, by all means let your customers in on the deal. Make certain that your menu enhances the theme and image of your restaurant from cover to cover.

Write Descriptive Copy

A menu should be "good reading." That is, people should be able to quickly and easily find the items they want, including relevant information about those items. The era of the cute menu full of ads, stupid stories, and lengthy descriptions is passing away. And it's not a minute too soon. Printing a Mexican restaurant menu entirely in Spanish may be "clever," but cleverness soon wears out when the patrons can't figure out what they're reading. Worse still, the time eaten up by the wait staff in making translations slows down the entire process of serving the customers.

The public these days is better educated. They don't want or need a bunch of poorly written or inane copy getting between them and their entrée. You can and in some cases you should be clever, but don't overdo it.

Descriptions are fine, but maintain some control over their length. Avoid fancy language unless you're operating a very upscale facility. Use descriptors such as fresh, crisp, chilled, ground daily, kosher, smoked, baked, broiled, spicy, hot, mouth-watering, special, and the like.

Proofread!

Proofread your menu again and again. Have other people proof it. If you have a sister-in-law or a cousin teaching English, have him or her pore over the thing, too. A simple typo can ruin the effect of an otherwise very well-done menu. A crossed-out item, such as a price, replaced by a hand-written notation is unforgivable. Your menu is your image. Make sure it is a professional one.

Seasonal versus Year-Round

Should your menu be static so that you always have a pretty good idea of how much to order of any given item? Or should you go with a seasonal menu that changes? Will the costs of those changes be offset by the additional profits brought in by using seasonal menus? There are positives and negatives to both approaches.

Buy When the Buying Is Good

One real advantage of a seasonal menu is that you can make your food purchases when there's a lot of the product around. Prices are lower when supplies are high. No one wants to hold out for high price and risk getting stuck with too much inventory. So when the shrimp is being hauled in,

Your Menu Is Part of Your Marketing Mix

A restaurant menu should secure your concept. It should tie all the elements together for your customer. For example, the Iguana Joe's menu was very colorful and used lots of corals and greens. It also incorporated many design elements from the building. For example, the interior walls were decorated with stripes, X's and circles, pink flamingoes, and even suitcases. The background of the menu was blue stripes with graphics of pink flamingoes, old suitcases, and old beach posters. Of course, the restaurant's menu was used.

when the strawberries are ripe, or when the "corn is as high as an elephant's eye," that's the time to buy. Good deals lead to good food on the menu.

On the downside, you lose the consistency of your menu. Supplies of seasonal items are notoriously fickle. For example, if the shrimp fishermen don't bring in the expected haul, you might not get all you need to meet customer demand. On top of that, the prices of what you do get will probably be higher. Customer disappointment can cause problems. Of course, you can't control the migratory patterns of shrimp in the Gulf of Mexico, but your customer really doesn't care. All he knows is that last week he came in and enjoyed a plate of tasty shrimp nachos. The item is still on the menu this week, but he can't get it. The dictates of supply and demand are nothing to the dictates of a man who wants a big plate of nachos.

Most of your customers will usually understand. The problem is that they've still experienced a disappointment, and that feeling becomes associated with your restaurant.

Another factor is the cost of redoing your menu. Every change in seasons demands new typography, new art elements, new paper and ink, and new printing. Another seasonal menu calls for writing another seasonal check.

Budget for Year-Round Savings

The opposite situation applies to a single, year-round menu. Basically, you print up an order and forget it. If you need a new menu, just grab one from the supply back in the office. Write one check, record it on the books, and that's pretty much it until you decide to change prices or the menu wholesale.

Having a single menu also pretty much ensures that you'll always have what the customer wants whenever he or she wants it. Naturally, there will be a few shortages now and then, but these should be rare events. Planning, scheduling, and budgeting is enhanced because you're dealing mostly with known factors. You'll take advantage of the lower prices when the shrimp harvest is in, but during the rest of the year you'll have made provisions to meet your needs and will have a well-stocked freezer.

Prices Always Fluctuate

You still have to stay on top of your supply situation. Droughts, floods, El Niño, snow melt, and dozens of other factors can affect the supply of meat, poultry, vegetables, and beverages. In any given year, prices can fluctuate wildly. Your cost/profit ratios can fluctuate right along with them. That's why restaurants need managers.

In summary, keep in mind that the core of your business is and will remain your menu. It is the bedrock of support upon which everything else will be built. Make certain that you start out with a solid foundation.

Keep in mind that the core of your business is and will remain your menu.

Chapter 12

Purchasing Supplies

Part One

Part Two

Part Three

Part Four

Part Five

Part Six

Presentation Is Key

Color is an important factor in selecting your dinnerware. Here's an example of someone who learned the hard way. A very talented chef in Tulsa, Oklahoma, opened his own restaurant. Almost immediately, he started getting complaints about the quality of his food. The complaints were hard to understand and equally hard to take. The chef really was good at his chosen profession.

He investigated and finally discovered the true source of the problem—food presentation. He had opened using very fancy, very expensive black china. People just hated the way their food looked on those shiny black surfaces. The dissatisfaction had nothing whatsoever to do with the quality of his fare.

The chef made a change to twelve-inch white dinner plates with colorful rims. Complaints from his customers virtually dried up.

Deciding on Dinnerware

Dinnerware is defined as your tableware, glassware, and silverware. How much you need depends on the nature of your operation and the number of customers you serve. A mom-and-pop Mexican restaurant can get by with a few of the basics: heavy plates and saucers, knife, spoon, fork, teaspoon, coffee cups, beer mugs, one or two styles of glasses, and paper napkins. A restaurant featuring fine European dining will require a much more varied and inclusive set of dinnerware items, such as a specialty spoon designed for eating snails or a demitasse cup for after-dinner coffee. What you need depends on what and who you serve.

Two key factors should be considered.

Choose a Style

Just like clothing, automobiles, and music, popular styles of dinnerware change. If your marketing plan embraces following the most current trends in the business or culture, you could be purchasing a lot of dinnerware on a fairly regular basis. Whenever possible, choose a style that will remain in style for some time to reduce your initial cost and your cost of replacement.

Look at Replacement Costs

Even if your style of dinnerware remains the same, waiters and waitresses will drop plates, which will shatter on the floors. Patrons will bump into glasses and send them to the same destination and an identical fate. Bussers, dishwashers, and cleaning equipment will take their toll, too. To keep these costly-but-inevitable accidents to a minimum, buy sturdy dinnerware.

Expect to invest $3,000 to $5,000 for china, glassware, plates, etc. Smallwares (pots, pants, scales, cutlery, tongs, spatulas, trash cans, can openers, ladles, and other kitchen prep and cooking items) will require another $1,500 to $3,000.

Purchasing Guidelines

You will need to purchase your tableware, glassware, and silverware based primarily on your seating capacity, with some consideration given to the type of place you operate and the needs and expectations of your clientele. Don't forget to include such items as salt and pepper shakers, salad bowls, tea pots for hot tea, side dishes (sometimes called "monkey dishes"), condiment holders for sugar and other sweeteners, creamers, and ashtrays. Getting that number is fairly easy. For example, if you have twenty tables, you'll need to order twenty sets of salt and pepper shakers, plus spares for back up.

Table 12-1 illustrates the dinnerware requirements for a typical restaurant. Plug in your numbers, customer expectations, and budget figures, and you'll have a pretty good base for making your initial order.

TABLE 12-1: TABLEWARE, GLASSWARE, AND SILVERWARE PURCHASING GUIDELINES

Item	Number per Seat	Item	Number per Seat
Dinner plates	2–3	Water glasses	3
Salad bowl/plate	2–3	Juice glasses	⅓–½
Side dish/monkey dish	3	Tea/beverage glasses	1–1½
Coffee cups/saucer	2–3	Forks	3
Soup bowls	2	Knives	3
Salt and pepper shakers	2¼	Steak knives	½–¾
Sugar holders	2¼	Tea spoons	3
Creamers	½	Iced tea spoons	1
Hot teapots	¼	Soup spoons	¾

You can allow your imagination to run free with all the different types of bar glasses that are available. Of course, you must keep in mind your budget and the needs of the folks who will be "bellying up" to that bar. Table 12-2 gives a list of basic glassware that should get you started.

TABLE 12-2: BAR GLASSWARE PURCHASING GUIDELINES

Type of Glass	Per 100 Seats	Type of Glass	Per 100 Seats
Cocktail	96	Wine—white	36
Highball	96	Cordial	8
Rocks	96	Margarita	36
Whiskey sour	48	Brandy snifters	12
Shots	48	Beer mugs/glasses	24
Wine—red	36	Frozen drink	24

The preceding figures are based on national averages, but Randy has used them successfully in a number of restaurants and bars for years. Your quantities will probably vary, but, initially, these will set you on the right course. Keep in mind that some tableware, especially china, is for decorative purposes only. It does not meet health code standards. Be sure that all the items you order meet or exceed the applicable local codes. Your vendors and suppliers can be very helpful in this area.

When to Replenish

Breakage happens in every restaurant. No matter how careful you, your staff, and your customers are, the sound of breaking glass or china will at some time grab everyone's attention. How many times have you been sitting at a restaurant and heard that shattering sound (sometimes followed by good natured applause)? While crossing your fingers in the hope that the tray currently sliding across the floor wasn't your order, haven't you thought, "Man, that sure cost the owner a few bucks!"

When that happens, more than the broken shards are tossed into the trash can. Some of your profits go in there, too.

No one can stop breakage. Like the rising of the sun, or better the falling (crashing, streaking, breaking) of a star, breakage will happen as long as you operate a restaurant. How do you stop it? Well, you don't, but you can institute some controls to reduce the damage.

Training is the key, and that's where you start the process. Begin with your wait staff and bussers. Educate them as to the proper way to serve and bus tables. Then show them how to correctly stack plates, glasses, cups, etc. on a bus table. Instruct them to never, never, never simply dump off a load.

Such careless behavior is guaranteed to break something. Keep a close eye on your wait staff and bussers during working hours to make sure they don't fall prey to bad habits as time passes. Show them how to stack items in the dishroom on the dirty dish rack. Not only will you prevent a lot of breakage, you'll also make the dishwasher's thankless job a lot easier. That will prevent even more damage and save you a few payroll dollars at the same time.

Teach your staff to separate the plates from the glassware and to put the silverware in a soaking container such as a bus tub. If you have a restaurant with bar service, it is highly recommended that you have your stemware and other delicate glassware washed in the bar. Have your bussers drop them off separately. This simple allocation of resources will save you money every day.

Breakage and replacement will be high if you do not set a policy on handling of your bar glassware. If you use a lot of stemware, your breakage will be higher than if you use big-base glasses. Bar glasses will usually run ½ to ¾ percent of your sales in replacement costs.

Food and Beverage Supplies

This area of purchasing is so varied and so wide open that it is virtually impossible to dictate specific guidelines. A good and competitive supplier of hamburger patties is far easier to find and to negotiate with than a supplier of truffles or the makings for a good batch of papabote. Cows are nearby and plentiful, and there are a lot of suppliers. Truffles are an entirely different matter. And when was the last time you saw a good papabote down at the supermarket?

Create your menu and settle on a specific set of recipes and stay with them. Change or make adjustments as you need to, but be very judicious in the process. Change just for the sake of change can be very expensive.

Two basic guidelines can apply across the board.

In the Bar
Less Is More

A fine-dining restaurant caters to a knowledgeable customer base. They know, appreciate, and expect to be served their drinks in the appropriate style of glassware. The more upscale your bar, the more specialized glassware and more storage space for that glassware will be required. Consider your patrons before ordering. For example, if your restaurant is a sports bar, you'll need more beer mugs than if you were running an upscale operation featuring fine wines and liqueurs.

With that exception noted, it is in your best interests to keep your glassware as simple as possible and your storage spaces under control. In fact, the faster your bartender has to open, mix, pour, and smile, the fewer types of glassware he or she should have to handle. Simplicity is speed, which translates directly into profit.

1. **Be specific.** Purchase only the exact ingredients that you need and only in the quantities that you need for a given period of time. If your menu and recipe calls for a twelve-ounce bone-in rib-eye steak, that's the criteria you use to evaluate your supplier's abilities to supply and their price for doing so.

2. **Buy quality.** Anything less ends up costing you more in the long run. Naturally, "quality" is a relative term. The meat ordered for a sports bar featuring hamburgers must meet all the health code standards, be pleasing to the eye, fresh, and tasty. However, it will also be covered with mustard, mayonnaise, and ketchup. There's no need to purchase a load of expensive cuts just to grind them into hamburger meat. Also, the egg-like products that look and pass for the real thing probably won't pass the taste test of an experienced diner. The quality may be superior, but in some cases that's still not good enough. If customers demand the real thing, then supply them with the real thing.

Work closely with your chef, your suppliers, and your customers. You'll get the hang of it soon. Your mastery of the science of purchasing will enhance the art of your cooking.

Choosing Suppliers

Choosing good suppliers who can provide quality at reasonable prices has gotten somewhat easier in recent years. The Internet has quite literally opened up the world to restaurateurs. There's still the challenge of shipping, delivery, receiving, and storage, but if you want thousand-year-old eggs from the Far East, you can log on and process your order in a matter of moments.

Clearly, those restaurants in larger markets have more variety of choices and more immediate access to suppliers. Yet trucks speed deliveries all across the nation every day to a country lined by efficient highways and roads. If you need something in the way of supplies, chances are it can find its way to your door with little trouble at all. So how do you select the people and companies who will be doing all that shipping?

Checking All Possible Information Sources

One of your first stops should be to fellow restaurateurs. Which suppliers are they using and for what supplies? Which ones deliver quality products? Are there any delivery problems? Have they encountered any regular problems or questions with billing and/or payments? Do some of the suppliers provide additional services, such as employee training? Can they relate any horror stories? Do they have any warnings? Recommendations from people in the same business will provide some of your best leads. Be sure to visit with your restaurant association, too. The organization probably has an approved supplier list.

Attend regional and national trade shows. These meetings are full of suppliers all anxious to earn your business. Meet with the representatives. Take home their literature. Get references and check them out. Lack of sources will never be a problem at a trade show. The only hassle you'll have is keeping some of them at bay as they pitch their wares.

Read your trade journals. They'll be full of advertising, which will provide products sold, names, addresses, Web sites and e-mail addresses, and other useful information. Check out the articles for featured suppliers. Take notes or clip articles and ads and then make contact with the most likely prospects.

> Attend regional and national trade shows. These meetings are full of suppliers all anxious to earn your business.

Asking Questions

Each supplier will have to address a number of issues unique to each restaurant. Still, you can help that supplier address your needs by asking very specific questions. During the give and take of research and pitch, you'll each come to a better understanding of how to best supply your needs. Here are a few to help you get the ball rolling.

- Can you provide exactly what I need for my menu and recipes?
- Can you provide those items consistently?
- Can you do so at a consistent price?
- What seasonal changes should I expect?
- Will you provide proof that your organization meets all appropriate government rules, regulations, and codes?

- When may I tour your facility? (If you can't take a tour, you'd better take a pass.)
- Have you failed any safety or sanitary inspections?
- How is your delivery fleet holding up? Any delivery complaints?
- Are your refrigerated trucks up to current specifications?
- What is your pricing structure? What are the bulk discount breakdowns?
- Have you received any industry awards, certificates, honors, etc.?
- What are your minimum order requirements?
- What are your terms of payments? How do I set up an account with you?
- Will you provide me with a list of references?

Ask these questions to every supplier. As you look around and ask questions, more and more specific questions will come to mind. Ask them all, and if you don't get adequate answers, look around some more. Remember that few organizations can deliver 100 percent satisfaction across the board. Just be sure that overall you will be satisfied with the service you receive for the prices you're charged.

It's a sound business practice to have at least two suppliers for each item you need. Competition is a healthy thing. Also, if one supplier unexpectedly has material or delivery problems, you have someone else in line to take up the slack.

The Role of a Good Supplier

The role of a good supplier is to supply. But if you work with them and allow them to work with you, they can supply a lot more than stoves and ovens, pots and pans, and meat and vegetables. Suppliers can be of tremendous value in planning your menu. For example, they serve a lot of different restaurants across a wide territory. They know what the customers are buying and what they are not buying. Knowing that twice-baked potatoes (or rib-eyes, chocolate mousse, spiced tea, etc.) are suddenly increasing in popularity at family restaurants can not only help you add an in-demand item to your menu, that information can also help you streamline your orders and thereby enhance your profits. These people have to stay on top of matters you might not even consider. For example, the supplier could warn you that orders for oysters will be down significantly in the coming year due to last season's hazardous waste spill that polluted the oyster beds. A good supplier, well connected to the industry, may even be in a position to spot major trends before they arrive. "Mediterranean fare will still be hot this year, but with more of a Moroccan flavor than Italian" may provide you with some inspiration to try out a few North African specials to verify public reaction to that trend. In other words, the supplier can help you stay ahead of your competition by helping you develop and adapt your menu to customer desires.

Remember the distributor who provided the chef to help Randy develop the Iguana Joe's menu? Many of your suppliers will be more than willing to help you in the same and other ways. Helping a new restaurateur works in everyone's favor. You get the help you need when you most need it. The distributor or supplier cements a relationship with someone who can become a good long-term customer. Suppliers are great resources. Don't hesitate to ask for help and advice.

Your vendors talk to a lot of people in the business and a lot of people in other businesses. If they like you and your operation, they'll spread the word. Be nice to these people. They are in a position to do you a great service. Many of them operate by the wise principle of "I do business with people who do business with me."

> The supplier can help you stay ahead of your competition by helping you develop and adapt your menu to customer desires.

Kitchen Equipment

One of your most important suppliers will be the company providing you with your kitchen equipment. It is essential that you conduct extensive research, check prices and resources, and shop competitively. A well-equipped kitchen will probably be on of the most expensive capital outlays you make. Make sure you plan your layout well so that every appliance fits properly and is conveniently located to all who will use it.

Take your time in making your equipment purchases. Really talk to your suppliers. Let them know exactly what you need, but also be open to better ideas. These are big-ticket items, and a simple suggestion could save you thousands of dollars. Restaurants such as Chilis, Applebee's, Outback, and others can invest $100,000 to $135,000 in kitchen equipment alone. Even a small pizza restaurant will require an investment of $25,000 to $40,000 in new equipment. Used equipment will still run from $15,000 to $21,000.

Keep an eye out for auctions, which are a great source of used equipment, as are bank repossessions, foreclosures, and going-out-of-business sales. Always check the equipment thoroughly to make sure you're getting something you can actually use over time. A good deal isn't such a good idea if it breaks down during a rush hour. And when shopping with suppliers, get competitive. Comparison shop, negotiate, and get the best deal possible.

Walk-In Cooler

If you're building a new restaurant or if the place you're buying or renovating doesn't have a walk-in cooler, you'll need to buy and install one. It will prove to be one of the most important parts of your kitchen operation. They vary in size and design, so make sure you design the area for its placement well. Plan on investing $8,000 to $15,000 for a new cooler.

Don't neglect to evaluate the shelving here, either. Some companies manufacture shelving especially designed for use in coolers and freezers. It's a wise investment, because they do not rust. This keeps the health department happy and off your back. The cost averages about $125 to $145 for a five-foot section with four shelves. Check it out, because the purchase will probably save you money in the long run. It's certainly more convenient than cleaning rust or buying new shelves when the health inspector says, "Uh-uh. That's got to go."

Beverage Equipment

Depending upon the supplier you chose, Coke or Pepsi, for example, you might be able to convince the distributor to install and maintain your beverage dispensing system. These units are very costly to purchase and to keep in sound operating condition. If the company does install the unit at no charge, they will expect loyalty on your part and that you purchase only their brands. That's a fair deal for both parties.

Be sure to check with your state government before attempting to negotiate such an arrangement. In some states the loaning of equipment may violate certain laws or regulations.

Bar Equipment

Work very closely with your suppliers. Tell them what you want, but also solicit ideas that might be better or more cost effective. Be open to new and better ideas from people who know the business. Always shop around and get multiple bids or prices.

A typical bar will need a jockey box. This is an ice bin with an area for juices and mixes used in mixing drinks. You will also need a three- to four-compartment sink, a drain board, refrigerator(s), draft beer box, or remote dispensing unit, blenders, mixers, and other related items. Plan on investing around $10,000 to $20,000 for bar equipment. Again, by working closely with your suppliers, you can probably save some significant cash or get more for your money.

Inventory Costs

Inventory is tied-up money, a resource sitting on the shelf and not earning you a dime. Inventory monitoring and control is essential to profitability. Remember Just-in-Time inventory? That's your target. It's a mistake to overstock anything out of fear that you'll run out. Emergency situations do develop, but they are rare and can usually be handled with a minimum of frantic activity. A little planning can take care of most such hassles. Have a list of "emergency" suppliers or phone numbers ready for just such an event.

Knowing What You Need

Figure out as closely as possible what supplies you need on a daily, weekly, and monthly basis. This primarily applies to food and related items, but keep any eye to the silverware, plates, etc., too. For example, if you determine that you need twenty-five steaks for Friday nights, make sure that you have twenty-five steaks in your inventory on Friday. It's okay to

Get the Right Equipment First

Sometimes trying to save a few bucks by getting by with existing equipment is more troublesome and costly than buying the right equipment at the start. Randy's restaurant Iguana Joe's was converted from a facility that had formerly housed a Lone Star Steakhouse.

Randy decided to use as much as possible of what was already in place. The grand opening was extremely successful in terms of the number of patrons who showed up. Unfortunately, the staff couldn't feed those folks as quickly as they deserved. Through no fault of their own, the kitchen staff just couldn't get the food out fast enough.

Plan your space and select the right equipment for the job or face the consequences in slow service, disappointed customers, poor reviews, and lost revenue.

plug in a fudge factor just to be safe, say 10 percent. This pretty much applies across the board. If you usually require ten bottles of red wine to go with those steaks, make sure you have ten (eleven with the fudge factor) on hand. If an unusual number of customers shows up and increases demand, you can always run to that emergency list or down to the Safeway or the corner liquor store to bail yourself out of the temporary shortfall. The point is to avoid having fifty T-bones tying up your capital when you only need twenty-five. That goes for beer, whiskey, salad dressing, dinner rolls, eggplants, and everything else.

The one exception might occur when you have an opportunity to make a great deal on a bulk order. Make sure the savings represent real savings. You'll have to factor in shipping and delivery charges plus the additional cost of storage. If the numbers, *all the numbers,* tumble in your favor, then go ahead and forget the Just-in-Time rule—this time.

Checking Supplies at the Door

Someone must be assigned to handle receiving of goods, especially food and beverage items. Receiving is a major focal point for lost profits. Make sure you receive precisely what you have ordered. Have someone check in each item, verify that it is the proper item in the proper quantity, and that the item is stored in its proper place. This procedure is essential to controlling inventory costs and therefore in controlling loss. You'll discover that it is amazingly easy to "lose" some merchandise on the loading dock or just inside your kitchen door.

Compare the delivery sheet with the purchase order for those goods and make sure they're an identical match. Real eggs and egg-like products may look and even remotely taste alike, but they are not one and the same. Their pricing is different, too. The person assigned to receiving must also make sure that the items ordered match the quality needed. An order of a dozen heads of lettuce should have a dozen heads of useable lettuce. Spoiled or very soon-to-be spoiled merchandise is a waste of money and inventory space. All of that comes out of your pocket. A sloppy or careless person in charge of receiving can over time cost you a fortune.

Creating Storage Space

Once you get it, you have to put it someplace. Storage space costs money, and that's another good reason for ordering just what you need. Your inventory storage should be conveniently located to the receiving area, easy to get in and out, easy to work in, and temperature controlled as necessary.

Well-organized storage also makes conducting inventories much easier, faster, and more accurate. If you don't appreciate that fact now, you will the first time you attempt to conduct one.

People must be able to get in and out of the area quickly and with the specific item they need. Obviously, put the more commonly required items nearest the door and in the most exposed areas. Hamburger meat will be sought after a lot more than those truffles or papabotes. Make sure it's handy. Store similar items together. For example, all produce should be in the same area. The same for dairy products, meat, canned goods, dry ingredients, and so forth. How you lay out your storage area is up to you, but make sure your people can get precisely what they need when they need it.

Point-of-Sale Materials

POS materials add marketing support to your menu by promoting specific menu items, such as special drinks, brand-name liquor, or desserts. These items can be high-profit dishes or loss leaders (dinner items that actually cost more than you sell them for) to attract customers who will hopefully order more profitable items. POS materials are frequently supplied by distributors and suppliers at low cost or even free to their customers. Again, this is a win/win scenario. The restaurant owner gets a lot of advertising and promotional material he or she could never afford. The supplier gets a lot of free advertising at the point where people order the products the company provides. You'll see a lot of these items

Are You Being Served?

Poor inventory procedures can lead to legal action against a restaurant owner. Here are two key guiding principles for your storage area.

Store cooked above raw. The reason is simple, raw food items drip. If any of that matter falls on cooked food and is served to patrons, a call to the ambulance company may be necessary later that evening. The trip to the hospital is usually followed by a call to the lawyer and an unwanted knock on your front door.

First in/first out. The first items stored should be the first items used. This is especially true for fresh food items. When that new batch of lettuce (or meat, eggs, milk, etc.) arrives, store it so that the older lettuce will be picked up and used first.

when a new snack or new drink is being introduced. Many times the materials are produced in conjunction with product rollouts from national brand name companies. The quality can be quite good.

Point-of-sale materials promote menu items before the customer even starts reading. They also remain in place, selling throughout the meal long after the waitperson has removed the menu. POS materials also offer your waitpersons an unobtrusive means of selling more items. They can simply point to the obvious POS item on the table and ask if the patron has tried it. The materials can provide a real boost to the impact of your menu.

POS materials include tent cards (folded ad cards placed on the table), items such as flags or banners to hang on walls and ceilings, colorfully designed balloons and blow-up toys, and all kinds of advertising materials. Some of these items border on junk (which is entirely appropriate for some operations), but a lot of it is really top quality, suitable for a wide range of restaurants. Some suppliers will even produce POS materials for your restaurant, complete with your name and logo printed on the item. As favorable as this might be, keep in mind that the supplier has other customers. Don't be offended if you find identical materials with another restaurant's name and logo in an operation across town.

> Point-of-sale materials promote menu items before the customer even starts reading.

Chapter 13

Securing Permits

Part One

Part Two

Part Three

Part Four

Part Five

Part Six

Go Along to Get Along

If you are new to the business or new to the city, remember that you will get further along the licensing/permit process if you have a good attitude.

Arrogance begets arrogance, or at least something called "payback." Guess in whose favor the deck is stacked? If you thought "inspector," then you guessed right. We all have different facets of personality. Why not use the pleasant ones? Randy often approaches people with the "good ol' boy" aspects of his nature. He's found that it works quite well and that many of his inspectors turn out to be some of his best customers.

Many people live by the motto, "It's better to ask for forgiveness instead of permission." That works sometimes and in some cases—never with the health department.

Getting to Know the Bureaucrats

To open a restaurant, you will have to apply for, meet the requirements for, perhaps make adjustments for, and eventually obtain a number of licenses and permits. Throughout the process you will be working with a number of government regulatory officials. Rules are rules, and you will have to comply if you want to open your restaurant and keep it open. How quickly and easily the application process goes depends to a considerable measure upon your own attitude and willingness to jump through the bureaucratic hoops placed before you.

Bureaucrats have been criticized for centuries as bumbling, inept, power-mad, insecure, paper-pushing bean counters. In some instances there is just cause for the description. Shakespeare's Hamlet speaks of bearing the "law's delay" and the "insolence of office," and that was written 400 years ago! Nevertheless, most people you meet in the license and permit departments of the various governments will be good people trying to do a good job.

It is in your interest to get to know these folks. Meet them in person whenever possible, even if you don't like dealing with government agencies or people. Put a face on the "faceless bureaucrat." People like to do things for people they like and admire. The government agent works every day with people just like you. From his or her perspective, you could all be the same person. It therefore becomes your job to stand out positively in the representative's mind. Of course there are no guarantees, but as he or she sits at a desk piled high with applications, isn't it more likely that the applicant that is known and liked will earn a high spot on that pile?

Consider what you know about human nature and act accordingly. Never go into an office or a meeting expecting the worst. A bad attitude on your part can create an atmosphere that will create the very scenarios you want to avoid. When you approach the license and permit process with an open mind and friendly demeanor, most people will respond in kind. And when you encounter the power-mad, insecure, or inept "faceless" one, just remember Hamlet. Bear the insolence and delay and get on about your business as quickly as possible.

Knowing the Cost of Delayed Openings

Delays aren't worth whatever caused them, which is usually an effort to skirt an issue or get by with something. Government agencies have inspectors, and it is their duty to find violations of permits and licenses. They're frequently very good at their jobs. Trying to pull off a "fast one" on these folks usually backfires.

For example, let's say it's the afternoon of opening night. An inspector walks through the kitchen and notices a roach, a bug, or some ants scurrying across the floor. He or she follows the trail to your walls. There the inspector finds a pipe or a door or an opening that isn't properly sealed against pest entry, an item the owner (certainly not you) bypassed to save a few hundred bucks during construction. The inspector shuts down the kitchen until the opening is sealed. With the kitchen down, the owner can't prepare food for the customers beginning to arrive in the parking lot. They'll be disappointed, frustrated, perhaps even a bit angry and may choose to take their patronage elsewhere for the rest of the year. Employees, even if sent home, have to be paid for the time already put in. Food and beverage will be wasted. The owner will have to pay for a costly reconstruction job, which will further delay the opening. All the opening advertising has gone to waste. And it goes on and on and the costs rise and rise.

This is a nightmare scenario but one that can easily be avoided. All you have to do is understand the process and play by the rules.

Understanding the Process

Before you actually make your applications, explore the ins and outs of the process. Find out which department you'll report to. Get the name of the person in charge or information you will need to present and in what form. Be fully prepared when it's time to make that application. You'd probably be surprised at the number of business owners who approach their license

Do You Need an Expeditor?

An expeditor is someone who knows the application process, the agencies, departments, and people involved. It's his or her job to take the paperwork for you and push it through the process as quickly, as easily, and as painlessly as possible. You can also hire an expeditor to handle a particularly challenging license or permit.

The decision to hire an expeditor depends on a number of factors. Do you have the experience and knowledge to research, fill out, and file all the paperwork? Do you have the necessary time available to carry out the process? Can you afford to hire an expeditor? As with many business decisions, it eventually revolves around time, energy, money, and the best allocation of resources.

or permit contact without the necessary information. All this does is create frustration and extra work for the contact. Again, consider human nature. Who will get preferential treatment, the disorganized and ill-prepared applicant or the person with all his or her papers in order?

Contact Good Resources

Good resources for getting this information include your lawyer and accountant, the office of the county clerk, or the city's office of economic development. Your local restaurant association is sure to have a lot of valuable information, too. Remember that licenses and permits may be required by local, state, and federal governments.

If you're building or remodeling, contracting and related license and permit applications should be the responsibility of your architect, designer, and or contractor. The individual or the firm you select should be fully up-to-date on all procedures and current requirements. You can, of course, verify these regulations yourself by contacting the health department, fire department, and the agency responsible for building codes.

Working Within the System

When working with bureaucrats it helps to remember that you aren't outside the system. You are an integral part of it. In essence you are all on the same team. Yes, you will always encounter arrogant and incompetent people within the bureaucracy. Don't allow their negativity to affect the way you treat people and bring you down to their nonproductive level.

Most people in most bureaucracies are overworked and underpaid, so they're in place out of a sense of duty, pride, and a sincere belief in what they are doing. Treat them that way and you'll be amazed at how cooperative people can be.

One of the best ways to deal with someone is to simply pick up the phone and call him or her. You may be in California and the person you need is in Washington, D.C., and you'll never meet face to face. You can still punch in a couple of numbers and contact that person with surprising ease. Don't be intimidated or hesitant. If you need help or information, get on the phone immediately while the idea or concern is "hot."

Don't Do Lunch

Here's another tip. Americans are infatuated with the business lunch. This may sound strange coming from a book on restaurant management, but avoid lunch meetings with bureaucrats, business partners, or associates, or anyone else if the get-together relates to business. You'll both waste time driving to and from the meeting, and the efficiency of that meeting will be impaired by the lack of privacy, limited time frame, and the constant bustling of restaurant patrons and personnel. Again, pick up the phone, solve the problem, and then dine out for the purpose of enjoying a good meal.

Contacting Your Top Three Bureaucrats

Your first three areas of business (regarding permits) should be to the following departments and agencies.

Visit the Health Department

Sanitation and safety is a special responsibility for restaurant owners, managers, and employees. The public deserves a clean and safe environment, as do those employees. Find out the local regulations on health and safety codes. Determine whether your employees who handle food and beverage will be required to get special certifications. Many of these considerations will affect the design of your layout, particularly the kitchen area. Make this visit early so you can incorporate those specifications into your designs (see Chapter 8 for more on timing). That's a lot better and certainly more cost effective than having to make changes after you've failed an inspection during construction. Ask first so you don't have to answer questions later on.

Address Environmental Concerns

This is a very local matter. Check with the state department of environmental quality and any corresponding local agencies. Areas of concern could include smoke from your ventilators, garbage and waste disposal, sewage, drainage, storage of chemicals, disposal of chemical wastes such as cleaning fluids, and even eye and ear pollution from signage or loud music.

Acquire Your Tax ID Number

Your business will need a federal Tax ID number from the Internal Revenue Service. This is a simple process and takes very little time. It's best to go ahead and take care of the matter early on so you'll have the number available when it is requested. Your attorney or accountant can provide you with information, or you can contact the IRS directly at ✆ 1-800-829-1040 or ✐ *www.irs.gov*. Getting a federal tax ID number is simple, painless, and— best of all—free!

Sample Permits and Certificates

> Every state and every community is different and will have different sets of rules and regulations, licenses and permits, agencies and bureaucracies.

Every state and every community is different and will have different sets of rules and regulations, licenses and permits, agencies and bureaucracies. The following material is from the State of Louisiana, where Randy owns a number of restaurants and clubs. Use the material as a guideline for your own research into your own state and community. There will be variations, but this is the type of material with which you will be dealing.

Food Permits

Food permits for food and beverage outlets are governed by the Louisiana Sanitation Code, which is administered by the Sanitation Services Department. Its offices are within the Louisiana State Office Building. Relevant information is contained in the code, which is readily available to interested parties. The permit should not be requested until all requirements for the retail establishment are complete.

Food Safety Certificate

The state requires all food-service licensees with annual sales exceeding $125,000 to obtain a Food Safety Certificate. Applicants must complete an education and training program, which is approved by the Council on Food Safety. Areas of concern addressed in the program include the nature, prevention, and control of food-borne illnesses, transmission methods, identifying and monitoring critical control points to enhance the safety of food production, processing, and serving.

A certificate is issued by the Department of Health & Hospitals or its designated agent and remains valid for five years statewide. It also supercedes any mandated certification courses in local communities. Compliance inspections are conducted by the same department. When an establishment is found in noncompliance, it has ninety days to rectify the situation. If the situation is not corrected to the satisfaction of the inspector, the food-service license can be revoked. See Appendix B for a food safety check list.

Responsible Vendor Program

This is an educational program for owners, managers, and employees concerning the sale, service, and consumption of alcoholic beverages. A retail license holder is required to earn a certification as a responsible vendor by placing all employees working with alcoholic beverages in the program's training course. Applicants must do so within forty-five days of employment.

In Louisiana, an employee is required to take the course if he or she is "involved in the serving, selling, mixing, or dispensing of alcohol." Employees who check IDs are also required to take the course. Bussers or greeters who do not take or deliver drink orders are exempt. This definition is according to the Office of Alcohol and Tobacco Control.

Responsible Vendor Program certificates are written in the name of the individual who takes and passes the course. It, therefore, is not associated with any given restaurant and may be taken with the employee to other restaurants. It remains valid for two years unless revoked or suspended. Restaurant owners/managers are required to keep up-to-date training records of certified employees.

This program is derived from a relatively new law in the state that shares the legal burden between the owner and the server. For example, if a server breaks an alcohol-related law, a criminal charge could be filed against that server. Time in jail, fines, and revocation or suspension of the employee's server's permit are possible. The program is regarded as one very favorable to owners.

Alcoholic Beverage Permit

A restaurant or a bar must have a beverage permit to sell alcoholic beverages within the state. Louisiana does not have a dram law. That means if someone who has consumed alcohol causes injury, property damage, or even death due to that consumption, the individual is responsible for his or her own actions. The restaurant or bar is not responsible even though the alcohol was purchased and consumed there.

Although the drinking age in Louisiana is twenty-one, an employee eighteen years old or older may serve or sell alcoholic beverages. An employee can be under the age of eighteen and be employed provided that the sale of alcoholic beverages isn't the main business of the establishment and provided that the employment does not directly involve the sale of alcoholic beverages for consumption on the premises.

A restaurant is required to run an ad in a local newspaper for two days prior to making an application for an alcohol permit. The ad must read as follows.

I am or we are applying to the Commissioner of Alcoholic Beverage Control of the State of Louisiana for permit to sell beverages of high and low alcoholic content at retail in the Parish (county) of _____ at the following address: Business name, street address, city, owner's name or the name of the corporation and the corporate office and his or her title.

After the ad has run, the newspaper issues an affidavit verifying that the ad has run.

Child Labor Laws

Minors ages fourteen and fifteen working in most states must have work permits, while minors age sixteen and seventeen must have employment certificates. Minors under age sixteen are usually prohibited from operating the following:

- Motor vehicles
- Power machinery
- Grinding machines
- Mixing machines
- Meat slicers or meat saws
- Elevators
- Automatic elevators

They are also prohibited from cooking and baking except at soda fountains, lunch counters, snack bars, or cafeteria serving counters.

Employees under the age of eighteen are not permitted to operate power machinery, meat slicers or meat saws, or elevators. An employee must be eighteen years old or older to serve alcoholic beverages.

Minors under sixteen cannot work in any gainful occupation except street trades for more than eight hours per day. They are not permitted to work more than six consecutive days in one week. They cannot be made to work more than forty hours per week except in agriculture, domestic services, or street trades. Minors under sixteen are not permitted to work more than three hours a day any day school is in session. Any minor working five consecutive hours must be granted a thirty-minute meal break.

Minors under sixteen are not permitted to work before 7 A.M. or after 10 P.M. except in street trades. Employment in street trades is prohibited during school hours; before 4:30 A.M. or after 7 P.M.; and April 1 through Labor Day—not after 8 P.M. Minors under fourteen cannot work on Sundays before 6 A.M.

When in Doubt, Check It Out

Even such a mundane task as changing your china serving dishes can become a major hassle if you don't check them out with your local health department. Here's an example of the nightmares that can develop.

A restaurant owner in Tulsa ordered a lot of new soup and serving dishes that were not approved by the local health department. The owner's suppliers should have informed him of the fact, but they didn't.

During the next inspection, he was told to get rid of the noncomplying dishware or shut down. The owner had to invest an additional $3,800 in new china that was in compliance. This was on top of the $4,500 he'd already spent on china he could no longer use and that the supplier wouldn't take back.

Chapter 14

Recruiting a Support Staff

Part One

Part Two

Part Three

Part Four

Part Five

Part Six

Finding the Right People

A restaurant owner is in touch with a lot of people: patrons, employees, suppliers, and even people from various governments. Owners and managers need all the help they can get. Fortunately, a lot of help is available. Chief among the members of your support team will be your lawyer, accountant and bookkeeper, insurance broker, financial advisor, and your marketing, advertising, and public relations advisors. This section gives you a brief job description of each.

Use the same basic process for finding a good lawyer as you'll use for finding a good accountant or marketing advisor. Start by getting recommendations from friends and associates, especially those in the business. Call them and set up an appointment. Usually the first visit with these professionals is at no cost. They view the meeting as a new business call. Conduct a serious interview and ask pointed questions. Ask for references and call those references. Leave nothing to chance, because you will be handing over the responsibility for a major portion of your business to these people.

Rallying Professional Support Early

Every restaurant has its in-house team: cook/chef, wait staff, business staff, and people fulfilling various functions for the business and the customers. These are essential services, but there are outsourced professionals who make equally valuable contributions to your operations. Unlike a chef or a bartender who can be hired fairly late in the game, it's important that you

How's Your Confidence?

You don't have to become pals with the professionals who serve your needs, but you should have a certain level of comfort with them. Do you feel confident in their abilities? Does he or she return phone calls promptly? Is there a sufficient level of trust? Does the professional treat you as a valued client? What are the fees involved? Are there additional charges for certain services? What will be the fee structure for your relationship?

bring these outside professionals inside as soon as you can. This section gives you a brief rundown. You can then find out more in the specific sections about each member of your support team.

Ignoring the Law Is Dangerous

Some states do not have "dram shop" laws. Legally, the consumption of alcoholic beverages is the cause of any injury, including death and/or damage to property to self or others that is caused by someone who is intoxicated. The sale of those beverages is not held to be the cause of the damage. In other words, the bartender who sold the last drink to an individual involved in a traffic accident is not responsible for that accident. The drinking driver is considered at fault. In other states, just the opposite is true. The bartender is considered a guilty party in the event. Legal penalties and damages for the bartender, the restaurant or lounge, and the owner of the establishment can be severe.

What's the law in your state? If you don't know or if you're unsure, then you've just experienced one of innumerable reasons to have a good attorney as part of your professional team. He or she can inform you up front about potential liabilities and legal concerns relating to your restaurant business, inform you as to the various legal permits and related matters you'll need to acquire, and keep you apprised of the inevitable changes in local, state, and federal law.

Restaurants are involved in many touchy areas of the law, public health and employee safety to name a couple. Laws and regulations can be stringent and expensive if violated. When getting into this business, it's wise to develop a good understanding and feel for applicable law and regulation. But it's practically impossible to run a successful restaurant and stay on top of the complex and ever-changing legal world. You need a professional active in that business to watch your back.

Interview a number of qualified attorneys. Find someone (or some firm) that is experienced, interested in you and your business, and is someone you can relate to and with whom you feel comfortable discussing important matters. Your attorney should be accessible, especially when you find yourself in a bind. He or she should provide a list of services, the fees and related costs for services, and a list of items or services that could generate additional costs. Place everything out on the table, come to an agreement, and then both of you work like crazy to make sure the only legal services you need are for routine matters.

Accountants Are More Than Bean Counters

You'll want to bring in the skills of a professional accountant within this time frame. You'll be making financial decisions from then on, so it's essential to have an expert at hand. Of course, you can find any number of basic accounting programs that you can insert into your computer drives, programs that will cover most or all of the basics of accounting. You can do the same thing with bookkeeping programs or you can hire out the services. Those conveniences do not replace your need for a topnotch accountant on your team. The restaurant business can change almost overnight. A restaurateur needs to be able to make swift financial judgments to handle a crisis or take advantage of a big opportunity. The guidance, advice, and counsel of a financial expert is invaluable at those times. It's valuable throughout the year, too. A good accountant will keep you posted on changes in regulations and the law that could have a dramatic impact on your business. Often an accountant can bring a new or little-known article to your attention that can save you far more money than you'll ever pay that accountant. An equally important service is to bring to your attention matters that if left untended could create serious problems for your cash flow, savings, or the health of the business.

Interview a number of individuals or firms. It's okay to provide some basic services on your own. After all, those computer programs can be right handy. Still, you'll need the services of a professional to make sure all the i's are dotted and the t's crossed at the correct height of the stem. Your accountant shouldn't be a passive receiver of documentation or someone that just spits back out your raw data in proper form. You want someone who is aggressively looking out for your interests, someone who brings you new ideas, suggests better ways of conducting business, and who isn't afraid to apply a little chastisement when you leave the financial straight and narrow.

> A restaurateur needs to be able to make swift financial judgments to handle a crisis or take advantage of a big opportunity.

Acquire Access to Capital

Some of that money needs to be placed in your hands, and the key to that transaction is your banker. Note the wording there, "your" banker, not "a" banker. The restaurant business is built on a thin margin of profit. Changes in the public tastes require changes in restaurant operations, menus, and methods of doing business. Shifting population bases may require a move to a different location. Opportunities arise when least expected. All of these events, and others, require infusions of capital.

Establish a personal relationship with a good banker in a solid bank. See that your banker gets to know you and your business thoroughly. You want a relationship so comfortable that you can make a phone call, state your need, and get a "come on in and we'll run the numbers" answer right away. Many smart businesspeople have a business lunch with their banker at least once a year. Outside of both offices, they meet and discuss what's going on, what's good, what's bad, and what might be coming down the road. The meeting isn't to blow smoke; it's to keep a valuable human asset up-to-speed and on your side.

Insure Your Restaurant

During your six months/one year set-up time frame, you should make time to investigate your needs for insurance coverage. As with most needs, specific requirements vary according to the type of restaurant and the market it serves. Regardless of those variables, you'll have to address two key areas:

1. Make certain that you don't overinsure your business so that you do not pay more than the value of the coverage you're getting.
2. Be equally certain that you are not underinsured. In the event of a loss, you could get less than you need to rebuild or, worse, no settlement at all. These and other considerations require an investment of time with a qualified insurance agent, preferably someone with experience in the restaurant business.

Insurance coverage you should consider includes business interruption insurance, property, liability, equipment, food spoilage, automobile, employee dishonesty, and crime. Other areas that may be appropriate for your operation are hired and non-owned automobile liability, playground coverage, valet parking, deductible and coinsurance options, fine arts coverage, and perhaps higher limits on any or all of the above.

Lawyer

You need a very good lawyer, preferably one with some experience in the restaurant industry. We live in a litigious society. People will sue other people at the drop of a hat. Sometimes it appears that all rational thought is tossed to the wind as seemingly normal people turn vicious, greedy, or vengeful over some perceived wrong. You may be able to avoid such an unpleasant encounter, but you will still need a good attorney to guide you through all kinds of situations.

For example, you'll need someone to review your lease agreements or your documents to purchase land, a building, or major equipment. If you make an agreement with your general manager offering a percentage of your profits, an attorney will need to draw up or at least review the paperwork. You can find a lot of do-it-yourself legal kits for setting up your business. Many of them can be purchased off racks in bookstores. You can do this, but be aware that the law can be a very complex matter. At least have an attorney review your do-it-yourself paperwork.

Your attorney should be "on call" whenever you need a legal opinion, and you should never be shy about making that call. Paying your lawyer for an hour of his or her time is far more cost effective than living with a bad

Don't Overlook Insurance

Insurance is a matter for serious consideration. A lack of coverage, even in a seemingly "small" area, can turn into a huge problem if you lack proper insurance or are underinsured in that area. Talk to the professionals. Get all the coverage you need at the right levels for full protection. In the long run, that's the most cost-effective way to buy insurance.

agreement. Make sure your lawyer reviews all legal documents, including contracts, letters of intent, leases, and employee policies and procedures.

Accountant

An accountant is essential in setting up the structure of your business and then in helping make sure that business stays on track. It's very expensive to have an accountant or an accounting firm keep your books on a daily basis. It's better to have someone keep the books and then turn the figures over to the accountant each month and at the end of the year.

Someone with bookkeeping experience can put in the sales figures, count the money, and organize the invoices. Management conducts all the inventories, and the owner has exclusive control of the checkbook. At the end of the month, all the paperwork is put together and shipped off to the accountant, who prepares the financial statements.

There are advantages and disadvantages to this system. For example, using an outside accountant puts an objective pair of eyes on your financial situation. It's possible for an owner or manager to be so close to a situation he or she can miss a problem obvious to an outsider. A major disadvantage of the system is that it gives management a significant amount of control. Whatever the accounting firm gets is filtered through the manager in charge of the restaurant. The manager can "cook the books" by sending in false or inaccurate data. An accountant can only work with the information provided. If it's off-base, then the financial statements will be off-base too.

Additionally, it's often difficult for someone working under a general manager to check up on that general manager. As the owner you will have to institute a system of checks and balances to make sure everyone is doing his or her job properly.

Bookkeeper versus Accountant

It's far more cost effective to have a bookkeeper manage the books on a daily basis. This individual can be an employee or an outside contractor. He or she handles the monthly statements, daily postings of sales and invoices, payroll, and payroll taxes. The inventory is handled by management and the figures checked by the bookkeeper. Tax returns are then handled by the accountant or accounting firm. The accountant is then available to answer questions and to review the financials with the owner if necessary.

Be sure that your bookkeeper has some formal training. Usually the first two accounting courses offered at the college level are enough. Find someone with restaurant experience or at least experience in dealing with inventories. Always ask for references and conduct a thorough background check. The potential for financial mischief is enormous in the restaurant business.

Again, set up a series of checks and balances, as many as your budget will allow. For example, have the day shift check the night shift's deposits. Have two people conduct your inventories. Divide the responsibilities. See that one individual handles the paperwork and another handles the money.

Accountant as Tax Advisor

In addition to setting up your business structure, an accountant should serve as a tax advisor, come to you with financial advice and suggestions, and help develop and implement an overall sound financial strategy. You'll want to involve your accountant in major purchases, investments, and other financial matters.

Banker

Bankers are primarily concerned with three questions:

- Where is the bank's money going?
- How will we get it back (with interest, of course)?
- What happens if we can't get it back?

No matter how solid your relationship, you will have to provide satisfactory answers to those questions. Respect your banker's time and expertise. Whenever making a loan application, have all your financial statements and documents in order. Anticipate all questions, have the answers at your fingertips, and be able to respond with confidence and enthusiasm.

You will probably be applying for one or more of four basic types of loans.

Mortgage loans are for long terms, such as fifteen years, and are used to finance large purchases such as land, a building, or major equipment.

Equipment or working capital loans are for shorter durations, perhaps seven years at the maximum. For example, if you borrow money to purchase a new stove, the loan will be designed for a payout on or before that equipment's useful life ends.

Inventory loans are designed to cover short-term needs, usually ninety days or less. The lending institution receives its payback from the sale of the inventory purchased.

A line of credit allows you to borrow short-term funds with reduced paperwork. Lines of credit are generally paid in full yearly.

The important factor is to consider your banker as an important member of your professional team. It's equally important that you make sure he or she feels the same.

> Consider your banker an important member of your professional team.

Insurance Broker

Seek out an insurance professional representing a number of insurance companies, someone who can provide you with a number of options. He or she should really know the business and be in a position to offer and explain all of those options. Your agent should be interested in your specific needs and the specific needs of your business. Insurance is a serious matter. You can't pick and choose as if reading a menu. You'll need general liability, employee benefits, and coverage specific to your environment, business operation, and individual needs. Here are a number of types of insurance you should consider.

For Fire/Extended Coverage

Fire/extended coverage insurance protects against loss of your property and contents in the event of a fire, natural disaster, or vandalism. Remember that replacement usually costs more than the original purchase, so buy enough protection to get your business up and running.

Document Everything!

During his twenty-eight years in business, Randy has been sued hundreds of times. Fortunately he's never lost a case. One of the reasons he's been so successful was he learned from a mentor. The man's advice was simple, "Document everything." Otherwise the judge and/or jury has to decide a "he says/she says" case.

Train your managers to document everything, too. Make it a policy to document everything, including slips and falls, calling a cab for a customer who had too much to drink, thefts, and any confrontations with customers. Take photos when appropriate. It only takes a few minutes, and it can save you so much grief. Make notes of who was working when the incident happened.

For Liability Insurance

Liability is particularly important for a restaurant. General liability provides protection if a patron, guest, or visitor is injured on your property. Product liability covers you in the event that someone becomes ill after eating in your restaurant. Liquor liability provides coverage in cases where an inebriated patron causes an accident or commits a crime after leaving your establishment. The cost of liquor liability will depend upon the amount of liquor business you do. The more bar business you have, the greater the risk and the higher the premiums.

For Auto Insurance

Auto/truck insurance will protect you should an employee have an accident while making a pick-up or delivery.

For Theft Insurance

Theft insurance is important because there are so many opportunities for thievery in a restaurant. Money, inventory, even smallwares can be "pocketed" and taken away quite easily. Restaurant equipment is often a valuable commodity on the black market. Even your supplies can be targeted. Ask about obtaining a fidelity bond to cover losses from employee theft.

For Business Interruption Insurance

Business interruption insurance protects you from the loss of business revenues. For example, after the tornado rips through your facility, you won't be able to conduct business until you rebuild, yet your expenses, such as the mortgage or equipment rentals, continue.

Marketing, Media, and Public Relations

In addition to the four core support areas, you'll likely need some help with marketing, media, and public relations. Choosing professionals in marketing and the related fields is a matter of your own personal expertise or the expertise of an employee, your available time, and your budget.

Media salespeople can certainly provide valuable information, suggestions, promotions, and even help with production of your ads or spots. Of course, these folks are salespeople and quite naturally will promote their own media above the competition. There's nothing wrong with that. It's just a factor to add into your equations.

Using an Outside Firm

Professional marketing, advertising, public relations, and design firms are an option, but they can be expensive. It's not essential that the firm have restaurant or club experience, but it is very helpful if they do. Previous experience can really shorten the learning curve. Make sure that any professional or professional firm you hire sees your restaurant's concept just the way you see it. Randy hired a top designer to create a logo for one of his restaurants. It was beautiful and very professional. Unfortunately, it looked "expensive," which meant that people thought the restaurant was expensive, too. It wasn't, but a lot of people never discovered that fact because they never walked into the door. As with all your professional

Training for Too Much Success

Randy hired a marketing and PR agency to help launch a fun Cajun seafood restaurant. The ad agency was instructed to start a teaser campaign twenty-eight days out to raise awareness about the new restaurant. The agency generated so much attention that during the opening week they were overcome by eager patrons. The restaurant ran out of food by 7:35 P.M. the first night and around 8:30 P.M. the next night.

He was afraid that the public would not be so forgiving and be upset that they couldn't be served, never to return. Fortunately, the ad agency turned a negative into a positive and convinced the public that the restaurant was the place to be. The overwhelming response to the grand opening the first few days was proof that the dining-out public was in for a true treat, if they could just get in.

suppliers, make sure that your marketing firm is a good fit for you and your restaurant.

Hiring an In-House Promotions Director

Many restaurants have a full-time person assigned to handle promotions, even when a marketing firm is part of the overall mix. If this person is good, well-motivated, and a creative thinker, he or she can be a tremendous asset to building your business. Here is a look at the criteria Randy uses to find the right people for this critical position.

The promotions director must show skills at constantly creating, organizing, and executing promotional activities designed to enhance revenues in food and beverage outlets, while remaining within budget guidelines. He or she must constantly control aspects of each promotional activity to ensure a smooth execution. Duties will include completing twenty-five solicitation phone calls each day to include new contacts, follow-ups (inquiries and current promotion guest responses), etc.

The director will constantly organize and execute frequent sales blitzes with tightly targeted markets. He or she must frequently create and distribute event calendars for in-house and local community use while researching existing vendor-supplied events and create unique supplemental events in-house. The

Finding Out What Your Franchise Allows

If you've purchased a franchise, some of these details will be handled for you as part of the package. Usually a set percentage of your franchise fee is allocated to advertising. Depending upon your agreement, you may be permitted to advertise on your own. Be sure to verify your limits so that you don't violate that agreement.

director must frequently interface with local radio stations to maximize co-sponsorships and prize donations.

The director will frequently solicit co-sponsorships independently of liquor and local suppliers (beauty shops, other retailers). Weekly recaps of events will be prepared and reviewed with the general manager, food and beverage director, and beverage/ lounge manager as necessary. He or she will communicate to the supervisor on all matters relating to lounge promotions as frequently as necessary.

Other duties include ensuring the consistency of product and service; when applicable, exhibit menu and wine knowledge; maintain an open line of communication for the distribution of pertinent information to appropriate staff; complete all paperwork relating to lounge promotions; if applicable, determine and play music within approved format for the evening when required; promote other outlets and upcoming events over the microphone during the evening, or have the DJ make announcements (voice-overs); maintain and encourage a lively club; display knowledge of third-party liability; demonstrate positive leadership characteristics that inspire others; promote employee empowerment (incentives); attend all mandatory meetings; complete other duties as assigned by supervisor to include cross-training; report all unsafe conditions immediately; and keep the work area clean and organized.

Some of those duties are basic, requiring only common sense. Others require a high level of skill and knowledge. All requirements mandate a desire for total customer dedication and, ultimately, the success of the restaurant.

Chapter 15

Hiring Employees

Part One

Part Two

Part Three

Part Four

Part Five

Part Six

PART FOUR STAFFING YOUR RESTAURANT

■ CHAPTER 14 Recruiting a Support Staff ■ CHAPTER 15 **Hiring Employees** ■ CHAPTER 16 Establishing a Good Work Environment ■ CHAPTER 17 Training and Coaching Employees ■ CHAPTER 18 Understanding Labor Costs

Understanding Which Employees You Need

Just who are the employees you need? Well, the staff varies from restaurant to restaurant according to the skills necessary to keep the individual operation functioning smoothly. Generally, the occupations will be pulled from among the following categories:

- The *host* or *hostess* greets the customers, seats them, and coordinates service and workstations to make sure each patron receives constant and thorough service.
- Your *cashier* collects payments, controls checks, answers the phone, and works the walk-up window. He or she can't let busy moments or stacking up customers to detract from a pleasant demeanor.
- *Bussers* assist waiters and waitresses, and maintain cleanliness and organization in the dining areas.
- The *cook* or *chef* prepares food and works with the manager to keep the menu up-to-date and in-demand.
- *Dishwashers* and *utility personnel* maintain a clean stock of service-ware and equipment for use by other personnel.
- Your *head waiter* or *head waitress* sells and serves the entire menu and is basically responsible for the entire dining room experience.
- The *bartender* prepares cocktail orders for waitpersons and also serves customers directly.
- Your *restaurant manager* is responsible for all restaurant operations.
- The *bar manager* is responsible for all bar operations.
- Your *general manager* holds the responsibility for all club/restaurant operations.
- The *manager on duty,* a position rotated among managers, is responsible for the entire operation during his or her shift.

You will also want to have a small force of *part-time employees* waiting in the wings when business picks up or if someone isn't available to handle his or her shift.

Seeking Out "People" People

The restaurant business is a people-pleasing business. If customers aren't pleased with the atmosphere, food, presentation, and service, they'll find someplace else to enjoy life. A smart restaurant manager hires friendly, outgoing, "bubbly" people for this reason.

It's tough to teach "bubbly," so look for that quality during your interviews. Another trait to look for is flexibility in the hours people can work. Sales trends in this business fluctuate wildly, and staff has to be in a position to "go with the flow." We've all been to restaurants where the wait staff seemed indifferent, yet somehow the business thrives. Any number of reasons could account for that survival; a long history in the community, for example. Don't gamble on your establishment by making that place a role model. Make a safe bet and hire employees who like, appreciate, and want to serve other people.

When conducting your interviews, keep in mind various positions the individuals may fill. For example, someone applying for a busser's position may have the personality to become a member of the wait staff. Don't limit your possibilities to the one-line job description on an employment application. Set up a pay rate that is different for full-time and part-time employees. Most employees will be paid on an hourly rate. Managers and the chef and/or kitchen manager are the exceptions. Let your candidates know up front what type of compensation they can expect.

Building Your Management Team

The heart of your restaurant will beat according to the strength of your general manager and your chef. Opinions are divided as to which is the most important position. Randy comes down slightly in favor of the chef (or kitchen manager). Both are essential positions, and both must be filled with people of the highest abilities.

> The heart of your restaurant will beat according to the strength of your general manager and your chef.

Hiring a Flexible General Manager

Take care in hiring a general manager (GM), especially if you plan on being an absentee owner. If you plan on being actively involved in your operations, find someone who complements your skills, abilities, and style of management. Hire someone with strengths to counterbalance your weaknesses. If you're an accounting whiz, but aren't very outgoing, find a general manager with a lot of personality. Of course, the GM should also have a solid foundation in accounting, and other management skills, too.

Look for someone with restaurant experience and make sure that the experience is relevant to your business. A great manager of a fast-food chain restaurant doesn't have much of a background in managing a Victorian-style establishment catering to the upper crust. Your GM must have a lot of experience in a lot of very different areas, such as selecting suppliers, working with vendors, scheduling, opening and closing procedures, training staff, conducting inventories, and managing cost controls, just to name a few.

Your general manager must be willing and able to promote the image of the restaurant and the image of a strong leader to the staff.

Leadership and communications skills are essential in an effective GM. How can you lead if you can't communicate with the rest of the team? A general manager must be able to direct traffic and keep the operation flowing smoothly in the back of the restaurant as well as in the front of the restaurant. He or she has to support the hostess in keeping the dining room calm while at the same time making sure that the restroom is clean and stocked. The GM has to see the lounge patron who has had one too many shots of tequila is cared for while handling a "We're out of eggs!" crisis in the kitchen. This person must understand that the job requires long hours and work on the weekends and must be willing to accept those conditions. Remember, you will do about 70 to 80 percent of your business during about 35 percent of your open time. Your GM has to be on the scene during those hours regardless of how early, how late, or how scattered throughout the work week.

Do not overwork your GM. Managers should have at least two days or four shifts in a row off whenever possible. Burnout or a high manager turnover rate can follow. Also, you don't want someone who is "wiped out" from overwork representing you and your restaurant to your patrons and suppliers. They're under an incredible amount of pressure at work. Make sure they take the time to let off a little steam.

Bringing in a Chef or Kitchen Manager

The person you need depends upon the service you offer. If you're opening a fine-dining establishment, you will most definitely need a well-qualified chef. If your restaurant is more of a kicked back family place or a deli, a kitchen manager should work out just fine. The chef or kitchen manager is one of the most important, if not the most important, managers in the restaurant. There are no management tricks, and no amount of slick sales or management "gab" will allow the individual to fake his or her way through the kitchen.

A smoothly running kitchen requires someone with a great deal of knowledge. Give the chef or kitchen manager the authority to hire his or her own cooks, prep people, and dishwashers. Handing over this responsibility isn't just good politics, it's good business. The manager knows what he or she needs to make the operation work well, probably more so than the owner. It is also the chef or kitchen manager's responsibility to schedule and train all of the "back of the restaurant" employees.

Ego is a major component of a chef's life. If you hire one, he or she will expect star billing. That's fine. Like a famous actor, rock star, or athlete, many chefs have a loyal group of fans. These fans will become your customers. Promote your chef within the restaurant, in your advertising, and in your promotions. When you have a star, let him or her shine. Chefs also like to create their own dishes. That's okay, too, and you can allow them to offer those dishes as nightly specials. If you want to stick with the same menu night after night, you might be better off hiring a kitchen manager or a good cook to avoid an inevitable conflict.

A chef will cost you more than a good cook or a kitchen manager. You'll be paying for training, talent, and perhaps some "star power." Salaries vary from region to region, so check with your local restaurant association for the applicable pay scales. Of course, a top chef may be in a position to demand a salary far above the norm for any region.

Should You Use a Headhunter?

The answer is easy: "That depends." Generally, you can fill just about any position from within. Sometimes the best candidate for the job is overlooked because of overfamiliarity.

When that's not possible, you may want to consider a professional recruiter to find the right person. When you find the right headhunter, work with him or her throughout the process. Write out in your own words a job description of the individual you need. Interview every applicant the headhunter recommends, even if the person doesn't appear at first fully qualified. Take careful notes and pass your comments along to the recruiter. Also call and speak with him about your comments. Eventually, your headhunter will start narrowing down his recommendations to candidates that more and more fulfill your needs.

Evaluating Managers

What do you look for in management talent? The mix of skill, education, knowledge, and personality will vary according to the needs of the restaurant and your needs as an owner/manager. Here are a few essential traits.

Personality: This is a business in which people must please other people. Regardless of their skills, if someone comes off as aloof or cold, they could turn away customers.

People skills: Can your managers actually manage? Barking orders is not leadership. How can a manager keep, train, and motivate a staff if he or she can't connect with people? Your turnover will be high if you don't have a manager who listens and gets along with others. These days, good employees know how easy it is to walk down the street and find a good job with a more understanding manager.

Honesty: This is an all-important trait. Your general manager will probably have unlimited access to your cash. He or she will certainly have access to your assets, trade secrets, staff, and ways of conducting business. This is why getting and verifying references is so critical. If you can't get any good comments from the owner or manager who most recently hired this person, consider that a red flag. You can't teach honesty.

Goal-oriented: Setting lofty goals is fine, but someone must have the drive and the ability to achieve them. Has the person being interviewed built a track record of reaching or exceeding goals? Managers should also have the ability to set achievable goals and to inspire others to reach them. Goals help you monitor the success of your managers and help with pay reviews.

Business sense: Does your candidate have any business experience other than being a fast-food cook or a star waitperson? Have they any experience in handling payroll, taxes, and reporting monthly sales forms to government agencies, or have they dealt with suppliers and vendors?

Experience: Nothing beats real-world experience. You will be incredibly busy in your restaurant, and you'll need strong backup. You'll have to take time for training in certain areas, such as your customer-service philosophy, but you don't have time to train a manager in accounting, getting along with people, government regulations, etc.

Marketing/advertising know-how: Has your manager any experience in this critical area? While not essential, some experience is important. You can certainly get qualified help from outside sources (See Chapter 14), but he or she will still have to oversee the production and execution of marketing programs. Even if someone else is doing the legwork, your manager has to know what's good, what's trash, what works, and what fails to capture the patrons' attention.

Recruiting Tools and Techniques

You have many recruitment tools available to you at all times. Use each one to ensure that you are always pulling from a large universe of the best-qualified people.

Use Traditional Sources

Traditional sources for finding talent include employment agencies, corporate headhunters, the chamber of commerce, job fairs, advertising in your local newspapers, and Internet Web sites. Of course, these are just the first steps.

Community colleges and vocational technical schools can be fertile recruiting grounds. Make contact with the teachers and have them keep an eye out for likely talent. Describe the skills you need, but also the personality traits that match your theme. If there's a culinary school nearby, by all means make and maintain contact.

Contact Vendors

Vendors are also excellent resources for qualified employees. These people get around. Who else other than a salesperson can get in the back of the kitchens or in the

Don't Give Up on a Winner

Sometimes you have to move people through different positions to find the right slot. Randy hired a waitress who was good at her job, but she could handle only three or four tables at a time, too few to serve all the people who needed to be served. Yet this employee showed up on time, never missed a meeting, had a great personality, and was a good worker, albeit with a limited capacity.

He invested the time to communicate with her, to speak and to listen attentively to her responses. She wanted to stay, and he wanted to keep her on. Randy tried her out in a number of different positions. She finally "clicked" as a hostess. The customers loved her, and she excelled at the position.

offices of restaurants in the region? Is there a faster, more efficient way to check the talent base at a competitor's operation? You'll soon learn that a lot of chefs, cooks, kitchen managers, general managers, and other employees often drop hints to suppliers that they're in a mood to make a move. See that you're first in line to receive these tips.

Open Your Eyes

The best recruiting tool of all is your own pair of eyes. Use them. Wherever you go, keep an eye out for good talent. Use your imagination and visualize where and how you could employ talented people you encounter throughout the day. That waitress with the sparkling personality working at the corner café might become a topnotch hostess with a little training. The hard-working number two man at a fast food outlet might be looking for an opportunity to move into a management position at a stand-alone facility. The young fellow mopping the floor with such diligence just might want to learn how to bus tables and maybe become a waiter someday.

Don't be ham-handed about approaching people working for someone else. Use a little discretion. This is especially true when dealing with potential management personnel. Just let them know that you like the job they're doing. Tell them a bit about your plans. If anyone is unhappy at work or if anyone is interested, he or she will show up at your door.

Good talent is everywhere. All you have to do is look.

Interviewing and Selecting

One of the real joys of the restaurant business is that management can take a good person, especially someone with a good personality, and with a bit of training turn that person into a really topnotch employee. Careers have been launched this way. Conducting interviews that discover the potential in people is an important skill required of a good manager.

Pay Attention to Details

You can tell a lot about a person from very few details. What is your first impression? How is the applicant dressed? You can probably achieve a lot more with a high school dropout who is neat, clean, and wants to work than with a sloppy college graduate who has a bad attitude. Someone who comes in with a "this is what I can do for you" attitude is far superior to someone who just wants a free ride on the corporation. Evaluate handwriting. If your people have to turn in written orders to the kitchen staff, this is a critical skill. Does the applicant look you in the eye when speaking? How is their personality? Does he or she have clean fingernails? Are there too many rough edges to work with, or have you discovered a true diamond in the rough?

List Your Questions

Different jobs obviously have different requirements. You'll want to draw up specific lists of questions to ask the different applicants. It's important to ask every applicant for the same position the same questions so you can make a fair evaluation. Don't rely on your memory. You could be swayed by a dynamic personality and hire someone who is deficient in some areas. Don't lecture about the job, your restaurant, or your business philosophy. Get the applicant to open up and expand on his or her skills, education, abilities, and even his or her plans for the future. Remember that some people who look good on paper don't work out so well on the floor. Conduct a thorough interview so that you select only the best people.

> Remember that some people who look good on paper don't work out so well on the floor.

Write Job Descriptions

You will want to have specific job descriptions available so your applicants will know their exact responsibilities. Each candidate will want to know the pay scale for the job, so make sure you have these figures settled before the interviews begin. Each job should have a minimum and a maximum amount paid. This will vary according to the applicant's experience and abilities.

Use Courtesy

Everyone deserves courtesy and respect. During the interviews, let the applicants know what to expect. Tell them when you expect to make your

Firing Is as Important as Hiring

Every once in a while a manager has to become an ogre, or some kind of monster in the eyes of his or her staff. Firing a nonproductive employee is just as important as rewarding someone for doing an excellent job. It's an unpleasant task, but one that shouldn't be ignored. Neither should it be delegated. Keeping someone around who just isn't performing is unfair to the other employees, to the company, to your customers, to your own success—and to the nonperformer. He or she might just shine in another environment. A smart manager will do the right thing—fire the appropriate individual, spend a few nights tossing and turning in bed, and then get back to the business of managing.

final decisions. Let them know how to find out whether they made the cut. Will you call, or should they contact your office? Will you be calling applicants back for secondary interviews? How you handle these interviews is a direct reflection on you and your business. Remember, too, that virtually everyone you meet is a potential customer, including job applicants. Even those who don't get the jobs will probably come around as customers if you have treated them properly.

Hiring "Too Many" People

When opening a new restaurant, it's a good idea to hire 18 to 22 percent more people than you need. Some of the new crew will inevitably become no-shows. Others will not measure up to your standards and will be let go during the training period. Sometimes you'll feel like it's a full-time job just keeping qualified staff around. That's another reason to make a maximum effort during your interviews to select the best people around.

A well-trained and seasoned staff takes time to develop. Don't expect to hire a competent group of people who can function like the proverbial well-oiled machine from the first day of work. Invest the time, energy, and money to train a great staff. Then take good care of your people. They'll respond by taking good care of you. As your restaurant and its reputation grows, word will get out that your place is a great place to work. Soon, you'll have the best people knocking on your door.

Making an Offer

If you want to attract good employees, you have to offer good pay. Period. End of discussion. Of course, pay means more than a salary or an hourly wage. Pay includes any benefits or perks offered. It can also include other factors, such as training, working with experts in the field, or building a reputation within the industry.

To attract and hold a top management team, you will most likely have to provide at least health insurance benefits. Other fringe benefits will probably be necessary, too. This trend is rapidly becoming the norm. Many "benefits" are no longer thought of in that manner and are often expected to be part of any job offer.

Turnover in employees should be expected. That's a challenge faced by all businesses. Try to keep yours as low as possible. Turnover drains resources better used to serve customers and keep the business running smoothly. Hiring good employees in the first place and then taking good care of them is one of the best ways to keep your turnover rate low.

In summary, your offer depends upon your needs and the needs of your customers. Market demand for labor, an individual's skill or prestige, your budget, and the abilities of the talent pool will all have to be factored in. Think beyond today. In the long term, making good offers to good people and having them accepted is the most cost-effective method of building a top-flight staff.

Dealing with Employee Turnover

Employee turnover is inevitable. In good times and in bad times some people will just pack up and leave. Turnover is very expensive. It costs you in training time. It costs you in customer loyalty, because some customers become attached to certain members of your staff. It costs you in service, because a new employee is not going to be completely up-to-speed on your customer-service philosophy. The best way to ward off turnover is to hire right—the right people, the right personality, the right attitude. Once you hire those folks, be sure to treat them right. Pay them top wages, give them good hours, and be flexible with their schedules. Build loyalty by getting them involved in the business and into the decision-making process.

Several restaurant chains offer employees a piece of the

Recruit People on Their Way Up

The best employees are those who want to improve themselves and their positions in life. They're hard working, dependable, willing to learn, and frequently a source of good ideas. Fortunately, upward mobility is practically built into the system in the restaurant business. Statistics provided by the National Restaurant Association support this statement. For starters, the industry provides the nation with 1.4 million managerial jobs.

The picture is bright for women and minorities. More minorities are at work as managers in the food and beverage industry than in any other. Women were employed in more than two-thirds of all supervisory positions in the food preparation and service industry in 1999, according to an industry overview on ✑ *www. restaurant.org*.

According to the Web Site ✑*www.restaurant.org,* the food and beverage industry is predicted to employ 13 million people by the end of this decade.

Ask for Complaints

Randy oversaw a manager who turned out to be too inflexible for his own good. For example, when the manager posted a work schedule, that was it. He would not allow any discussion of shifting the schedule to meet legitimate needs of the rest of the staff. His attitude was, "My word is law."

After some time, Randy noticed that the restaurant was slowly losing a lot of good workers. He asked around and, more importantly, he listened to what was said. Soon the problem was rectified, and the schedules became more flexible to employee needs.

Remember that pay is just one factor in what an employee wants from a job. Sometimes "small" details, like courtesy or respect, are quite high on an employee's "want list."

You'll never get the full story unless you ask.

action. For example, if you stay with the organization for five years, you could earn 5 percent of the restaurant's business. After that five years, they might offer an additional 5 percent if the employee stays. Other perks include signing bonuses and immediate thirty-day vacations.

Some employee turnover is inevitable. In good times and in bad times, some people will just pack up and leave. You can't stop it, but you can be ready for it. The best way to be prepared is to have a solid training program in place. People go and new people come in to take their place. Have a system set up so that they can be brought up-to-speed as quickly as possible. Have a training video ready and a policy book, but most important, have an experienced trainer on hand.

Incentives are a good means to reduce turnover and to find the right employees. For example, you could offer a bonus if an employee recommends a new employee. Establish a benchmark, such as ninety days continuous employment, before you pay the bonus. The advantages are obvious. First, your employees probably know other people around town, people in the same profession. Restaurant/bar workers tend to be a tight group, so they can bring in some topnotch talent. If someone recommends someone else, he or she probably already gets along well. The only possible setback is that some employees may be more loyal to other employees than the company.

Finally, one of the easiest, most cost-effective "bonuses" you can offer is to simply treat people well. Use that "thank you" we keep mentioning. It works. The gestures cost nothing, yet they make people feel like part of the family.

Chapter 16

Establishing a Good Work Environment

Part One

Part Two

Part Three

Part Four

Part Five

Part Six

PART FOUR   STAFFING YOUR RESTAURANT

■ CHAPTER 14 Recruiting a Support Staff ■ CHAPTER 15 Hiring Employees ■ CHAPTER 16 **Establishing a Good Work Environment** ■ CHAPTER 17 Training and Coaching Employees ■ CHAPTER 18 Understanding Labor Costs

Knowing Why You Should Worry about Your Work Environment

Randy once defined quality as fun. "Good service, consistency in our food and drink, and cleanliness of the club are all important and contribute to the quality experience, but unless you've provided an atmosphere where people feel special and equate their visit with having a fun time, they won't be back. A quality experience is the customer's memory of a good time," he said. For the most part, a fun experience is not what the customers brings. The experience is what they are seeking, and that's the reason they're coming through your front door.

People come to a restaurant trying to fulfill a need—maybe to relax, to get together with family or friends, or to experience food from a faraway place. Your employees are a major component of that experience. They are the "front-line troops" that customers see and with whom they interact. Your food is what you sell, but the experience customers have is created by your atmosphere and your employees. Who among us hasn't experienced poor service from an impolite or careless waitperson? We might chalk that up to a bad day and we might even come back. If the experience is repeated, chances are we'll refuse to return anymore, and we'll spread a very negative word of mouth about the whole place.

Your employees are an intricate part of your total image. Make sure they are happy and well-trained. Marketing starts from the inside and goes outward. Your employees should be your biggest fans. Treat them well, ensure that they take pride in their work, and they will respond by treating your customers well.

> Your employees are an intricate part of your total image. Make sure they are happy and well-trained.

Committing to Employee Welfare

The strength of your restaurant is to a considerable extent found in the arms, legs, and brainpower of your employees. It is in your best interests to consider what is in their best interests. Often, they'll disagree with you on some of the definitions, but you have to look at the long-term success picture for everybody concerned.

This may sound way off base, but it is true. When you ask employees why they like their jobs, the answer is rarely pay. More than salary, most employees are interested in three things.

Personal Fulfillment

Employees want personal fulfillment. They want to be recognized for doing a good job. Praise is a severely neglected form of compensation. They want to be appreciated. A simple and sincere "thank you" goes a long way toward building employee satisfaction. People want to know that they are individuals in the eyes of management. A good manager is concerned and gets to know his or her staff as individual *people*.

Training

Employees want to be well-trained. It is important that you invest serious time and money to ensure that your employees know how to do their jobs well. You will also need to train them on your philosophy, the need for real customer service, and on your expectations.

Benefits

Employees want benefits. Health insurance, paid vacations, access to higher levels of responsibility, and a percentage of business are great inducements, provided you can afford them. If not, see what other types of low-cost benefits you can provide. Benefits give you an edge on attracting and holding good employees because they prove you're willing to invest in them.

Establishing a Team

Your staff is a team and must see itself as a team. This means everyone from top to bottom must commit to employee welfare. It is important that the owner/manager instill a drive to create win/win situations and to be happy when one member or group within the team achieves success. Do everything you can to avoid an "us versus them" situation in your operation or within any part of it. No truer words were ever spoken than "we're all in this together." When one part of the team suffers, all the others suffer, even if indirectly, and the entire operation is affected. It is your responsibility to create and maintain this spirit.

Inform your staff that success is built on hard work and sacrifice and that as members of a team, each one makes a commitment to mutual goals. Their rewards will be financial and personal.

Make All Employees Responsible for All Aspects of the Restaurant

It's easy for employees to define their work area as their own little world, which eliminates responsibilities in other areas. This lazy attitude doesn't enhance teamwork, and it can leave customers feeling somewhat out in the cold. Nobody wins. Here are a few tips Randy uses to foster teamwork among the bussers.

Encourage Helping Coworkers and Their Customers

If a member of the wait staff is overloaded, don't ignore the situation because it's not within your specific area of responsibility. Pitch in and offer to help. If you're not busy with your own customers at the moment, help carry out large orders regardless of whose table it's headed to.

If someone else's customer is looking around for help and that waiter or waitress isn't around, approach the customer. Ask if you can be of assistance and volunteer to find their waiter. When going to a bus station empty-handed and you pass a table with empty plates, help your teammates out by picking them up. If you are refilling coffee or tea for your customer, why not see if other stations nearby need service as well.

Establishing Policies That Reinforce Your Commitment

Start from the beginning. Make sure your job descriptions foster a teamwork environment. Wait staff should help bussers clear tables, bussers should help dishwashers by stacking plates correctly, hostesses can bring around water or coffee. Put it in the job descriptions so there's no room for doubt. Train for and build teamwork from day one.

Management should reinforce the idea of teamwork through personal action. Pitch in to help a busser clear tables or bring coffee around to help the wait staff or help a dishwasher who gets behind.

> If a member of the wait staff is overloaded, don't ignore the situation because it's not within your specific area of responsibility.

Keep Everyone Informed

Ensure that all personnel know the menu, including daily specials. They need to be fully informed on all promotions. They should certainly know their way around all areas of the restaurant so they can find something when needed. A customer asking any employee about the menu or a promotion should get a complete and knowledgeable answer. That applies to the bussers, wait staff, and the hostess. It's management's responsibility to see that they have that information. If the wait staff is busy and a customer needs some extra butter, a glass of water, or whatever, a busser has to be willing to pitch in and take care of the situation. Every employee should know each menu item from taste to presentation.

Reward Correct Behaviors

When you see one of your employees going that "extra mile" to help a customer or fellow employee, offer a reward such as movie tickets, gift certificates, certificates for meals at another restaurant, recognition at a team meeting, or just a simple "thanks for pitching in." People appreciate being appreciated, and they respond well to the gesture.

Foster pride and personal fulfillment by involving employees in decisions. Ask "What do you think about ...?" often. Be serious and show that interest. Notice and reward initiative and always look for opportunities to promote from within.

Fairness Is Essential

Spoken policies have very little value if they're never enacted. Your policy needs will be dictated by, well, your needs. Whatever those needs may be:

- Put them in writing
- Be absolutely fair about enforcing them

Back up your words about teamwork achieving mutual goals, fairness, and opportunity by showing you mean business at every opportunity.

Relaxing Sales Quota Policies

You'll hear different theories from different managers, but as a general rule be wary of being too strict with your quotas. Management should have specific numerical goals to achieve as far as labor percentages, bar costs, and operating costs. Profit margins are so thin in the restaurant business that if you don't keep a close track of your costs, your profit can dwindle down to nothing in nothing flat. An owner or manager must, however, keep an eye on the big picture. A myopic view can start dwindling those profits, too.

Don't reduce cost if the reduction reduces quality and long-term customer satisfaction. The "savings" aren't worth the losses that will follow. Listen to your managers. If they can justify the higher cost in terms of customer benefits, then they're engaged in sound policy.

When policies call for rewards (promotions, raises, bonuses, recognition, etc.) see that the rewards are handed out fairly, openly, and quickly. When someone violates policy, see that the appropriate punishment is meted out just as fairly, openly, and quickly. That includes firing someone when the violation merits it. One of the worst things a manager can do is to allow someone who deserves to be fired to continue on the staff. If he or she isn't let go, the other staff members get a negative message and might start slacking off, too.

Know How to Handle Conflict in Advance

When conflict occurs between employees, get the parties together with management as the mediator. Set up a situation that allows them to resolve the situation together. Foster teamwork. Each side should have the opportunity to speak. Management directs the conversation toward resolution. "We need to work together. How can we make that happen?" Often just hearing the other person's side is enough to eliminate the problem.

Build relationships between your employees by having an occasional party or luncheon or outing where everyone gets together on a personal level away from the work environment. Provide a table where all employees eat so they can get to know each other. See that the employees have a break area where they can meet and get to know each other a little better on a daily basis.

Conducting Performance Evaluations

As a general rule, performance evaluations can provide owners and managers with necessary feedback. This information can then be used to improve conditions and make necessary changes in staff, facilities, and services. Evaluations enhance the manager/employee relationship by creating an environment for one-on-one conversation. Many employees who are shy in groups will open up in private. It's a good way to get sound information, hear gripes you wouldn't hear otherwise, and to gain insight into your people. Of course, it's a two-way street, and you have an opportunity to help an employee improve his or her knowledge, skills, and abilities.

You can also use performance evaluation time to reinforce the need for teamwork and the importance of that individual to the success of the team. Here are a few tips.

Give Periodic Pop Quizzes

Evaluate the menu knowledge of your wait staff through testing, even pop quizzes. "How many shrimp are in a fried shrimp dinner, and what size are they?" "What's the difference between a burrito and a chimichanga?" "Are there restrictions on substitutions?" "How long does it take the chef to prepare the special of the evening?"

Set Up What-If Scenarios

Evaluate cash register knowledge through further testing. Set up various scenarios and see how well they handle each situation. For example, have a "customer" order an item. Allow the employee to enter it into the register and then have the customer change his or her mind. How does the employee handle that? Here's another. The person in seat one orders an item. The person in seat two orders something else, as does the person in seat three. Now, have the person in seat one want to pay for his meal and for the meal for the person in seat three. Have the employee print up the ticket.

Use a Mystery Shopper

Use a mystery shopper to see how your people react in real-world situations. A mystery shopper is a person or series of persons who are "ringers." They're friends or associates of the manager who come in to test the staff by actually ordering food and beverage items. Their "payment" is often the free meal at your establishment. The staff should know nothing about this. After the shopping experience is concluded, go over the pros and cons with the shoppers. You can then discuss very specific problems or good behaviors with specific employees.

You can also evaluate an individual by looking at his or her sales per hour.

Personal Policies and Procedures

The following policies and procedures document was developed especially for one of Randy's restaurants. Feel free to implement it as is, or use it as a base for developing your own personalized program.

Time registration: All employees should report to work ten minutes prior to their scheduled shift time. Misinterpretation of a time card and/or punching another employee's time card is grounds for immediate termination. Check with a manager before closing out. Your workstation must be approved before your departure is authorized.

Smoking: Due to the raised level of awareness of smoke-free environments, smoking will not be allowed in any of the dining areas or kitchen areas of the restaurant. The smoke break area is located at the end of the kitchen hall near the manager's office. Only one person will be allowed to break at a time and only with prior management approval.

Horseplay and profanity: Horseplay is not permitted. The use of profanity and/or obsessive loud tones and outbursts cannot and will not be tolerated. Foul or abusive language toward peers, management, or customers is unacceptable and grounds for immediate termination.

Phone calls: The telephone is off limits, and there are no exceptions. Emergency phone calls will be taken by a manager. All other messages will be distributed at the end of the shift. The pay phone is available to employees while off the clock. In extreme circumstances, with prior management approval, the pay phone may be used during the shift. Additionally, the bartender has priority over accepting incoming calls. Please answer the phone if the bartender is unable to answer the phone. When answering, use the following method: "Thank you for calling (name of restaurant), this is (name of employee). How may I help you?" If the caller asks to speak to a manager, please ask, "May I tell him/her who is calling?"

Cell phones are not permitted while on the clock. If you are expecting an important call, inform the management when clocking in. DO NOT carry cell phones on your person.

Paychecks: Paychecks are issued on the 8th and the 23rd of each month between 4 P.M. and 6 P.M. If you cannot arrive at this time, your check will be issued at the end of your next shift. Pay weeks run from Monday to Sunday. Company policy does not allow cash advances under any circumstances. Wages are not to be discussed with any other employee.

Absence, illness, or tardiness: Failure to report to work without notifying a manager is grounds for immediate termination. To be excused due to illness, management should be notified as soon as possible, but not less than two hours prior to your scheduled shift. It is at management's discretion to request a doctor's clearance before allowing you to return to work. Tardiness will result in a written reprimand. Excessive tardiness can lead to termination. It is required that all personal business be conducted off the premises and on your own time. Please make every effort to schedule doctor's appointments at a time when you are not scheduled to work Transportation problems are not a valid excuse for tardiness or absenteeism.

> Failure to report to work without notifying a manager is grounds for immediate termination.

Server banks: Each server is required to arrive at his or her scheduled time with a $30 bank. Your bank should include loose change. Please consider your bank part of the uniform.

Accidents: In case of an accident involving any person or group of persons, please notify management immediately. Do not attempt to administer first aid. Employees involved in an accident will be required to be drug tested at the time medical attention is administered.

Customer complaints: Notify management immediately. Show sincere concern and notify the customer that you will notify a manager of their dissatisfaction. Do not offer any guarantees.

Employee meals: Employees may order meals before their shift as long as they are finished ten minutes prior to the shift. Absolutely no food is to be eaten by any employee during his/her shift. Eating food during a shift will result in a written reprimand up to and including termination. When you order from the kitchen, retain your meal receipt until you have completed your meal. Employees receive a 50 percent discount. Certain items are not included. When off duty, you and one guest may have a 50 percent discount on food (excluding certain items). The chit for your food must be presented to the manager for authorization before the meal will be prepared. Alcohol is still full price. All to-go orders are at full price. Please tip your server graciously.

Breaks: Breaks are allowed with management permission only. Only one person at a time is to be on break. Breaks will be dictated by business.

Parking: Employee parking is the row of parking spaces immediately facing (STREET) due to the limited number of customer parking spaces. There are no exceptions. Security is on duty from 5 P.M. till midnight for your safety. When possible, please walk in pairs to your automobile.

Scheduling: Schedules are posted weekly. They will be posted on Friday of each week. It is each employee's responsibility to make a note of his/her schedule. Do not call in for your schedule. No one is excused from working holidays. A form for requested days off must be completed and submitted ten days prior to the Monday the schedules begin. At this time, it is only a request until authorized by a manager. If special circumstances exist, please notify a manager at least two weeks in advance.

Shift change: You will be allowed only one shift change per pay period. You must complete the shift change form and have it approved by management. Both parties must be present. Once the change is authorized, the person accepting the shift is responsible for the shift and will be held accountable. You may not ask for a shift change that might put someone into overtime. If this occurs, the party acquiring the overtime will have his/her schedule change privileges revoked. New hires are not eligible for schedule changes until they have been with the company a minimum of four weeks.

Dress code: If you are scheduled to work, you must be in your complete uniform while in the building. There are no exceptions. Your uniform must be cleaned and starched upon arrival. If you are dismissed due to a substandard uniform, you will be reprimanded. After your shift, you must leave the property to change out of your uniform.

Meetings: Periodically, staff meetings will be held. A notice will be posted at least ten days in advance, and attendance is mandatory.

Probation agreement: The first forty-five days of employment is considered a probationary period before permanent employment is offered. During this period you are under supervision. You will receive sufficient training. You will be evaluated at the end of the forty-five day period, and if your skills at this time are not considered adequate, you will not be offered permanent employment.

Tips: Tips are not to be counted or discussed in public. These tips are your gratuity from your customer and should be kept private. Tip-out to bussers and bartender are mandatory. One percent of total sales is tipped to the bussers and 5 percent of total bar sales is tipped to the bartenders. Tips should not become an issue for dispute at any time. Tips are to ensure proper service to our guests. If a problem arises, please bring it to management's attention. An automatic 15 percent gratuity is charged for private parties and parties of ten or more people. Any other arrangements must be approved by management.

Bar area: The bar area is off limits to all employees while on duty except when picking up drinks at the designated service area. Anyone caught behind the bar except the on-duty bartender will be terminated immediately. On your days off, you may drink at the bar at full price. At the end of your shift, you may have a drink in the bar at full price, but you must be out of uniform. No exceptions. The bar area is off limits to any customer under the age of twenty-one. This is the entire area with hardwood floors. The video poker machines are off limits to any employee while on the clock or in uniform or under the age of twenty-one.

Substance abuse: Use of narcotics is strictly prohibited and grounds for immediate dismissal. Drinking is prohibited while

Breaking Down Barriers

Here is a technique often used to break down barriers between the different staffs. It's also an excellent tool for eliminating fear and suspicion. It's called role reversal.

Every restaurant has a "front of the restaurant" staff and a "back of the restaurant" staff. Have each group switch places for a week. Randy has used this technique often and says that it increases teamwork tenfold. Role reversal fosters empathy for the other person's position.

Obviously, there are limitations. A busser can't really replace a chef. But a busser can work in the kitchen. After the last meal has been prepared, a chef can pitch in and help bus tables. A GM can learn a lot and even "remember when" by bussing a few tables. And who says the owner can't pitch in at the loading dock?

on duty. When off duty, all drinks are purchased at full price. Any comped alcohol for a guest must have the signature of the manager and server/bartender.

Sexual harassment: Any form of sexual harassment is forbidden and grounds for immediate termination.

Lost and found: All lost items should be turned over to a manager immediately. Customers can retrieve these items from any manager. All lost and found items will be locked in the office.

Chewing gum: Chewing gum will not be allowed in public view.

Vacation policy: Full-time employees (thirty-five hours a week or more) are entitled to one week paid vacation after the first year of employment. Part-time employees are entitled to one week's paid vacation after twenty-four months of continuous employment.

Employee restroom: The employee restroom is located at the end of the kitchen hall near the office. Smoking is not permitted in the restroom. Customer restrooms are off limits to all employees.

Employee interruptions: When the need arises for management assistance and the manager is in a meeting with another employee, manager, or guest, politely excuse yourself. "When you have a moment, I would like to ask a question." Please do not stand by the manager waiting for a response. If it is a very serious situation, mention the importance of a rapid response.

Involve Your Team in Decision-Making

Everybody on the team should have a say. Naturally, the owner or manager must have the final word, but you can certainly make time to listen to the words of your employees. Listening isn't just window dressing to make someone feel good, either. Your employees are out there on the front lines. They're often much closer to problems and opportunities than the management staff. Some of their ideas will be off base, but you'll also find many of them are home runs.

Do not assume that the manager's conversation is just "small talk." Please do not interrupt telephone calls.

Conduct Regular Meetings

Schedule them according to what is best for you, your employees, and the success of the restaurant. Many managers conduct weekly meetings with management staff and at least one meeting a month with the entire crew.

Weekly meetings can address the entire range of problems and opportunities or they can be targeted to a specific area. Randy uses a combination. For example, weekly meetings with management always stressed promotions. "What can we do next to keep our customers excited and coming back?" But each manager was also tasked with bringing up a problem area for discussion. He or she was also responsible for bringing a solution to that problem to the table.

Monthly staff meetings were used to get feedback and to specifically let everyone experience being an active part of the team. Regular meetings with management and staff are also a terrific means of proving your commitments and getting your employees involved. Discuss problems. Ask for opinions. Get a serious discussion going. Don't forget that the role of management isn't to dictate. It's to lead. Talk about upcoming promotions. Ask for ideas on making improvements. Offer incentives and get everyone involved in the conversation.

Treat them well and keep them informed. Be sure that they know you are interested in hearing their ideas. You're also interested in them as individuals. Show it. Employees can quickly make or break a promotion. Don't forget that your employees can be one of your most effective ways to advertise. Ask for information about any complaints they've received. Ask for the compliments, too. Are customers regularly asking for items not on the menu? What suggestions have customers made?

Mutually Beneficial Supplier Agreements

Treat your suppliers as extended members of your team. In fact, that's a pretty apt description. They can be of enormous benefit. For example, wine distributors can do a lot more than just deliver cases of red, white, and rosé. They can train your wait staff in the proper way to pour, which wine goes with what type of cuisine, how to handle wine tasting, what's the difference between dry and sweet, and the other areas of wine lore. Food vendors can also be extremely helpful in creating and refining your menu.

Suppliers can devise and run promotions for you. Often they'll even provide the promotional materials necessary. Well-designed full-color tent cards are a good example. In some cases they'll be able to provide giveaways, such as T-shirts, glasses, buttons, or product samples.

Chapter 17

Training and Coaching Employees

Part One

Part Two

Part Three

Part Four

Part Five

Part Six

PART FOUR   STAFFING YOUR RESTAURANT

■ CHAPTER 14 Recruiting a Support Staff ■ CHAPTER 15 Hiring Employees ■ CHAPTER 16 Establishing a Good Work Environment ■ CHAPTER 17 Training and Coaching Employees ■ CHAPTER 18 Understanding Labor Costs

The Mission of Training: Improving Customer Satisfaction

Customer satisfaction is the backbone of success to a restaurant. That's what keeps them coming back, bringing in their friends and family, and speaking well of you wherever they go. Thorough and ongoing training should be targeted toward satisfying your customers—at a profit. Everyone in your operation has an effect on your patrons' enjoyment of their experience (or the lack of it). That applies to employees that the customer never sees.

A plate with a bit of dried lettuce stuck on the rim presented to a customer as clean can ruin an otherwise perfect meal. You could lose the customer and all subsequent referrals and positive word of mouth over any number of unpleasant incidents. That customer dissatisfaction can be traced back through the system. The waiter or waitress who brought the plate should have spotted the unsanitary condition. Your dishwasher should have taken his or her job seriously enough to do the job properly. The kitchen manager who allowed some of the staff to shirk their responsibilities is also at fault. The chief culprit, however, is management—the people who failed to train and instill corporate values in their team in the first place.

Even experienced people need training. If nothing else, they need to understand your corporate philosophy, your customer satisfaction policies, and the way you run your restaurant. Training is necessary for everyone in the organization. Start at the top.

> Everyone in your operation has an effect on your patrons' enjoyment of their experience (or the lack of it).

Restate Your Mission Statement

Unless your brain gets stuck in some kind of permanent automatic loop, it's impossible to say your mission statement enough. This short and simple statement is at the core of your business and your business philosophy. The way the world, the economy, and trends shift these days it's incredibly easy to backslide. A mission statement is not something you write, post on a bulletin board or annual report, and then forget. It's the driving force behind your drive for success.

What is your mission statement (see Chapter 6)? Can you say it right now without looking it up? If you can't, think about how you're going to manage your restaurant without knowing your own guiding principles. It's a good idea to ask the same question of your management and staff from time to time. If they don't know it, there's no way in the world they can carry it out.

What is your image? Is it the image you want to project? Is it the image you've allowed yourself, your staff, and your restaurant to slide into? These are elemental questions. Their purpose is to make sure you're staying on course throughout the life of your business. Ask them often. If for no other reason than to avoid embarrassment, your employees will learn the answers, and those answers will stay with them.

Make sure that your service philosophy and your training manuals and materials are designed to make your mission statement happen. Keep your mission statement in the forefront of your mind whenever designing a training program, training materials, or a training session. Repetition is the key to learning, so say it often.

Communicate Expectations

You will use a variety of training tools, including lectures, show and tell, role-playing, pamphlets and books, and videotapes. Be sure that every employee knows and understands your expectations before they flip the first page or insert the first tape into the VCR.

Schedule meetings for the specific purpose of ironing out problems. Reiterate your expectations in clear and precise terms during each of these meetings. Keep those expectations at top-of-the-mind awareness levels by repeating them every so often one-on-one or in small groups. Make time every day to be on the floor. Offer guidance and encouragement to prompt correct behaviors. There's no way in the world employees can live up to your expectations until they know them. Again, communication is a must. It will help solve a lot of your daily problems and allow you to take proper care of other matters, such as talking to your customers.

Establish a Customer-Service Philosophy

If you don't have a practical, easy to understand customer-service philosophy, it's best that you develop one quickly. Otherwise, one will develop on its own, and you probably won't like it. Neither will your customers.

Like a child growing up without supervision, it will develop without control, discipline, or purpose.

Of course, you'll want to serve your customers as best as possible, but what does that really mean? A quality meal at Hector's Hot Dogs can be a totally satisfying experience, but standing under an umbrella squeezing condiments from plastic containers next to bustling traffic cannot meet the customer's expectations of quality at Chez Hector's Continental Bistro. Your definition of "best possible" service will then depend upon your concept.

- Does your customer order at one end of a counter and pick up the order at the other end?
- Are you creating a fine-dining experience in which time slows down between courses?
- Do you need to be polite while moving 'em in and moving 'em out as quickly as possible?
- Should a greeter acknowledge the customer at the door, or should the wait staff have that responsibility?
- Is everyone ultimately responsible for a given table or just the individual assigned to it?

Put the Philosophy in Writing

Regardless of the details in your customer-service philosophy, commit it to writing and then spread the word. A recent manual for one of Randy's restaurants includes these guidelines for ensuring customer satisfaction:

- Acknowledge guests within five minutes of being seated.
- Be sure to say "thank you," and when they leave, "goodbye."
- Personalize the experience by learning a customer's name, favorite drink, or favorite entrée. People like to buy from friends.
- Be aware of customer needs. Are they in a hurry and need fast service, or are they in the mood for a leisurely dinner?
- Stay close at hand without intruding. When a customer needs something, make sure you're in a position to meet that need quickly.
- Know your product and your promotions. What's in the vinaigrette? Is that a cream sauce on tonight's pasta special? Are those center cut

pork chops? Can an adult order off the children's menu? What time does the two-for-one enchilada special start? Does Happy Hour include bottled beer? Customers should never have to wait while someone dashes off to find an answer to basic questions.

Involving Key Personnel in All Training

Early on insist that your general manager, front-of-the-restaurant manager, and/or kitchen manager handle your training. Watch them carefully and evaluate their performance:

- Do they have the education necessary?
- Can they balance education with real-world experience?
- Can they convey that know-how to others?
- Do they motivate the employees or put them to sleep?
- Can they make the connection between every job and total customer service?

> Insist that your general manager, front-of-the-restaurant manager, and/or kitchen manager handle your training.

After you've observed and evaluated their performances, your "stars" will start shining. They won't be very hard to spot. Put them in charge of training from then on. Your most knowledgeable hand may not be your best trainer. Julius Caesar was brilliant at strategy, balancing politics and warfare and leading great armies into battle. He still needed drill instructors to get the troops into shape.

Involving key personnel from the beginning has several benefits. Handing over such a key responsibility is proof of your trust and your commitment to the manager's personal and professional growth. The manager responds with increased loyalty and commitment to the organization. That's basic human nature. Your trust creates pride in the instructor, which is a powerful motivation to do a great job. The instructor's confidence can be felt by the students, which builds confidence and comfort.

Preparing Manuals

Preparing your training manuals is a team effort. This team should consist of the owner, general manager, front-of-the-restaurant manager, and back-of-the-restaurant manager. You'll need this varied input to make sure all your training bases are covered.

Here's a list of items you'll most likely want to include:

- Job descriptions: Stress teamwork and customer satisfaction in all your job descriptions. Describe the proper attitude for the theme of your restaurant.
- Uniform requirements: If they're allowed to dress on their own, clearly delineate the limits of your dress code.
- Sanitation: Cover the basics, such as wash your hands after going to the toilet or sneezing, etc. Note any special considerations for your type of operation, too.
- Daily/weekly cleaning schedules: Draw these up in forms for assignments. Use written documents to spell out the standards and requirements for all cleaning tasks.
- Procedures: Include opening and closing procedures; check out procedures for bartenders, wait staff, and cashiers; and clock out procedures. Be specific and leave nothing to the imagination.
- Important days: Paydays, vacation policy if any, and your holiday policy if any.
- Parking policy: The best parking spaces are always reserved for customers.
- Tip policies: Carefully spell out any policy on shared funds.
- Legal information: This could include such subjects as tip reporting, video poker, or gambling laws where applicable; and liquor laws, such as alcohol awareness, the proper way to check IDs, and how to handle someone who is intoxicated.
- Security measures: Note the importance of keeping the doors locked when not open and closed except when in use. Tell what to do in the event of a robbery. State your policy for handling fights or when customers lose control of their behavior.
- Special policies, such as what to do if a credit card is rejected.
- A statement about theft.
- A simple, clear statement about behaviors that will result in termination: Be sure to have each employee sign a copy and place it with his or her employment file.

- Sexual harassment policy: Also have the employees sign a copy and place one with each employee's file.

Creating Service and Kitchen Training Schedules

The simplest and most efficient method for developing your service and kitchen training schedules is to break down the duties of the large jobs into smaller elements and then set up a training schedule. List:

- Each skill
- The time that skill will be addressed
- How much time will be devoted to that session
- When the testing will occur

Basic training should be completed by opening day. Of course, there's always room for improvement, and new people will be coming on line all the time, so training is a continuing management responsibility.

Front of the Restaurant

You're not without valuable training resources. You can order excellent training tools on a variety of topics from the National Restaurant Association Educational Foundation. Materials are available in virtually all formats, including manuals, books, videotapes, CDs, and multimedia kits.

Discuss every element of your own manual and do so in detail. Ask for questions and see that everyone understands everything. The moment an inebriated patron starts shouting Hamlet's "to be or not to be" soliloquy is not the time to discover your wait staff can't handle a drunk. Cover your philosophy of service, the importance of maintaining a consistent image, your mission statement, and the need for total commitment to customer service. These sessions are

Experience Isn't Everything

Randy opened a restaurant and lounge in Shreveport, Louisiana, a few years ago, and his management team just couldn't find enough employees with experience combined with a great attitude. He instructed the managers to hire only the best personalities and the people who already knew how to smile. They'd train everyone from scratch.

They thought he was crazy, but in retrospect it was one of the best things he could have done. The extra money it cost for the extra training was the best money he ever spent. The people who had never been in the business had not learned any bad habits, including the ones on how to rip off the store. Their lack of experience turned out to be a real bonus.

Help Dreamers Dream

An employee Randy had trained about eighteen years ago approached him one day not to long ago. He just wanted to thank his old boss for hiring him so many years earlier. More than that, he was grateful for all the training he'd gotten under Randy's guidance. He had really grown to love his job and that line of work. More than that, he had pursued a career in the business. The man is a partner in a very successful restaurant today. Of course, he and his partner have worked hard and have earned their success, but none of that might have happened if not for a very positive training experience. Randy says that nothing makes you feel better than to see former employees pursue their dreams and move up the ranks and own their own restaurant or club.

excellent opportunities for show and tell demonstrations.

Menu training is critical. Coordinate these sessions with your kitchen staff. Topics that front-of-the-restaurant personnel must know thoroughly include plate presentation, menu ingredients, tasting, and testing.

Cover register training thoroughly. Sometimes your training sessions will seem bit like flight training in a simulator. See how much you can throw at your students to determine how much they can handle.

Be sure to cover cleaning schedules, daily duties, and safety and sanitation procedures. Test them on these procedures.

Back of the Restaurant

Even though you'll have a trained and experienced chef, you'll still have to train the rest of your kitchen staff. Your chef will also need some training in your individual policies and procedures, so everyone gets to go to school. Topics that definitely must be covered include recipes, portions, plate presentations, sanitation, expediting line flow, cooking, tasting, and check-in procedures.

Forming Employee Committees

Employees want to feel that they are a valuable member of the family and an important part of the team. Involving them in the business is an excellent way to foster that feeling and to get some surprisingly valuable input. Employee committees are an excellent tool. Here are a couple of proven committees to give you an idea of how to start your own.

Explorer Groups: Just like Marco Polo, Columbus, or the astronauts, your team heads out to explore other regions. Specifically, they explore your competition. It's a version of "mystery shopping," only your people will be scouting another operation. Call a meeting afterward to discuss what the competition is doing right and wrong, their price structure, methods of doing things, and how the customers are responding.

Promotion Groups: The team can create ideas for upcoming promotions. Management can even assign specific and important duties to see that select promotions are carried out. Have your group get into the details, including execution of the promotion in-house, advertising and public relations, and the time line of events.

External Party Committee: Throw a party for your employees off-premises. Ensure that it is a success by assigning employees to specific duties. Create a time line and a list of priorities.

Internal Party Committee: Sometimes you'll want to hold a party for your employees and their families in-house. Set up an employee committee with real responsibility for making it happen. Again, set specific duties, create a time line, and set priorities for execution.

New Customer Committee: Set up this group with the specific task of promoting the restaurant in the outside world. They can bring in friends and family, take lunches to your corporate neighbors, target businesses for specific visits, hand out gift certificates, and walk through fairs and festivals promoting your facility.

Holiday Decoration Committee: You have more creative people on your staff than you realize. Give them an opportunity to show their imagination and skills.

Other Committees: Use your imagination, too. Which areas lend themselves to employee input by committee? Some restaurants go so far as to have scheduling and hiring committees.

Motivating Your Employees

Most managers know to search out errors, mistakes, and inefficient ways of doing things. But a good manager knows to also seek out the positive things employees are doing. "Catch" people in the act of doing a good job. Compliment them on the spot. Be direct, specific, and unconditional. "Beverly, you handled that rowdy customer just right. Keep up the good work!" You will be astonished at the motivational power of a few positive words. Be sure to tell your employees that you appreciate their efforts. Thank them for doing well and making your restaurant look good.

When you have to correct or discipline employees, don't do it in front of others unless the extreme nature of the offense so dictates. Most of the time it's best to issue your reprimands back in your office and in private. If at all possible, do this after the shift is over. That way other employees probably won't be around, the workday pressure will be off, and if you need extra time, that time should be available.

Lend a Helping Hand

A good manager volunteers to help out whenever and wherever a helping hand is needed. Randy always says that part of a manager's job description includes "Assistant to an employee who needs a little help or attention; that's the place for a good manager." It is always amazing that in any restaurant, or any business for that matter, the manager or management team that works to back up each other always seems to be a winner. He or she does whatever must be done so the employees can get on about serving the needs of the customers—priority number one. If that means helping with the coffee, prebussing, or pouring water, so be it. A good manager isn't above using a broom, mop, or dustpan if the act will expedite the business at hand.

Back Up Your People

Train them to handle customer complaints, but jump in every now and then to give someone support. Also, make sure your employees have and are taking advantage of breaks during the workday. If someone is in need of extra training, then take the time to provide it. The team leader is still a member of the team and is expected to do his or her part.

Use Motivational Tools

All kinds of things motivate all kinds of people. Before you start any type of motivational program, take some time to think about your different kinds of people. What will motivate the entire team? What would motivate the different teams, such as the kitchen staff or the front-of-the-restaurant group? What will motivate each individual employee? This bit of research shouldn't take an inordinate amount of time. After all, you should already know your people pretty well. Just make an effort to know them a little better in specific areas. Here are a few that have worked well in the past.

Run contests: For example, the employee with the highest sales for the month earns a prize.

In-house recognition: Recognize positive behaviors. You can do this right on the spot. "Nice job, Kevin. I couldn't have handled that better myself." You can then recognize Kevin in the next staff meeting.

Public acclaim: Employees who achieve an "above and beyond" performance can be made Employee of the Month (or week, quarter, year). Mount a framed picture in a prominent position so that your customers can see it.

Prizes: Award simple gifts for good behaviors. Movie tickets, gift certificates, and meals at other restaurants are a few good examples. You can make arrangements to trade for many prizes with other businesses. Naturally, you can combine recognition, public acclaim, and prizes.

Say "thank you": This is one of the most effective, most appreciated, and least used forms of compensation. It's fast, easy, highly motivational, and it costs nothing other than a breath of air.

Ask for opinions: Not only does this recognize the value of each employee, it's a good way to learn important facts about your operations. Your employees have a different perspective, and often it's a most valuable one. Randy always says, "I don't care if it's my idea or yours, as long as it is the best or a better way to do it."

Tips on Motivation

Train every employee to pitch in and help motivate everyone else. Everybody should aggressively seek out opportunities to give a "well done," an "attaboy," or just a basic "thanks." In a team, each member is responsible for enhancing and maintaining a high level of motivation in the other members.

Let your people know that management encourages the sharing of thoughts, feelings, and rationales. This isn't a "touchy-feely" exercise. It's a practical means of improving communication between team members. It should be policy that "there are no dumb questions" and that when people need information or help they should ask for it.

Give feedback on job performance. Even negative feedback can be placed in a positive context to encourage improved attitudes and abilities.

Involve employees in committees: Involvement translates into commitment. It doesn't cost much, if anything, and it works.

Throw parties: Some should be just for your employees, but some should be designed to include their husbands, wives, kids, and dates. Create an ongoing family atmosphere by extending your "family."

Awarding Promotions

Two main conditions must be met to award a promotion. One, a position must be opened or created so that it can be filled. Two, someone qualified to handle the responsibility must be available to do the filling. Promoting from within is a sound policy. You already have information on the individual. You have seen him or her perform in working conditions, and you've already formed some opinions about his or her abilities. A working relationship is already in motion. Why bring in a stranger when qualified people are already in the restaurant?

The guidelines for selecting someone to move up to a higher realm of management are the same for selecting your midlevel and senior managers. Find someone who:

- Exhibits the viewpoints necessary to promote your restaurant
- Cares about the success of other employees
- Is self-motivated
- Is detail-oriented
- Has initiative
- Is people-oriented
- Has sound business sense
- Shows a willingness to put in the time required to earn a management position

Follow the same procedure, too. Evaluate the individual first. Increase their responsibilities gradually. Evaluate again and promote when you think he or she is ready.

Developing Senior and Midlevel Managers

These people will be exercising considerable authority, and authority that is in your name. You'll be wise to take extra care in selecting your midlevel managers and senior team. The time you invest early pays off later in ways you may never experience, see, or even hear about. The goal isn't to recreate yourself. There's only one you. Find people who understand, accept, and will support your philosophies and set up a framework that allows your managers to carry them out.

Recognize Positive Behaviors

Superior work habits and work ethics can indicate a potentially superior manager. You'll want someone with initiative, a self-motivated achiever who isn't afraid to take action. Seek out those people who go beyond their job description and who do a little bit for the company on their off hours. You want to hear, "Your bartender (chef, dishwasher, busser, etc.) said I should check this place out. I'm glad I did."

You want people with sound judgment and who can handle themselves and others in tough situations. Some of the role-playing during your training sessions will reveal the top contenders for upper levels of management. Listen to everyone's opinions, but look for those people who have a grasp of the picture or at least understand that there is a big picture. Managers don't have to be best buddies with their people, and as a general rule they shouldn't be. But managers must have the ability to get along with other people during all kinds of situations.

> Some of the role-playing during your training sessions will reveal the top contenders for upper levels of management.

Let Your Stars Shine

The stars are those few individuals who show real personality and real potential during your training sessions. Take note. Many will be management material. You'll want to give them an opportunity to become team leaders. One of the best ways to test their abilities is to assign them to training positions.

See how they handle responsibility, leading others, setting an example, imparting knowledge, and motivating people. Take note of the bean counters and the ones who really care about their fellow employees. You want people who want their team members to succeed.

Increase Responsibility

Once you have your stars working in positions of responsibility, start adding to that responsibility a little bit at a time. You're not trying to find someone's breaking point. You just want to see how they handle people, additional tasks, and pressure. For example, you can authorize someone to make special purchases, allow him or her to authorize giveaways, or handle the checkouts. A good manager looks for ways to show trust while discovering more about an individual's management potential.

Those who don't measure up to the challenge aren't total washouts. You still have some talented, hard-working, and valuable employees in the restaurant.

Expand Their Capabilities

Train people to handle responsibility in other positions. Widen the range of skills of as many employees as you can. This is a good policy in general and it's an excellent method of training good managers. Your highest-level managers should know how to do every job within the facility. In a crunch, they shouldn't hesitate to pitch in and handle one, either.

Loan out your library of restaurant books, videotapes or CDs, and trade publications. Send promising managers to seminars, lectures, and college courses. Another good technique is to involve people in some of your management meetings. You might even rotate people through different meetings to give them a bigger, more complete understanding of the operation.

As your managers increase their skills and as you increase their responsibilities, you should intervene less and less in their decisions. Watch them closely. Watch them grow, but also let them grow. Sure, they'll make some mistakes along the way. We all have, and we all will continue to make errors. That's how we learn. Just be around to help pick up the pieces, point out ways to avoid the error next time, and offer encouragement.

Creating Mentors

Soon your trainers will expand their capabilities and become mentors to your staff. They instill good work habits by instruction, but knowing that the person being mentored is watching, they continue to improve their own performance. The mentor relationship encourages open communication both ways. The instructor can provide positive and negative feedback comfortably. The student is also less intimidated and will feel more comfortable asking tough questions. Staff and management job performance is enhanced across the board.

Make sure that the person selected to handle your training is thoroughly versed in your corporate philosophy and that he or she understands the type of image you're creating:

- Do you want your wait staff to introduce themselves?
- Should the wait staff be mostly seen and not heard?
- Do you want to encourage friendly banter or polite accommodation?
- Do you want your hostess to put reservations in the database?
- Is your desired atmosphere eclectic, relaxed, open and friendly, or reserved?

Train Your Trainers

Everything and everyone affects everything and everyone else. You can't afford to have elements of your staff working at cross purposes, so make sure each employee is on the same page as the rest of the staff.

Randy's experience with his Kingfish Restaurant is a case in point. The concept was to promote a really exciting and fun time for all patrons.

Unfortunately, the GM trained the wait staff for a reserved, fine-dining establishment. Customers would walk in expecting a good time only to be faced with a tight-lipped escort that resembled a firing squad. Their training-based behavior worked against the theme of the restaurant and made the customers uncomfortable.

Make sure your training staff understands *and agrees with* your concept so your staff is trained appropriately.

Chapter 18

Understanding Labor Costs

Part One

Part Two

Part Three

Part Four

Part Five

Part Six

PART FOUR   STAFFING YOUR RESTAURANT

■ CHAPTER 14 Recruiting a Support Staff ■ CHAPTER 15 Hiring Employees ■ CHAPTER 16 Establishing a Good
Work Environment ■ CHAPTER 17 Training and Coaching Employees ■ **CHAPTER 18 Understanding Labor Costs**

Understanding the Cost of a General Manager

The answer depends upon your own knowledge, skills, and experience. Can you run your own operation successfully? Even if the answer to that question is "yes," do you have the available time to actually manage the shop? Do you have other restaurants, other business obligations, or other demands on your time that would draw you away from the restaurant? Profit margins are slim in the restaurant business, and someone must be on duty to make certain those profits aren't squeezed any tighter. Knowledge, skill, and experience are useless if you don't have the time to put them to work.

If you lack the ability or time, then you will need the services of a good general manager, someone who will run the day-to-day operations under your overall guidance. A good businessperson who may have little or no restaurant abilities can still own a successful operation with the help of a good GM and a good staff.

Hiring a GM is a major decision and should be done only after extensive research, interviews, and reference verification. What are the strong and weak points of the candidate? If you're outsourcing your GM, he or she must be fully qualified in four key areas:

Front-of-the-restaurant operations: You need someone who can oversee the efficient ebb and flow around the wait staff and the patrons. That's a lot more complex than just saying "Table four needs some coffee, Bob." A good GM really *manages* the operation. He or she will have to handle many different and sometimes challenging chores, such as staff training, making register adjustments, authorizing complimentary meals or portions of meals, greeting guests, making sure the staff is performing at the expected level, handling surprises and emergencies, and other tasks.

Back-of-the-restaurant (kitchen) operations: A key factor is the make-up of your menu. Is this a GM responsibility in your restaurant, or will you put someone else in that position? If your menu is fairly simple and basic, you might not even need the services of a well-trained and highly skilled chef. Or if it is more complex, you can hire a top-flight chef on a temporary basis to set up your menu, plate presentation, recipes, kitchen flow, and even assist in training your kitchen staff. Once everything is up and running, your GM or kitchen manager can take care of running the show.

Promotions: People can't show up to enjoy all that good food if they don't know where you are and what you serve. That's the job of marketing, advertising, public relations, and promotions, and you'll need someone who really knows this tricky arena. Some restaurants do all their own marketing. Can your GM write an ad, a radio commercial, a news release, a menu insert, a sign, or a special invitation? Can your GM buy media and work with advertising and promotional salespeople? Can he or she read a media rate card? Does your GM know where to get the best deals on imprinted T-shirts, coffee mugs, and other merchandising materials?

Finance: There are two schools of thought here. One way of thinking is the "put all your eggs in a single basket" approach. Your GM keeps the books. It is essential that the general manager be an individual of good character. In addition to lunch and dinner, there's the danger that your GM will cook the books. The other theory, based on checks and balances, addresses this possibility. It's generally a good idea to have two sets of eyes on your finances. The general manager has the responsibility for daily operations, but someone else, presumably the owner, is looking over his or her shoulders by keeping the books.

A good general manager must play multiple roles. If your GM is weak in any of these four areas, someone will have to pick up the slack. If that person will be you, consider how much a drain that level of support will take from your other responsibilities, and why are you hiring a GM in the first place? Naturally, some training will be required, if only to bring the newcomer up-to-speed on your management style and your objectives. Still, is the candidate worth the extra effort required to build up insufficient skills, or should you look at more candidates? The answer will depend upon the prospective GM's willingness and ability to learn, your patience and ability to teach, salary and benefits, and your timetable, among other things.

> A good general manager must play multiple roles. If your GM is weak in any areas, someone will have to pick up the slack.

Costing Other Salaried (Fixed Payroll) Employees

Salaried employees are easy to budget. You know the people, the number of salaried employees, and the salaries. All you have to do is plug the appropriate numbers into your break-even calculation to arrive at the correct budget figure. Since there are very few variables, there are very few if any surprises at the end of the month or the end of the year.

The convenience in preparing and checking budgets is significant because you can take hours out of the equation. Regardless of how many hours a salaried employee works, the amount of that salary remains the same. Salaries are based on the amount of money an individual is willing to accept for performing a task.

Setting Criteria for Salaried Positions

Your general manager will be a salaried employee. Presumably others will be drawing a salary also, but you need to decide how far down the "food chain" you want to pay salaries. You have two major considerations in making this decision.

- Overtime hours. If the individual's work hours will fluctuate a good bit, you might have to cover a lot of overtime. That can get rather expensive rather quickly.
- Presence. If the position requires the individual holding it to be present regardless of whether business is brisk or slow, you will want this person on salary. For example, your front-of-the-restaurant manager has to be on the job whether the place is packed or practically deserted. The duties must still be carried out.

Offering a Bonus

A goal-oriented general manager may be motivated to achieve even greater success if you offer a salary plus a percentage of the profits. Everybody can benefit from such a bonus deal. For one, as an owner you can offer a lower salary going in. If the relationship doesn't work out, you're not locked into paying a large salary. The lower figure isn't much of a "hit" for the GM to take because that big bonus is out there.

A percentage arrangement is a tremendous inducement for management to produce significant results. Pay your percentages on a quarterly basis. You don't want to wait till the end of the year, when your property taxes are due.

All of that out-go at once can create a real strain on the budget for the next quarter. It's far better to pay out those amounts during the year.

This should be a win/win situation, so don't fall for the trap of cutting a bonus when someone really succeeds. This is a common and very foolish management tactic. You see it a lot in businesses offering commission sales. When salespeople reach a certain level of sales, the company reduces the percentage of their commission. This is nothing short of punishing success. You want to do just the opposite. Regardless of how much you pay out in bonuses, you're still getting the lion's share of the profits. The more bonus money you hand out, the more you have earned. Reward success!

Remember that you *want* to pay high bonuses and profit percentages. That means your business is doing very well. Taking good care of your people can launch new careers for your employees. As they succeed and move out on their own, you build a network of proven performers, all of whom are in positions to help each other.

Looking at Your Variable Payroll

Wages, benefits, perks, and other employment factors are dictated primarily by the local market. Of course, the government sets certain standards, such as the minimum wage or the hours in a work week, but we still live in a supply-and-demand economy. If your competitors provide their employees with free meals, public transportation fares, bonuses based on performance, vacation packages, or whatever, you'll have to compete to find and retain the best people.

Part of your initial research should be to determine the wages for the hospitality industry in your area. The restaurant association, national publications, regional surveys, etc. can give you a general idea to start, but nothing replaces on-the-scene information gathering. Find out what the "standards of service" are around town.

Earning the Bonus

Be very careful about offering a bonus or percentage of the profits up front. People often talk a good game but aren't able to produce on the job. Give your people time to develop. Wait a year before offering the bonus deal. You don't have to present a reduction in existing salaries, just offer to forgo anticipated raises for a percentage of the profits at the end of each quarter. A motivated employee will jump at the opportunity.

You want to make sure that employee stays motivated. It's best to work up to the full amount of the bonus you're contemplating offering. Ease into the arrangement over a three-year period. This gives both owner and employee time to evaluate the benefits of the agreement.

Invest in Employees

Your employees are as big an investment as your building, equipment, parking lot, supplies, and materials. Take care of that investment.

Randy once had a location in a city experiencing very low unemployment, less than 2 percent. Good employees were very much in demand, and a few owners realized the value of offering valuable enticements to recruit and retain those people. Randy was among that crowd.

He became the only restaurant owner in town to offer his part-time employees vacation pay. That's quite a benefit, and people took notice. His philosophy is to have a pool of part-time talent always available. An excited group of part-timers waiting on your phone call is an invaluable resource, especially in an emergency situation.

- Self-service
- Casual
- Full-service
- Elegant

You might want to equal those standards or even play a game of one-upmanship. It's important to differentiate yourself from your competition. Hiring the very best personnel in town is one of the best ways to achieve that goal.

Define the local standards and then see where you can fit in. What atmosphere do you want to create? What type of personnel do you need, and where can you find them? Once you hire them, what set of benefits will not only retain their services, but will keep them motivated? The answers will be found in one place only—the local market.

Determining Your Wait Staff

You can use a basic formula to find out how many people are needed on your wait staff. There are only three steps:

1. Estimate how many customers you will have per shift.
2. Estimate how many tables one person can handle.
3. Multiply the cost per person needed times the hourly wage.

Bussers

Bussers for the most part keep your tables clean. This is an essential job because you can't seat a new party until the plates, glasses, and utensils from the last party are cleared. It's key that you get customers in and out quickly without looking as if you're pushing them. A good staff of bussers relieves a lot of pressure from the waiters and waitresses, who can focus their attention on personal customer service. Consider how busy you want to be and how many people will be required to maintain order and efficiency in that type of operation.

Greeters

Greeters should make patrons feel comfortable the moment they walk in your door. This is particularly important for your regulars who want to feel as if they're part of the "family." The job isn't always an essential one. People, after all, know how to seat themselves. Still, a greeter can really help control the flow of tables to make sure the kitchen staff and wait staff are not overloaded. Your greeter occupies a dual role. He or she must be able to help the wait staff with water, coffee, prebussing, etc. while keeping an eye on how fast the tables are being served. That often calls for a lot of "juggling," and you need someone whose job performance won't be thrown off balance by the act.

The downside to having an official greeter is that he or she is an unproductive cost when the place isn't busy. On the other side, a good greeter can contribute to keeping the restaurant busy. Also, there is never a shortage of tasks at a restaurant. When those slow moments arrive, the greeter can pitch in wherever needed.

Expeditor

An *expeditor* controls the flow in the kitchen. It's his or her responsibility to make sure that the food for each table arrives at just the right moment. A key element of the expeditor's job description is to review plate presentation to make sure that nothing goes out that does not meet restaurant standards. Food involves taste, but other senses are employed too; smell and sight, for example. Never underestimate the importance of plate presentation on the full enjoyment of the meal by your patrons. Again, the only real downside is that your expeditor isn't busy when the restaurant isn't busy.

Kitchen Staff

Your *kitchen staff* can be a single cook or a laundry list of stations that need to be manned, such as the fryer, the grill, or pasta station. Your menu dictates how many people you will need to properly staff your kitchen. Is your menu complicated or simple? How much food prep is involved? Does plate preparation require skills matching those of a floral designer or just someone who won't slop mashed potatoes onto the buttered corn? As always, *what will your patrons expect?*

Your kitchen design can also affect the number and qualifications of your staff. Arrange the layout so that one person can perform several tasks from one position. Cut down on the number of steps to be taken and the amount of kitchen cross-traffic by putting refrigeration units near where the ingredients will be used. Consider preparing as many items as practical ahead of schedule and then keeping them fresh on a steam table. If one person can do the job of two because of a well-executed kitchen design, you can cut down on the size of your staff without cutting the quality of your customer's dining experience.

If your volume of sales can justify the expense, it is highly recommended that your kitchen manager should be a salaried management position.

Dishwasher

A *dishwasher* performs an obvious and necessary task, but do you need this as a specific position? Examine your personnel and the demands on them to see if there's someone who can perform dual functions. A number of factors must be entered into the equation. How much china do you have? How fast does the china (glasses, cups, utensils, etc.) need to be washed so there is enough for the dining area? Bogart's in Colorado Springs featured a hundred gourmet sandwiches. The owner had his cook and a helper wash their own dishes. This was a lot of extra work, but with fewer people on staff, he was able to offer each person higher wages. The employees were happy. Labor costs were still low because the extra pay didn't equal the amount that would have been paid another employee. The dishes were always clean and ready on time, too.

Offering Benefits

The benefits you offer to your employees will be dictated by other businesses in the area. As with wages and salaries, it's all local. Remember, however, that you are also a member of that business community. You can set higher standards if you deem it necessary for employee recruitment and/or retention.

Benefit packages are one of the real advantages of franchise operations. They are regional or national in scope and have tremendous buying power compared to individual operations. Just as in making bulk orders of meat, vegetables, bread, or cooking oil, they can use the same approach to buying other things, such as health insurance. Obviously, the more and better benefits you offer, the better and easier it will be to attract and hold onto good employees.

Restaurant profit margins are and will remain thin. You have to factor that into your decision-making. You can offer a lot of different benefits, but generally the big two are:

1. Vacation pay. Even part-timers can be offered vacation pay. How much you offer and how many extras you attach to the package depends upon the demands of your local market.

2. Health insurance. This can give you a big advantage in the marketplace. You can set up your program as a co-pay, in which they pay a portion and you pay a portion. You can also set up a cafeteria plan in which payments are made with pretax dollars. Consult your accountant and your insurance provider for the best program for your restaurant.

Studying Employee Welfare Costs

Employee welfare costs and employer paid taxes fall into five basic categories:

Employer FICA (Federal Insurance Contributions Act) requires an employer to be taxed to fund the nation's Social Security retirement fund. The taxes are shared by the employer and employee at a set rate. As this book is being written, the rate

Size Matters

A large, spread-out kitchen is fine for a home, but it automatically increases labor costs in a restaurant. Arrange your kitchen layout so that the number of steps required to complete a specific task is as few as possible.

To determine the variable cost, create a grid with the number of people needed for each job. Color in the hours in half-hour increments, i.e., one square equals one half-hour.

Now just multiply the hours worked by pay per hour to determine hour variable labor costs. Note that this is a variable cost and will fluctuate with your volume of sales.

Understand that your kitchen costs are less flexible than some others. Be sure your staff is multifaceted so they can turn their attention to other tasks when business slows.

is 7.65 percent of gross payroll. According to this act, the employer withholds the employees' portion from their paychecks and combines it with his or her own contribution for payment to the federal government.

Unemployment taxes are paid according to **FUTA** (Federal Unemployment Tax Act). Taxes apply to every employer of one or more persons. There are stipulations as to how much money the employee must earn or how many weeks he or she is employed. Check with your attorney or accountant for the current rules and regulations. As this book is being written, the rate is .008 of the gross payroll.

State unemployment taxes are based on the industry and experience (how many claims have been made against you). Check with your own state to find out what rules and regulations apply to your restaurant.

Other taxes. The number of taxes, the different goods and services taxed, and the amount of those taxes will vary from community to community. It is essential that you check with the local authorities to make sure you are always in full compliance. Stay in touch, too. Government tax authorities love to find new things to tax.

Workers' compensation is a requirement for all your employees. Again, the situation varies state by state. In some cases a restaurant owner can acquire workers' comp through a government agency. In others, private insurance carriers can provide the service. Contact your state restaurant association. In some states they provide self-insurer funds. This type of program provides multiple benefits, including low rates, possible rebates if your claims are low, information, and training.

Reviewing Employee Education Costs

As an owner and/or manager you want constantly improving service. That means constantly improving the knowledge of your employees (yourself, too). Knowledge is power, the power to fuel profits.

Education is one of the major keys to success in the restaurant business. You can afford to hire inexperienced people if you are prepared to train them in proper procedures. In many cases their inexperience works in their favor, and yours, because they don't have to "unlearn" bad habits picked up

Chapter 18 ■ Understanding Labor Costs

at other operations. Training should include the skills necessary for the job for which they were hired, but you should also do some cross training. Should someone get sick or become a no-show, someone else can pick up the slack right away. Employees should be taught the company value system.

You'll notice that your good workers will want education, and they'll appreciate your efforts to train them. Continuing education shows that management is serious about quality, but also that they care about the quality of their personnel.

Management should regularly attend trade shows, trade association seminars, and other educational programs. The business changes at a remarkable pace, and you must stay on top of an ever-changing set of circumstances. Subscribe to the industry's trade journals and encourage your management team to read them. Managers should also be encouraged to make regular visits to other restaurants to see what the competition is up to and to pick up any new ideas that might work well in your place of business. Also, be sure to educate your managers in the various operations so that they can fill in at a moment's notice.

Generally, if an employee fails, that failure is the fault of management. Somewhere along the line, leadership failed to train that individual properly or failed to instill the company values.

Forecasting for Seasonal Changes

Seasonal variations are also a local phenomenon. If you're located in a ski resort, then you're heavily dependent on cloudy skies full of soft, white flakes. That's something over which you have absolutely no control, and you have to plan as best you can accordingly. Of course, you may also have secondary seasons, such as during the summer vacation months. Spring break down on the beaches may bring in enough business in a week or so to cover most of the rest of the year. Some places even shut down for months at a time

Education Means Training and Record Keeping

Training should include dissemination of your training manual, orientation meetings, seeing that personnel paperwork is completed and turned in, a full explanation of company policies and procedures, and a detailed discussion of your company's goals and attitudes. As an owner/manager, you should develop testing procedures to ensure consistency of service. Inform personnel of their duties and how they will be evaluated. Make sure your employees are fully versed on health department rules and regulations and that they follow them.

Your employee personnel files should include their job application, W-4 form, other appropriate forms, data sheets filled out, termination dates with the reason for termination, eligibility for rehire, any reprimand and evaluation forms, which should be filled out in full and signed, current address and phone number, and signed procedures and policy statements.

Streetwise Restaurant Management ■ 223

during the off-season. What you do or how you recast your business during the season and the off-season is entirely a matter of what happens in your own backyard.

Fortunately, you can do some estimating. You might not know how much snow pack will be on the slopes, but you do know that snow arrives in the winter. You know the tour buses start arriving in June and start disappearing from your parking lot as the leaves start turning. If your community is selected to host the Super Bowl, you'll have exact dates for planning. You'll know to expect an influx of people, traffic, and noise a few days before the event. You'll also know to plan for empty parking lots the day after the big game.

Know your town and its economic ups and downs. Know when the tourists generally first start arriving and how swiftly they depart. Know your business, how much you have to staff up, how many more supplies you'll need, and what you'll have to do to start attracting your regulars back after the season.

> Know your town and its economic ups and downs. Know when the tourists generally first start arriving and how swiftly they depart.

Considering Some Tax Problems

If you're thinking about changing the classifications of some employees to avoid tax payments, your thinking isn't very clear. Noncompliance is viewed as a serious offense by the U.S. Department of Labor. As this book is coming together, the DOL has announced plans to target three key areas of noncompliance with the tax laws regarding wages and hours.

Misclassification of Kitchen Personnel

You're asking for trouble if you attempt to reclassify your hourly chef or assistant chefs as salaried employees to exempt them from earning overtime. The federal government has strict guidelines as to who qualifies as a salaried or hourly employee. As a general rule, a salaried employee is one who is paid a salary and is classified as holding an executive, administrative, or professional position. The government's attention is focused more on the duties of the job than the fact that a salary is paid or title. This can get tricky when you have one person performing a specific task, such as your chef, and also handling a management responsibility. Before reclassifying anyone or any job description, verify your compliance with your attorney.

Computing Overtime Payments

Does an employee earning tips qualify for overtime? The answer is a qualified yes. The employee must work more than forty hours a week to earn that overtime. If you take a tip credit, the rate of overtime is not figured on the employee's wages but on the applicable minimum wage. The minimum wage is added to the overtime premium rate to get the appropriate rate of pay for those overtime hours. If your state does not permit the owner from taking a tip credit, overtime payment must be based on the regular hourly rate of the employee earning that payment.

Watch your books, hours, and employee's rights carefully. It is the owner's responsibility to ensure that all employees receive accurate compensation for their working hours, including overtime hours.

Kitchen Personnel Overtime

Some kitchen personnel are allowed to earn money from a pool funded by employees earning tips. Service charges are something different altogether. These are charges added to the bills for banquets. That's where the phrase, "A service charge of X percent will be added for parties exceeding X number of persons" comes from. It's accepted procedure for kitchen personnel to receive a portion of that pooled money. These funds are added to the employees' regular pay rate to compute the overtime rate.

It's surprisingly easy to overlook overtime compensation or portions of overtime payments. Double-check your figures to make certain you are in full compliance. It's your responsibility. Be sure also to check with your state government to get the exact rules applicable to your operations.

As an owner and a manager, you always want the best possible deal for your people. That's how you attract and hold the best people. Make certain that you are always in full compliance with the applicable laws, rules, and regulations. It's just as important to take good care of the people working with you. That's how you keep them working hard for you.

Chapter 19

Understanding the Basics of Restaurant Marketing

Part One

Part Two

Part Three

Part Four

Part Five

Part Six

Describing Marketing

Marketing is the big picture. It is the master plan controlling advertising (see Chapter 20) and public relations and promotions (see Chapter 21). Those are all important elements, but without the direction provided by marketing, they can be little more than wasted resources, missed opportunities, and lots of time, energy, and money working at cross purposes.

Marketing is the plan that takes you from where you are to where you are going. It is a process that pulls together various elements, organizes them into a cohesive action plan, carries out that plan, and adapts along the way as necessary to achieve those goals. Consider your marketing plan a "living" entity. Follow its guidelines, but change it whenever and however the changes in your market dictate.

Recognizing That Marketing Isn't Advertising, PR, or Promotions

Marketing is the umbrella, the overall plan, and the guiding force. Advertising, public relations, and promotions are all functions of marketing and are directed by that plan. They are valuable, but by definition are subservient to marketing.

> Marketing is the umbrella, the overall plan, and the guiding force.

Advertising

Advertising is the use of paid media to get your message to your audience. Vehicles include radio, television, outdoor, direct mail, newspapers and magazines, skywriting, and your neighbor's kid with a handful of fliers.

Public Relations

Public relations is working with the news media to reach the public, and ideally your segment of that public. PR is "free" media in the sense that you can't buy it. You have to work through the news departments of radio and television stations, newspapers, and magazines, which means you have significantly less control over the delivery of your message, assuming it gets out there at all.

Promotions

Promotions are generally internal events or sponsored events designed to bring in additional customers at specified times. It is a vehicle that can also be used to generate positive news coverage and generate good will in the community. Promotions often involve the use of paid advertising and public relations. Getting all this "free" media can be quite costly.

Defining Some Key Marketing Terms

The marketing and related industries have their own jargon. Don't ever be intimidated. Restaurateurs do it, too. People in the media probably don't understand what you mean when you refer to the "front-of-the-restaurant versus back-of-the-restaurant expenses." Just ask for definitions and explanations. Here are a few of the basics.

Reach is the number of people who see or hear your ad within a designated time frame. Reach is usually evaluated in terms of four weeks. Newspapers and magazines use the term *circulation*, but the meaning is the same.

Frequency refers to the number of times an individual is exposed to your ad during a set time frame.

Penetration is the percentage of the total population reached by a media vehicle. Keep in mind that your market may not be the total population or it may be rather narrow, such as college students or senior citizens.

Waste Circulation relates to broadcast as well as print media. These are the people you can reach with your message but who really aren't your customers. The larger the media's audience or circulation, the greater the likelihood of waste circulation.

Pass Along Readership is a print media term. Unlike broadcast ads, a newspaper or magazine ad can be passed along from one person to another. For example, there may be only one subscription to the daily newspaper for the restaurant, but when Dad finishes reading he passes it along to Mom, who may pass it along to Grandma, and so on. Therefore one subscription could represent two or more readers exposed to your message.

Positioning Your Restaurant: It's a Mind Game

Positioning is a mind game, and a serious one at that. Positioning is the art of creating a positive image in the mind. Positioning is pitting your business (product, service, etc.) *against* something else.

Perhaps the most famous cases, certainly one of the most successful, positioned Avis Rent-A-Car against Hertz. Avis came up with the now-famous "We're Number 2. We Try Harder" campaign. The positioning stated that you, the customer, will get far better service with us guys at Avis because we know we have to work a lot harder to earn and keep your business.

It worked. Over several years, Avis's internal sales growth jumped from 10 to 35 percent. The key was to recognize their position in the market and claim it.

You can play the game in your market. For example, if your competitor is big and fancy, you can position your restaurant as "down home and friendly."

A *flight* is an advertising run of limited duration. For instance, if you are promoting a big New Year's bash, you'd schedule a flight of ads a week or two weeks prior to the event and would end it the day of the event. Flights are often pegged to holidays or your own special promotions.

Continuity refers to a continuous run of advertising, such as the sponsorship of a weekly news or weather broadcast. Success depends on a lot of exposure over a long period of time so as to accumulate enough impressions to, well, make an impression.

Audience is the term for the group or groups of people reached by a media vehicle. This is primarily a broadcast media term. The print media call it circulation.

CPM means "cost per thousand," and it refers to the dollar investment necessary in a given media vehicle to reach a thousand people. The figure is helpful when comparing the effectiveness of different advertising vehicles.

Finding Your Unique Selling Proposition

Also known as USP, a unique selling proposition is what sets you apart from everybody else. It can be virtually anything, such as your chef, location, menu, an extraordinary wine list, theme or décor, you name it. To be effective in marketing, your USP must be something that creates a desire in the hearts and minds of customers to come in and enjoy that USP. "We're the only fine dining establishment located on Highway 9" may be unique, but if you're right next door to the hog rendering plant or the Air Force gunnery range, that's not going to bring in a lot of folks. "We offer the unmatched culinary arts of Chef Ferdinand" is a good USP. "The only place in town for authentic Chicago-style deep dish pizza" is another.

Be very careful in selecting the USP you want to promote. If Chef Ferdinand jumps ship and starts whipping up soufflés for the competition, you could have invested a small fortune promoting a competitor's new USP. Also, your unique selling proposition doesn't have to be all that unique. It can be something that competitors have but are not marketing. Be wary of this approach, too, because at any moment that competitor could start promoting the same thing. Uniqueness flies out the window. Price can be a unique factor, but it can also backfire on you. "Our steaks are just as good as those over at Billy Bob's Steak-O-Rama" may be a sound proposition, but old Billy Bob can blow you out of the water by cutting his prices for a while.

Defining the Marketing Plan

The marketing plan is your guidebook or road map that gets you from where you are to where you are going. It is essential that you know that destination and any important points in between. Your overall plan will have a definite timetable broken down into specific activities. You will also include a budget broken down into smaller elements. For example, you'll have a master budget, say total marketing costs of $50,000. One element will be the advertising budget, which could be $35,000 of the overall. You'll then break that down even further into subcategories, such as newspapers at $20,000, radio at $10,000, and direct mail at $5,000. (These figures are just for illustration and aren't meant as a guideline.)

Set Measurable Goals

Marketing goals need to be specific and measurable. "We will enhance customer value through strategic business initiatives empowering employees to work in new team paradigms" is neither specific nor is it measurable. It's certainly not a goal. "Randy's Rowdy Restaurant will increase net revenues by 10 percent in dining and 8 percent in the lounge by December 31, 2003" is a real goal. It is specific and measurable. You

Separate Features, Benefits, and Proof

You have to know the difference between these three concepts so you can promote them correctly, and you have to promote the third so people will believe what you say.

- A feature is a fact. Chef Ferdinand studied at the Culinary Institute of France in Paris.
- A benefit is what that means to the customer. Chef Ferdinand prepares delicious cuisine unlike any other here in Missoula.
- Proof is the factual basis for your claim. Mounting a copy of his diploma on the wall next to his picture for all to see would be proof. Preparing delicious meals unique to Missoula would also be considered proof.

Your restaurant will have any number of positive features. Align them with benefits in your advertising, public relations, and promotions. And always offer proof.

Conducting Marketing Research

By the time you're ready to draw up your marketing plan, you'll have completed a lot of your research. This is the "who am I" phase of your plan. By the time you reach this stage, you have already compiled a solid base of valuable marketing information. Think about all the market work you've likely already accomplished:

- Your business is defined.
- Your customer base is defined.
- You've studied the competition.
- You've studied the market (geographical, income levels, age, race, etc.).
- You've conducted a SWOT analysis (strengths, weaknesses, opportunities, threats).
- You've created your mission statement.
- You've created your menu.
- You've set your goals.

Your marketing plan is a key element in your ability to reach those goals.

should also include benchmarks along the way, such as quarterly or monthly goals designed to keep you moving toward the overall goal.

Create a Calendar

Things have a way of remaining unreal until they are put in writing. Make your marketing goals as real as you can. Look at the month, the quarters, the year, or even multiple years, and schedule the implementation of your marketing plan. You'll actually have several calendars. One will be the master document, and the others will break the master into smaller, more specific time periods. The smaller the time segments, the more detailed will be your calendar.

Your master calendar will include your advertising program, your public relations efforts, and your promotions. You can also create subcalendars for those specific areas.

Create a Budget

A budget is a fairly straightforward document. Virtually every element used to draw it up is a known factor. For example, you can get the price of a thirty-second radio or television spot, the cost of an inch of newspaper space, or the price of an outdoor billboard. Estimate how many of what you need and tally up the figures. Media representatives will gladly help you with this task, beefing up their portion of the budget, of course. You can also hire professional advertising and marketing firms.

When creating your budget, follow your sales curve. In the above example, business traditionally picks up as the flowers start to bloom. That's when the manager decided to grow his or her budget. That money invested in January or February, when business is typically slow, would have been a wasted investment, most likely. It is very unlikely that you can use advertising to change a traditional sales curve. Save the money and invest it at times when it will do you more good. Use it to bring in even more customers when they're in a mood to enjoy your fare.

Keep your budgets and compare them year to year. The more you do it, the better and more accurate you'll be. You'll learn what works, what doesn't, and what works best at one time and what works best at others.

Implement Your Plan

That's relatively simple. You just go about doing the things listed in your budget and on your calendar. You can do this yourself, have your GM or promotions director handle the responsibilities, or you can hire outside professionals.

If you decide to do it yourself and you find the experience a bit daunting, don't be concerned. You can handle it. First break down that list of chores into tasks that you can handle one at a time. For instance, if you want to advertise on the radio but know nothing about the medium, don't be intimidated. Call the stations and start collecting information. (We'll go into media in more depth in Chapter 20.) A little common sense will carry you a long way. If your customer base, called a "target audience" in media terminology, is senior citizens, then you'll know not to call the local stations featuring rap music or heavy metal. The easy listening, oldies, or news and information stations will be better suited as vehicles to reach potential customers. If your market is primarily college students, you'll need to call the rap station and/or the country & western and rock stations. Remember, you don't make a media buy based on your own preferences. You buy what your audience reads, hears, or watches.

When the media representatives (salespeople) call, get all the information you can. They subscribe to rating services, such as Arbitron, which monitor audiences. They can show you down to parts of an hour who is listening to which stations—male, female, age, etc. Describe your customer base and say "show me." Evaluate the rates, choose your stations, and make your buys. Follow the same procedure with the other media appropriate to your customer base. Take your budget one segment at a time, one media at a time, until you've completed the task.

Follow Up

Always monitor your budget and how well the public is responding to your efforts. Give the media time to work, but continue monitoring and evaluating. If things don't work out after a fair trial, move on to something that does work. Randy has a rule of thumb: He always gives an ad campaign or promotion at least six weeks before deciding if it was successful or not. Stay on top of things. Stations change formats, on-air personnel, and salespeople, and sometimes public taste just changes. All of these factors could affect the efficiency of your media buy.

If a particular media buy doesn't work, it's not enough for you to pull the plug. Find out why the buy didn't work. Perhaps you bought the right station(s) but at the wrong time. When is your audience actually listening? Did you buy spots in the less expensive midnight till 5 A.M. block even though your customers listen during the more costly drive-time hours? Why buy time when your audience isn't listening?

Did you buy enough spots to be heard? There are lots of advertisers out there. Your commercials have to be played a lot just to get noticed. Repetition of your message is essential. The rule of thumb states that a spot or an ad has to be seen or heard at least six times before the audience member even knows that he or she has seen it! And that's before the actual selling can begin.

> Your commercials have to be played a lot just to get noticed. Repetition of your message is essential.

Is your ad or commercial lacking in creativity? Ads in newspapers or magazines are stacked on top of and beside each other. Commercials on radio or television are bunched together in clusters. It's easy for the consumer to be overwhelmed by all of that information. Your ads have to be creative to be seen or heard. They have to become "cluster busters," or they'll never bust out and be noticed. Are your advertisements jumping out of the page, or are they being lost in the gray matter?

Treat the implementation of your marketing plan as a learning process. Keep learning. Keep fine-tuning and improving your skills.

Adapting to Changes in the Market

Change just for the sake of change can be dangerous. As they say, "If it ain't broke, don't fix it." Change to curry favor with the trendy set following the latest fad can be dangerous, too. By the time you've gone to the considerable expense of making over your restaurant, the fad could have already passed.

There are some changes that must be addressed. Even if you decide not to implement change, you're still better of having given the matter some in-depth thought. Markets change, and sometimes you have to change with them to survive. For example, people age. If your neighborhood customer base is aging, you might have to mature with them to keep those folks coming back. As the college kids become wage earners and parents, their taste for burgers and inexpensive sangria might grow into an appreciation for continental cuisine and fine wine. You'll have to adapt or find another bunch of college kids to attract.

Rise and Fall of Economies

Economies rise and fall. If the town mill has a bunch of layoffs, a lot of people lose a lot of discretionary income. You might have to make some adjustments. Adjusting doesn't mean sacrificing quality. If you're running that upscale restaurant featuring continental cuisine, you probably shouldn't change your menu to burgers and brew. But you might want to start adding some daily specials at lower prices. You don't want to alienate your existing customers who have the wherewithal to invest in a fine meal, but you should consider adding a few items to attract those folks who are a bit strapped.

Changes in Tastes

Tastes change. People at one time enjoyed strong whiskeys. Later they moved to lighter liquors and then on to wines. Red wines were all the rage, and then folks switched over to the whites. Not too long ago many people thought sushi was a something that attacked Godzilla in cheap Japanese movies. Now sushi bars are all around the country. Cajun food was hot for a while (pun intended), but the trend cooled off. Who knows what the next trend will be. If you want to follow it, consider adding items to your menu rather than renovating your entire restaurant. That way you can follow the trends without being dominated by them. It's far easier to print up an insert to your menu than to do a makeover on a restaurant.

Of course, if you own a Mexican restaurant and really want to open a sushi bar, why not? That is, provided you've conducted the appropriate market research to determine that the change is feasible. Most of the time, however, the real key to handling change is to adapt to it rather than allowing change to dictate the direction you go. After all, that direction might not be pointing to your ultimate marketing goal.

Marketing is the big picture. Handled wisely, with plenty of thought and careful follow-up, it can be "picture perfect."

Chapter 20

Advertising Your Restaurant

Asking Preliminary Advertising Questions

When it comes to advertising, ask basic questions and ask a lot of them. Use this simple rule as you enter the world of advertising: The less you know, the more questions you should ask, such as the following:

- Who is my market?
- Where are they located?
- What media vehicle best reaches that market?
- How much does it cost to reach them?
- Can I afford it?

You don't want to advertise on the most popular station in town if that station doesn't reach your customers. Their high numbers are irrelevant because of the significant amount of waste circulation. You would be better off with a smaller, more affordable niche publication or station that appeals more to the people you want to attract.

Until you get the hang of it, you may decide to work with advertising professionals, such as salespeople or your own advertising firm.

Understanding Advertising and Developing Goals

Advertising is purchased media. You buy newspaper space, radio time, outdoor panels, etc. just as you would buy meat and vegetables, tables and chairs, or refrigerators and stoves. As noted in Chapter 19, advertising is a function of marketing and must be carried out under a well-conceived overall marketing plan.

Make your goals very specific. "We want to reach X number of customers/potential customers X number of times per week (or month or length of the advertising campaign)." That's really all there is to it. Look at the media rate cards. Select those vehicles that have the highest number of readers/listeners/viewers in your target audience and allocate the appropriate resources.

Allocating Funds to Your Advertising Budget

How much budget should you allocate to advertising? That's a question impossible to answer here. Every market, every customer base, and every restaurant is different. A new restaurant will probably have to invest many more ad dollars in many more vehicles than an established restaurant with a loyal customer base. Some well-established restaurants run a bare bones "maintenance" ad schedule just to keep the name out there. The schedule may be augmented by additional media buys for certain promotions such as a Mother's Day special. A highly competitive market will require more advertising expense than a more stable one. Smaller markets have fewer media vehicles, and prices are lower than in major markets.

Evaluate your situation, your competition, and your budgetary resources, and come to a reasonable figure. As a rule of thumb, a typical restaurant will invest 1.5 to 3 percent of its overall sales in its marketing program.

Evaluating Media Effectiveness

A good manager or owner will continually monitor his or her advertising and public relations efforts. Is it working? Sometimes it's remarkably easy to evaluate media effectiveness. If you've advertised a St. Patrick's Day special and business picks up with a lot of happy people wearing green, then you can attribute your success to the ad/PR program.

Sometimes it's harder to make an evaluation. There's that famous quote attributed to the great entrepreneur John Wannamaker that half of the advertising budget is well-spent—he just didn't know which half. Well, if your advertising efforts are bringing in customers, chances are that at least that powerful half is working. You will also run into the curiosity of someone coming in because "I read your ad" or saw your spot, heard your radio ad, etc. when you haven't

Grand Opening Expenses

Every time Randy opens a new restaurant, he allocates from $10,000 to as much as $25,000, depending on location, competition, and the overall market, for a pre-opening ad campaign. His goal is to not only alert the immediate neighborhood but the entire city that a new restaurant is in town. If the location is on a very busy street (hopefully so), he will use a banner or even a portable sign to let the thousands of cars passing by every day know that a new restaurant has opened.

His opening ad budget is always based on overall sales. From 2 percent to as high as 5 percent is a good range for budgeting advertising and marketing. Some areas have been highly competitive, which naturally costs a little more to penetrate.

advertised at all. That may still be a credit to a residual effect of your earlier advertising efforts.

If there's no increase, chances are something is a bit off. (The exception would be when you're just running a maintenance schedule and just want to keep the status quo.) Any number of reasons could cause a lack of response. Here are some of the top contenders.

You bought the wrong media. Your customers were listening to talk radio instead of reading the city magazine.

You bought the wrong medium. Your customers were reading the shopper instead of the daily newspaper. They watched the local news instead of Fox or MSNBC.

You bought at the wrong time. The middle of the night is a great time to get very low advertising rates. But is anybody out there listening? Try to target not only the right media but the best time.

You bought the wrong audience. That billboard out on the interstate has an audience in the hundreds of thousands, but it's 20 miles from your restaurant, and those people eat close to home. Tens of thousands of those readers aren't even local anyway.

You sent the wrong message. Perhaps your appeal to your market wasn't very appealing.

Correcting Ineffective Media Decisions

A good manager asks the hard questions, gets to the source of the problem, and makes the decisions that correct it. Work with your advertising outlet: Don't make accusations, but get their help in getting to the real cause of the failure. Sometimes the lack of response can be laid at the feet of the media. Sometimes it will be your fault, and often failure is the child of both parents. The main point is to learn from the experience so that you won't repeat it, and continue fine-tuning your efforts.

Your message just didn't cut it. Ads and spots appear in clusters. Your approach has to be simple, easy to remember, and creative enough to cut through all of that clutter.

Reviewing the Major Media Types

The following sections discuss very briefly the major types of media. There will be some shifting of categories in different markets. A small circulation weekly newspaper or the small wattage radio station up on the hill may be considered major media in Smallville, USA. In New York, Dallas, Phoenix, or Los Angeles, these options would be considered secondary because of the vast number of media options bringing in large audiences that are available. Whatever your market, it is important that you select the medium/ media that best reaches your specific audience affordably and effectively and with the least amount of waste circulation.

Television

Television is considered the most influential medium in terms of numbers of people reached. In times past, an advertiser could purchase one, two, or three network-affiliated stations and cover huge markets. Today, television broadcasting is fragmented like never before. Cable and satellite providers have been added to the mix, and now there are hundreds of networks on which to advertise. In a sense, modern television has evolved into something akin to radio. There are now many, many narrow markets from which to choose. Broadcasting is becoming narrowcasting.

Don't get too caught up in playing the ratings game. Of course, you want high numbers of viewers watching your TV ad, but make sure those viewers are your customers. A program with "low" numbers might actually have a significantly higher number of potential customers than a much more highly rated and expensive program on another vehicle. Television is generally an expensive medium, but it can be affordable in smaller markets or on specialized stations catering to limited audiences.

Get Close to Remotes

Another product radio stations usually offer is the remote broadcast, usually called "remotes." This is where station personnel come to your restaurant and broadcast live for a couple of hours. They will send a radio personality to talk about your business and will usually discuss whatever you want them to.

Another thing that Randy always tries to do with radio stations is to set up a trade account with them. This is where you allow the radio station to bring clients to your restaurant and sign for the meal. Track the amount that was "comped" for the month, and that is the amount of free radio spots you should receive for the trade. Yes, it costs something for the food served.

Radio

All kinds of formats are available, and one is sure to match the profile of your target audience. Your buys on radio can include: country & western, pop, rock, oldies, classical, rap, heavy metal, gospel, news and talk, etc. Locally, you can have many options within a single format. For example, if your restaurant features a "heart smart" menu, you might consider advertising on the weekend health show.

Prices vary wildly and reflect the number of listeners, but many restaurants find radio a very effective way to reach specific audiences. Again, buy your audience, not the station or the format, regardless of its numbers.

Newspapers

Despite dwindling circulations and the loss of most evening papers, this medium is still the most read of all print media. Depending upon the size of your market, you can select from a major metropolitan daily, a weekly, a community newspaper, and papers catering to ethnic or specialty audiences. Which one best reaches your audience? Furthermore, which *section* of which paper best reaches your audience? Is your ad better placed in the entertainment section, the business pages, or in main news?

Many newspapers run special pages or sections devoted to dining out. These can be particularly effective because they are read by people who are actively looking for things to do and places to go. Check into the rates of the tabloid sections of larger newspapers. These are frequently devoted to arts and entertainment, including dining.

Magazines

The national publications are pretty much out of the picture for the majority of operations. Most restaurant ads in national magazines are for the chain operations. However, some national publications offer statewide or regional buying options. If you have a significant ad budget and can draw customers from such a large area, this might be an effective option.

Most medium to large cities have one or more city magazines. These are generally slick publications in full color. Ads can be reasonable for local restaurant advertisers. Production costs can be higher, especially if you want to use color or photographs in your advertising, which for the most part is a good idea. Large markets will have many magazine options to reach many specialized audiences, such as the business community, general interest readers, upscale readers, and readers interested in arts and entertainment, sports, tourism, and so on.

Direct Mail

As a rule, direct mail is an expensive medium in terms of cost per contact. That's balanced by the fact that it is also the most effective in reaching a specific audience. For example, if you want to send a mailing to your existing customers, just have folks who want to receive mailings fill out an address card. If you want to reach the members of the chamber of commerce, you can purchase the chamber's mailing list. If you want to reach the residents of a specific neighborhood or even part of a neighborhood, a list is available from any number of list suppliers.

There are two keys to success in direct mail.

1. **Your mailing list:** If you want to reach an audience, there is a list that will do it. Just make sure that the list does that. Make sure it is current. Also, don't think you can buy a list once and use it again without paying. List suppliers "salt" their lists will employees, family, and friends just to catch people in that act. A name list is more expensive than an "occupant" list, but it will also generate higher readership. Names printed on the envelope draw more responses than labels but are more expensive. If you can define a market, regardless of how specialized, there's probably a list for it.

2. **Your creativity:** People get lots and lots of direct mail every day. You have to make the effort to create something that will stand out

from the crowd. Otherwise, you'll end up in the "round file" along with the brochures for credit cards, insurance plans, retirement homes, and Alaskan real estate. Direct mail is typified by letters, brochures, and fliers, but for the imaginative there are no limits. If you choose direct mail, work hard on "thinking out of the box." You have to break out of the clutter in this medium, too.

Outdoor and Transit

Outdoor refers to billboards and outdoor posters you see along the highways and roads throughout the country. Transit ads are those signs on the sides of buses and tops of cabs. They're usually bought for a month at a time or even for a year, which over time makes the medium pretty cost effective.

Outdoor and transit advertising has to be designed for fast reading. After all, either the reader or the medium will be in motion during the exposure to your message. Sometimes they're headed in opposite directions. Simplicity combined with creativity is essential to readability.

Telephone Directory Advertising

This used to mean the yellow pages, but in recent years many more directories are available. Evaluate your budget and your message carefully, because you will be living with it for a full year. Many businesses consider directory advertising an essential ingredient in their marketing mix. Avoid overspending. A very creative small ad can dominate a much larger but poorly designed one. That philosophy applies to all advertising media as well.

Looking Over the Secondary Media

Most markets, even the smaller ones, have numerous options for advertising. These generally serve smaller and more specialized audiences.

Community Newspapers

These are basically smaller, more limited versions of the metropolitan daily. The differences are that they serve a specific geographic area, such as a town, a community within a larger metropolitan area, or even a neighborhood. Their focus is generally on local people and events. Rates are usually quite affordable and are attractive for a restaurant pulling from the local market. The opportunities for public relations are generally greater, too, because the restaurant is a member of the community.

Shoppers

Shoppers feature products and services for sale. Some are specialized, such as used cars and boats, and others are more general. They're inexpensive to purchase and are often given out for free. It's hard to know just how many readers actually use a shopper. Still, there wouldn't be so many of them around if people weren't reading them. Rates are usually very affordable. Some publications even have a policy of printing news articles, always positive, about their advertisers.

Point of Purchase

This is a broad category, but in the restaurant business point of purchase (POP) generally refers to tent cards on the table. They are used to promote specific menu items, specialty drinks, or upcoming events. Often a supplier will provide the restaurant with POP materials free of charge. Sometimes the supplier will cover the expense of printing your name or logo on the card. Signs, even homemade ones, placed in strategic locations are also considered point-of-purchase items.

 ## Using Comment Cards

It is highly recommended that you use comment cards. From the first day you open, you should place comment cards on the table, or better yet have the wait staff present them as they present the check. You will find out the good things as well as the bad. Put a place for the patrons' address. You can then write or phone them and start building a valuable database (mailing list) as well.

Knowing Where to Begin

Begin with your customers. Define your customer base as specifically as possible. Describe them by age, race, marital status, income, education, etc. This information will help you decide which advertising media to buy and what type of message to send. Once you know your market, the advertising salespeople can tell you how many of those folks read, watch, or listen to their medium. They can surprisingly accurate. Just buy the medium or the media mix that best reaches your customers.

Really get to know your customers. Discover what makes them "tick." That way your advertising messages can be targeted to the emotions that motivate them to dine out. Always think in terms of those motivations. Put yourself in their place and see the world through their eyes. Find the emotional buttons and push them (gently, of course) in all of your advertising.

Really get to know your customers. Discover what makes them "tick."

Chapter 21

Doing Public Relations and Promotions

Part One

Part Two

Part Three

Part Four

Part Five

Part Six

Establishing Public Relations Goals

PR is often referred to as "free" media. Nothing could be further from the truth. Sure, it's free in the sense that you don't pay money directly for time or space, but be clear on this: Public relations is an expense. It doesn't have to be a big expense, but you'll need to allocate some resources and track them just as you would inventory. As you might expect, there are many variables. To evaluate the costs of free media, you'll need to establish how you want to use that media.

As with your advertising goals (see Chapter 20), make your public relations goals specific. "We want to reach X number of potential customers through (PR vehicle) within the time frame of (days, weeks, promotion)." Knowing whether or not you've reached this goal is fairly easy to determine. If the news release is carried on the local radio station during a specific newscast, you can get the number of listeners to that broadcast from the station. They'll be happy to provide those figures (and try to sell you time within the program). If a section of the newspaper or local city magazine carries the release, you can get the circulation figures. It's all pretty straightforward. You either reached X number of people or you did not.

Developing a Public Relations Budget

Your biggest publicity expense will be the salary of your PR person or your payments to your advertising agency or public relations firm. You really shouldn't have to deal with too many unknown factors, so budgeting should be fairly easy and accurate. Your staffperson's salary is obviously a known figure. When working with your PR firm, you have several choices. You can pay them per project, or on a flat rate per month, or a combination of the two. Whichever route you go, be sure to get an estimate of costs before authorizing any expenditures. Review the figures and expect some variations between the estimates and the actual costs. Get clarification on any items that appear to be out of line.

A lot of your publicity expenses will be covered by existing supplies. For example, you'll write your news releases on your letterhead and will use your envelopes to mail them in. You'll already have a supply of stamps or a postage meter. The phone lines used to call media representatives are already in place. The salary of the person handling public relations, even on a part-time basis, is already established.

That being said, you should still develop a specific PR budget to help you track these costs. Even with "free" media you'll need to see where your money is going, how much good it is doing you, and where to trim or beef up the budget.

Working with the News Media

Public relations involves many of the same media vehicles, with two major distinctions. You will be working with the news rather than the advertising department, and you can't buy space or time. Promotions are events that you create in or concerning your restaurant to attract customers or create good will within your community or targeted elements of that community.

Your public relations and advertising efforts may involve the same media vehicles, but you will be dealing with two entirely different departments. The advertising department is in place to serve your needs because you pay them money. The news department views its role as serving the public, and you can't pay them to do anything. In fact, the more pressure you try to bring to bear on the news department, the less likely are your chances of success. The media likes to say that there is a wall between advertising and news. Regardless of your power in advertising, up in news they don't believe they owe you a thing.

A news editor is faced with a stack of items, and in his or her eyes many or all of them have equal value. Space or time is limited, and only so much of it can be devoted to news. If there's only room for one story, which is more important, the grand opening of Ralph's Seafood or Reginald's Seafood? Often the difference is simply in how the material is presented.

Write up your news in proper form. You'll use the same format for print and broadcast media. Here are the key items of every news release.

Assign Responsibility for PR

Someone must be responsible for coming up with marketing ideas, implementing them, and working with the media. Large facilities will have a full-time staff person in charge of this task. The owner or general manager may handle it on a part-time basis in smaller facilities or in operations that do little promotion.

Check with your vendors and salespeople, especially the beer and liquor companies. They have people on the payroll whose job it is to go out and help promote. They know that the more successful you are, the more product you will order, so their sales will increase. Use them and let them help with table tents, decorations, fliers, or posters. Sometimes they will even participate in certain forms of other advertising. Ask, you never know.

Make Personal Contact

Whenever possible, hand deliver your news release—it's also a great way to create beneficial relationships that can provide additional and even unexpected PR benefits. For instance, if they're doing a story or feature on the restaurant industry, you could get a call for a quote simply because the reporter remembers your name.

Always maintain a professional demeanor with any news media contact. Never threaten or try to intimidate a reporter or editor. If you have a legitimate beef, try to work things out peacefully. When it comes to news coverage, the news department has all the power.

Letterhead: They have to know who sent in the release. Your business letterhead will do just fine. You don't need to print up special forms just for releases.

Contact person: This should be someone the reporter can call back to verify facts, get a quote, or to help beef up the story. This person has to be knowledgeable about the subject of the release. He or she also has to be available.

Date of release: Most releases use one of two basic forms. "For Immediate Release" means that the editor can use the story right away. If you send in a release that you want held to a specific date, just write "For Release on (date)."

Headline: Many people like to write a headline, but it's not really necessary.

The release: Write it in descending order of importance. The most important item goes right up in the first paragraph. Don't pad the material. Also never use superlative descriptions. "The lavish establishment that is Reginald's Seafood announces a splendid new addition to this popular eatery, a delightful new banquet facility" will be headed straight for that round file. That's not news. It's puffery, and the editor will not want to waste time in a rewrite. Ralph wrote a better story. "Ralph's Seafood opens a new 50-person capacity banquet room Friday, announced general manager Ralph Junior" imparts the message in a professional manner and is more likely to make it through the editorial process.

Make sure every news release is about real news. When you send in non-news items to the news department, you waste the editor's time. He or she will remember that. Some of your legitimate news items may be ignored because you've "cried wolf" too many times in previous efforts.

Promoting with a Business Solicitation Letter

Draft a letter offering the services of your restaurant. "We've been in business X years and have made a lot of friends. We'd like to make a lot more." Include some pertinent information such as menu changes, a new chef, or physical improvements that would attract new customers. Mail to a list developed from your business card drop-off, addresses collected from customers at events during the year, or to a purchased mailing list targeting a specific audience. Here's a good tip: Personal checks are a terrific source of names and addresses.

Soliciting by Phone (Direct Sales Calls)

Telephone solicitation will prove to be one of your most effective promotional tools. But before you can start punching in telephone numbers, you have to have those numbers. There are numerous ways to build a list. You can buy telephone lists from suppliers. You can look up people in your city directory, or you can use the regular phone book. All these methods are inefficient, because you'll be contacting so many people who will never be patrons of your restaurant.

Realistically, the best place to start is with your patrons. Work the crowd all the time. Trade business cards. Provide opportunities for them to win prizes in such a way that they have to provide a name and telephone number. You can even provide a sign-in sheet for people who would like to be informed of upcoming events or specials. Use your imagination to get names and numbers. These people are a prime market. They're people who know where you are, what you serve, and the kind of excellent customer service you provide. They're already "sold." You just want to bring them back more often.

Once you've decided on a marketing promotion, start making calls. Be sure to call any new leads you have along with the existing customers. If you're contacting businesses for a major promotion, be sure to fill out a call sheet that includes the company name, contact person, address and phone numbers, fax number and e-mail address, date of the call, booking date of the promotion, comments from the contact person, any impression you feel important, and date of your next planned call.

Let's put this into work in a real marketing promotion.

An Example: The Free After-Work Party

A free after-work party is a great way to reward loyal customers and attract new customers in groups to your restaurant. Plan an affordable menu, know your available dates, coordinate everything with the other managers before making the calls, and then start punching in those numbers. A phone solicitation should be brief, friendly, and informative. Here's how a good one should sound. Of course, you'd adapt it to your customer and the specific event.

> A free after-work party is a great way to reward loyal customers and attract new customers in groups to your restaurant.

"Hello, my name is John Smith from Your Friendly Neighborhood Restaurant. I am calling to thank you for your recent visit and to let you know that you have won an after-work party. Do you have a moment for me to describe all that you have won?

"Great! You have won a reserved decorated area in our restaurant (club or bar) for you and ten to twenty of your employees (or friends) next Tuesday evening. Everybody attending will receive a complimentary beverage of their choice and half-price appetizers. We'll also give one complimentary pizza for every five people in your party.

"Is next Tuesday a good day for your party? Fine, then I'll just book that to make the event official. Again, thank you for your recent visit. Do you have any questions?"

Again, the specifics will vary according to your bill of fare, your customers, etc., but you get the idea. Work closely with your food and beverage manager and your chef to design party fare that is cost effective yet pleasing to your customers. If the individual can't commit to a date, say that you will call back in a few days to allow him or her time to consult with others in the company. Once a date is set, be sure to mail or deliver a confirmation immediately and to follow up with a phone call two days before the party.

Use Solicitation Reports

When you make the number of daily telephone solicitations you should be making, you'll find it impossible to keep all that information in your head. Use the following solicitation reports to keep accurate records and valuable information. They're all quite simple, and you can draw up your own forms. All that is required are spaces for such information as name, company, date, phone number, and lines for the caller's comments. A couple of examples will be provided. File them for convenient reference on follow-up calls. Many people keep such records in three-ring binders.

The *Weekly Sales Activity Report* is use to record each daily call. Include the date, contact name, phone/fax/e-mail numbers, call status, and follow-up date.

The *File Status Sheets* record a detailed account of each contact. Keep them in a one to thirty-one day file folder, placing them behind the date of your next follow-up call. Once the promotion is booked, the office party for example, record the information on the sheet and put it in a three-ring binder. Use the forms as a reference for follow-up calls.

A *Qualification Sheet* is used for recording information on more detailed promotions, such as a very large office party.

Follow-Up Fax Sheets are used to forward information (via fax, mail, or e-mail) to your contact once the event has been agreed upon. Record the date and details of the event.

Provide your contact with an *Employee Sign-Up Sheet* so that he or she can sign up the friends or coworkers who will attend the event. Once the sheet is completed, the contact person can tell you precisely how many people will attend.

Weekly Tracking Sheets help you set a goal of how many events to book as well as how much revenue you want to bring in.

Party Information Sheets are used to inform your staff of the details of the booked events so that they can prepare for them. Note such information as the name of the organization, how many people will attend, what food and beverage specials should be provided, the hours of the event, etc.

If a DJ will be employed, provide a *DJ Party Information Sheet* with information that he or she will announce, such as birthdays, anniversaries, food and beverage specials, people to thank, upcoming events, and people to be recognized.

Reviewing Unique Promotional Ideas

Options for promoting your restaurant or club/restaurant are limited only by your imagination. This section gives you a list of idea starters for other promotions. Put your creative mind to the task, and there's no limit to the number of good marketing ideas you can create.

Reward Loyal Customers

Say "thank you" with a gift certificate for a free meal or a certain amount off their next meal. You can also provide a delightful surprise by giving a loyal customer a free drink, appetizer, or dessert. The cost is minimal compared to the good will generated.

Keep the Juices Flowing

Your ideas for promoting your restaurant are only as limited as your imagination. Try out different ideas. Drop the ones that don't pan out. Repeat the ones that work well. If you're clever enough, you might even start your own traditional promotion. A clip file of your ideas, magazine articles, and information on promotions will be very helpful for those days when the ideas just don't flow. Start clipping now.

Offer Cooking Lessons

Your chef can prepare a special meal with recipes to be handed out to the participants. The chef introduces the meal and has a follow-up session to answer any questions. Schedule the promotion once a month at a fixed price and by reservation only. This event is also a great way to have a test run on new menu items.

Promote National Days

Every month has a number of "national days" within it. For example, September is National Chicken Month, National Piano Month, and contains National Grandparents Day. Use your imagination. How about a month of chicken specialties or a grandparents special complete with a free photograph of the entire family?

Institute a Grazing Menu

One night a week offer a significant amount of new dishes at low prices and in sizes just below your appetizer sizes. Customer get to experience a lot of different types of food at one sitting without overstuffing or breaking their budget. Make sure that the grazing menu is of equal quality to your regular menu. Don't try to cut corners by cutting quality, or the experiment will blow up in your face.

Start a Wine Club

Once a month, host a wine tasting. Set a fixed price and offer a variety of wines plus appropriate hors d'oeuvres. A wine expert or someone knowledgeable about wine can make a presentation to help educate the public. A good time to schedule the event is roughly 5:30 to 7:30 P.M., a time frame that could lead a number of the club members to stay on for a meal.

Potential Events That Draw New Customers

Here's a list of potential events that will promote your restaurant: corporate breakfast, lunch, or dinner meetings, class reunions, engagement parties, weddings, wedding receptions, showers, anniversaries, birthdays, graduation parties, bar mitzvahs, bat mitzvahs, baby showers and christenings, family reunions, holiday parties, company parties, happy hour parties, retirement parties, company anniversaries, luau parties, coming out parties, chamber of commerce parties, church retreats, Sunday brunches, charity parties, school meetings and conferences, bereavement luncheons and dinners, bachelor/bachelorette parties, and employee promotion parties. And that list only scratches the surface.

Timing Your Promotions

With promotions (and nearly everything else in the restaurant business), always follow your sales curve. Smart fishermen fish when the fish are biting. Smart restaurant managers promote their businesses when the customers are coming in. If your business is traditionally slack in July and August but picks up in September, allocate your promotions budget so that July and August expenditures are low. Increase your budget just before the season picks up in September. When business traditionally drops back off, follow that trend.

Create a yearlong budget broken down into months and even weeks. You can always make adjustments to changes in the market as you go along. Be sure to track actual versus estimated costs so you don't "bust your budget" before the year has ended.

Work the Tour Bus Crowd

Contact the people organizing tours through your area. Provide a special meal with something extra special. For example, for folks taking a historical tour, provide a meal with a presentation by a local historian.

Offer Seminars with Other Businesses

For example, you could have a seminar on flower arranging conducted by a florist in your building, shopping center, or immediate area. Provide the seminar and the meal at a fixed price.

Turn the Tables on the Boss

Work with local businesses to arrange a party in which the boss is the server to the employees, serving food and beverages, bussing the table, etc. Check the local liquor laws if drinks are to be served. Assign someone to assist the boss and to make sure that he or she feels special and enjoys the event, too.

Chapter 22

Dealing with Unruly Customers

Part One

Part Two

Part Three

Part Four

Part Five

Part Six

PART SIX   RUNNING YOUR RESTAURANT DAY-TO-DAY

■ CHAPTER 22 Dealing with Unruly Customers ■ CHAPTER 23 Creating a Plan for Burglary, Fire, and Other Disasters ■ CHAPTER 24 Reducing Employee and Supplier Theft and Other Losses ■ CHAPTER 25 Conducting Inventory ■ CHAPTER 26 Finding Additional Sources of Revenue

Serving the Deserving

Every customer deserves excellent service—until he or she proves unworthy of it. Most customer confrontations in a restaurant usually involve misunderstandings or a slight overreaction to a legitimate request. These are simple situations and can usually be straightened out with a little firmness and customer sensitivity.

The other kind of customers, the troublemakers, should get an entirely different kind of treatment. After someone has proven himself or herself to be a problem customer, have the wait staff change their level of service. Never ignore a customer, but give the problem people the absolute minimum of service. Don't allow them to get away with anything. Continue the process every time these people show up. They'll soon get the message and move on to another establishment with looser rules.

Reminding Servers That They Have Responsibilities

Let your waiters, waitresses, and bartenders know that they have a responsibility for the condition and safety of their customers. Any situation that is unusual or potentially dangerous should be immediately reported to a manager so he or she can step in and diffuse the situation. The ability to serve and at the same time monitor your customers is an acquired skill. You have to train, and they have to practice, and it's well worth the effort. Customers will appreciate the attention without ever knowing they're being so closely monitored.

The wait staff should report any of the following behaviors:

- Use of profane language
- Verbal arguments
- Yelling
- Loud whistling
- Someone bothering another customer
- Inappropriate touching/feeling of a female customer
- Intoxicated persons

If a situation gets out of hand or appears to be getting out of hand, several things should happen. A manager must be notified right away. Any employee involved in the incident should refrain from interfering with the manager's handling of the situation. In the case of an intoxicated patron or a patron who is bothering another customer, it is the manager's responsibility to ask that person to leave. No one else should make this effort.

Empowering Within Limits

Employee empowerment is getting a lot of press these days. Within limits, that's a fine philosophy. The owner or manager has to establish those limits. For example, everyone should be trained to handle customer conflicts on his or her own. Often speed is essential in keeping a touchy situation from becoming an unpleasant or violent one. Employees must know what to do, and they must have the authority to do it. Of course, they should also be trained to know when it's time to bring in bigger guns and go get or send for the manager.

Committing to Training

Make sure the employees know how to handle problems, such as a rejected credit card or a customer who has had one too many drinks. The customer isn't always right, and it's important that management backs the employee when he or she is in the right. Provide register training so they know how to quickly fix a problem. Inform them of the circumstances in which management authorization is required. The more you can prepare your employees ahead of time, the less stress they'll experience when something happens.

Hiring a Security Manager

A security manager should be thoroughly familiar with every area of the premises. He or she has the responsibility of explaining the security codes

Continuing Empowerment

Empowerment can also work, again within limits, in other areas. Employees could provide important input on making decisions in such areas as how tips are to be distributed, setting up cleaning schedules, or in handling other responsibilities. For instance, if it doesn't really matter in what order Bob, Ted, Carol, and Alice sweep the dining room, what's wrong with allowing them to set their own rotation?

Whenever giving even limited decision power to employees, it is still essential that the manager keep an eye on how the process is working.

to other security personnel and the staff. He or she should maintain a professional bearing at all times, even when confronted by a touchy situation.

The security manager should fill out a complete report immediately after any incident or accident. If the police or an ambulance is called to the restaurant, a copy of the report should be procured and attached to the security report. If a situation comes up that the security manager is not trained or equipped to handle, he or she should be trained to contact management.

The security manager should also conduct monthly meetings to discuss and explain procedures for various situations, such as hold ups, fires, or evacuations.

> The security manager should fill out a complete report immediately after any incident or accident.

Establishing Security Codes

You know that it's foolish to shout "fire" in a crowded theater. It's just as foolish to shout "fight" in a crowded restaurant. Set up a code system so that your employees can know what's going on in a troubling situation without having to alarm your customers. For example, "Code 2 in the parking lot" means nothing to a customer, but the staff will know how and where to respond. Here is a system Randy has used.

Code 1: A fight may be starting. The bartender may have trouble with a customer. A patron may be sick.

Code 2: A fight is in progress. The tip jar has been stolen. A customer has passed out.

Code 3: A fight has actually broken out. A security guard is in trouble. There is a fight or a wreck in the parking lot.

Code 4: Weapons are involved in an actual fight in the facility or the parking lot. Call the police. Possible weapons include a knife, stick, beer bottle, gun, or mace.

These are pretty typical. If you have specific situations, you can add your own special codes. For example, if you're in "tornado alley," Code 5 could mean "get everyone into the basement now!"

Controlling Uncontrolled Customers

You don't have to call out the militia or start unrolling the fire hose to control an unruly customer. Here are a few techniques to help you and your managers deal with troublesome guests in the restaurant.

Use Aggressive Listening

That means seeking to find out what the other person is really saying. It involves listening for underlying meanings or hidden meanings. It also requires the listener to physically show that he or she is listening, for example nodding your head, saying "I see" or "I'm listening."

Allow the customer to blow off a little steam. Sometimes that's all he or she wants in the first place.

Refuse to Argue but Avoid Negative Words

Sometimes a customer just wants to stir up trouble. He or she may be angry at a spouse or the boss and has decided to take out that frustration on you. The customer may be trying to impress someone by being tough or demanding. The patron may just be a jerk. Whatever the situation, don't give the other person more energy by trying to fight back. After a while, the unruly patron may just get tired and give up.

Try not to say "no" or "you can't" or similar words and phrases by using different terminology. "That's not such a good idea, sir" is much less of a challenge than "No, you won't!" This can't be done in every situation, but use the technique whenever possible.

Provide Options

Salespeople often close a sale by giving a customer two choices, each of which signifies a purchase. "Would you like that delivered Thursday or Friday?" You use the same technique to handle tense situations. "Might I suggest that we do this or that? Would you then feel satisfied?" Use your imagination. It's possible that your customer has realized he's gotten himself in an awkward situation and would jump at the first opportunity to get out.

If at all possible, allow the patron to exit the situation with some dignity. The strategy helped solve the Cuban Missile Crisis. It can certainly help prevent a crisis in your dining area.

Explain the Rules

If the situation doesn't seem to be getting resolved, point out that you must follow the established rules and policies of the restaurant. In some cases you can say that you're only following the law. For example, if an inebriated customer wants to continue drinking, you can state that you're prohibited by law from continuing to serve him. It's a good way of shifting the emphasis from the manager confronting the situation onto something or someone else. Try to get away from the "me against you" mentality. Depersonalize your answers by using "the bar" or "it's our policy." It's much less emotional to the troublemaker than your "Because I said so!"

Don't Buy into Negativity

Even if someone is in your face cussing like Yosemite Sam from the Looney Toons, don't descend to that level. You'll only make things worse and perhaps even ignite a physical confrontation.

Keep Other Customers Out of It

If a customer is causing trouble, other customers may want to pitch in to put more muscle on your side. This is especially true of your regulars. There are two very good reasons to avoid help from your patrons. First, they're not trained to handle these situations. The problem is part of your job. Secondly, a patron could get hurt. You don't want that on your conscience, and beyond that, you don't want to face the lawsuit that could follow an injury.

Stick to Your Guns

Rules are rules, and you can't back away from them no matter how much the other person pushes you. Breaking the rules opens the flood-gates for others to rush in and start breaking them, too. At some point you might have to use a phrase such as, "I've explained our policy several times, sir. We have to drop the subject now." Your voice and demeanor has to be cool and calm for this to work, or you might just set the other guy off. In a good many cases, however, the unruly customer will realize that his behavior is inappropriate.

Walk Away

Provided the situation isn't very tense and the customer is merely fuming rather than tearing up the furniture, you can buy a little time by leaving. Point out that you have to review your policy manual or consult with the owner. Waiters or waitresses faced with the same problem can simply move on to serve their other customers. That extra time may allow the unruly patron to cool down or even leave in a huff. Either way you and your customers are better off without the annoyance.

Tell 'Em to Go Away

Everyone has seen those signs reading "We have the right to refuse service to anyone" posted in bars and restaurants throughout the country. Well, provided you're not violating someone's civil rights, you do have that ability. "You'll have to leave now" or "If you don't leave immediately, I'll be forced to bar you permanently from this restaurant" is perfectly appropriate. Don't use such phrases as a bargaining chip when trying to negotiate someone out of an unruly state. Use your right to refuse service only when you really mean it.

Call in Your Bouncer—or the Police

If the use of physical force is required, then by all means use it. Make sure your bouncer and your support staff are well trained in handling violent

Practice Customer Sensitivity

Happy and satisfied customers don't create problems. One of the best ways to maintain high levels of customer satisfaction is to train your staff to be sensitive toward their patrons.

Sensitivity is the ability to notice or become aware of a certain situation that is not correct. For example, if the music, temperature, or lighting level is too high or too low. Crumbs on the floor should also be swept up right away. Replace any dirty or stained eating utensils or glasses before a customer has time to make that request.

A restaurant staff must do all it can to anticipate customer desires and to be aware of the positive impression made by paying attention to details. Everyone must make a total commitment to customer service. Customer sensitivity is a direct and visible expression of that commitment.

or potentially violent customers. Obviously, this is a measure you take as a last resort. Most restaurants don't need a bouncer, although those larger businesses with a lounge might require one. It's a good idea to consider some bouncer training for selected members of your staff just in case a situation does arise.

If you can't handle the situation, there are trained professionals who can. Sometimes you have to call in those authorities. If you genuinely believe the situation warrants that kind of action, make the call immediately. Tell the offending party that you have called the police and then calmly walk away. Chances are he or she will head out the door before the police arrive. If he's too hot to trot away, his friends or associates may be persuasive enough to get him out the door. You can also use this treat as a bluff, but be prepared to actually make the call if your bluff is called.

Controlling Unruly Crowds

Crowds are generally a good thing. Lots of happy patrons make for a very happy owner. As anyone who watches television news these days knows, crowds have a way of getting out of control and wreaking havoc, or at least wrecking the evening. Loss of revenue, loss of customers, and loss of valuable property can follow. Crowd control must be part of your training regimen.

Watch the Crowd

Managers should spend time on the floor observing what's going on. They should always be looking out for problems or potential problems. Some actions or activities that may require attention include:

- An obviously drunk person
- Someone who cannot walk straight

- Customers who sway back and forth when standing
- Someone who has passed out in his or her chair
- Loud or obnoxious behavior
- A patron who manhandles another customer or member of the staff
- Someone making threats or threatening actions
- A customer ordering only water or soda (and possibly mixing drinks from a hidden bottle)

Pay particular attention to any crowded areas. Keep an eye on places where people might have to squeeze through, such as stairways, tunnels, near the restrooms, the front door, or near the bar. People brushing up against each other, even accidentally, can start a conflict. Managers should be trained in "people skills" and in handling touchy situations.

Establish a Door Policy

Dress codes are entirely appropriate for many establishments. If yours is one, set a policy. It's a common experience that people who are poorly groomed or inappropriately dressed cause more trouble than well-groomed, appropriately attired customers. That's not an absolute rule, but you'll find that it holds up over time.

If you institute a dress code, allow your customers to violate it at first. Give people a few weeks to get used to the idea. Use those weeks to educate your customers as to the appropriate mode of dress. Then start politely enforcing the rules.

Refuse Service to Inebriated Guests

Alcohol is at the center of many problems. Serving someone who has had "a few too many" is more than bad judgment. It's bad business, and serious repercussions could follow. In some states it is against the law to serve alcohol to someone who is drunk. Your door hostess or greeter must be trained to prohibit anyone who is drunk or on drugs to enter your facility. The inebriated person can't create a problem inside if he or she is restricted to the outside. And if there is a scene, at least it will be outside and will not disturb your customers.

If you don't have a greeter, or if someone gets past the greeter, or if a patron becomes drunk while at your establishment, have the wait staff or the bartender bring the situation to the attention of a manager immediately. Your policy must apply across the board. A customer who is a "regular" should not get special treatment. It's better to lose the business of a single customer than risk losing your entire business through a lawsuit.

A customer who is a "regular" should not get special treatment.

Thwarting Customer Theft

Your customers are members of the public. Thieves are members of that same public, and some of them will wander into your restaurant, their eyes glassy with greed. You have to see that when they leave they exit with nothing more than satisfied taste buds. Pay careful attention to your customers. You want to do this anyway, because it's a necessary element of customer service. But train your people to keep an eye out for any theft at the same time.

Believe it or not, a lot of people steal drink glasses. Train your wait staff to quickly remove glasses from the table after the customers are finished. This also holds true for napkins, silverware, and tableware. Sometimes people are just looking for trophies from your restaurant to show off to friends.

As a general rule, don't allow customers into the back of the restaurant for any reason. There they'll have access to potentially stealable items. If you have to break the rule, see that the guests are escorted at all times.

Chapter 23

Creating a Plan for Burglary, Fire, and Other Disasters

Part One

Part Two

Part Three

Part Four

Part Five

Part Six

Making Security a Priority

Unfortunately, security is a big concern in today's business environment, even in the restaurant business. Big concerns don't have to become big problems. A little foresight, planning, and training can help eliminate many problem situations before they develop. Those that can't be eliminated can at least be controlled so that they don't escalate into serious or threatening situations.

Security is a full-time concern. Obviously, you think about it in terms of your customers' health and safety and the enhancement of their total dining experience. You also need to give the same consideration to your employees and guests. Also, it's important to think of security when your business is closed and there's no one in the restaurant. That's the way to make sure that there's no one in the restaurant. Lack of preparedness could lead to inconvenience for you, your employees, and your customers. It could also lead to a lot of terrible situations. The best way to handle security problems is to prevent as many as you can before they can happen. You can do a lot and you can start now. Planning, preparation, training, and practice will do the job. As the owner, it's your responsibility to see that it does.

Putting a Stop to Credit Card Theft

Credit card theft is a common problem faced by restaurateurs. Train your staff to examine every card to see if it has been altered. Anyone handling credit cards should automatically match the face on the card with the face of the customer. They shouldn't stare, which could make the customer uncomfortable. A quick glance is all that is required. The staffers must look carefully at the signature. The handwriting on the card must match the handwriting on the credit card form. People using someone else's card often misspell the name. For example Smithe can become Smith or Dan can become Don. Train your people to look for such errors.

People sometimes go on a "buying binge" when they get a new credit card. It's a celebration. Others binge because the card belongs to someone else and they intend to run up a huge bill that they'll never have to pay. Unusually large tips or heavy buying on a newly valid card may be cause for concern. If these situations arise, make an authorization call.

Ask your POS or electronics supplier about purchasing a check verification system. These units can be free-standing or they can be a part of your POS system itself. The expense of purchase and installation will surely be surpassed by the savings realized through catching invalid credit cards.

Preventing Burglary

Make sure that all doors are locked when the restaurant is not open to the public. You'd be amazed at how quickly a skilled thief can dash into a building, grab something valuable, and disappear down the street. Do all that you can to see that you are not amazed in that manner. You'll need operating cash on hand, but keep ready cash at a minimum. Word gets around, and thieves are always listening. Even the most honest employee can be a big mouth. Crooks are well known for probing talkative employees. "Yeah, the boss takes the daily cash receipts right to the bank every night at midnight." A blabbermouth is like a gold mine to a thief.

Never open your safe in front of employees or anyone else who does not already know the combination. Some people are quite good at memorizing number combinations. Prevent problems by removing temptation. If you have to open the safe in front of others, maneuver the door so that they cannot see the contents of the safe. Whenever you must open the safe, shut the door to your office and keep it locked until you have closed and locked the safe.

After closing your restaurant, you or your security personnel should walk through the entire building. Look closely at all rooms, stairwells, bathrooms, storage areas, and any other spaces where someone could hide. Use your imagination, too. The crooks will be using theirs.

Acceptance of credit cards and personal checks cuts down on the amount of cash on hand, which can cut down on the desire to burglarize your safe. In any event, when carrying cash to the bank, take proper precautions to see that

Call a Manager

All employees handling customer credit cards should check the card against the cancellation bulletin to make sure that it is still valid. This duty should be standard operating procedure every time a card is used.

Bad cards, suspicious cards, or cards used for a bill of more than $50 must be brought to the attention of a manager. Depending on the size of your operation, you may want to raise or lower this figure. The point is to have a set figure and train your staff to respond appropriately when it is reached.

All credit card vouchers must have a code written at the top of the voucher if the amount of the bill is $50 or more. That figure includes the tip. Again, you may want to raise or lower the amount for your restaurant.

you are not robbed on the way. Always assume that the company blabbermouth has been at work.

Facing Violent Crime

Violent crime is an ugly reality in the food-service business. Many factors are involved. Restaurants are public facilities, and the public is full of unpleasant characters. Some of them come in to eat and drink and some just come in to cause trouble. The availability of alcohol in many restaurants can also be a contributing factor.

Sadly, most people who commit violent crimes are people the victims know. Coworkers or former employees are common attackers. Signs of potential trouble include drunkenness, illegal drug use, drug abuse, a deteriorating job performance, or making verbal threats or threatening physical actions (shaking fist, obscene gesture, punching, etc.).

Train Managers for Conflict Resolution

Managers are authority figures, and many violence-prone individuals have a negative reaction to authority. Some attackers may strike out with little or no provocation, especially if drugs or alcohol are involved. Managers have the responsibility to correct behaviors, criticize, and fire employees. Many of those employees will focus on the alleged offense until they start causing problems. Lastly, managers are the people most likely to be dealing with troublesome customers or any criminals who show up. Training in conflict resolution is highly recommended.

Clues to violent outbreaks are often telegraphed days and even weeks ahead. The soon-to-be perpetrator may not even realize that he or she is sending out those signals, but a trained and observant manager can easily read them. Watch for the following clues in employee behavior:

- Regularly uncooperative with managers, other employees, and/or your customers
- Angry, resentful, or surly without any cause
- Shows an inability to handle disappointment or frustration either on the job on in his or her personal life (brings problems at home to work)

- Threatens coworkers verbally or physically
- Regularly violates rules and policies
- Overreacts to changes in working conditions
- Shows signs of alcohol or drug abuse: violent temper outbreaks, chronic absenteeism, poor work performance, an unusual number of trips to the restroom, or examples of violent behaviors, such as kicking trash cans or throwing tools around violently

Reduce Your Risk

An owner can set in motion a series of policies to eliminate some problems and reduce the likelihood of many others. Have every applicant for every job fill out an application. Items left blank require inquiry and perhaps an investigation because they may be attempts to hide a problem. An application may reveal hidden problems. For example, someone who has worked at numerous jobs during a short period of time may be a writer gathering research for the great American novel. It is more likely, however, that he or she is a problem employee. Every prospective employee should provide several references, and these references should be checked. Ask specific questions. "Would you hire this person if he or she returned and asked for the job back?" If a former employer gives a negative reference or even is hesitant to provide any answer at all, you may be facing a troubled worker.

Institute Mandatory Alcohol and Drug Testing for Employees

The problem of alcohol and drug abuse is so big these days that drug testing is becoming a common and even expected procedure. The potential problem will probably walk away and seek employment elsewhere. Also, if you don't have such a policy, you'll probably attract your fair share of applicants with such problems. When it comes to crime and criminal opportunity, word gets out.

Fight Panic During a Fire

Practice helps. Also, tell your people that an evacuation should take place quickly, but it's not a sprint at the Olympics. Awareness is as important as speed.

Try to stay calm even if you think you're trapped. Close the doors between you and the fire. Keep the smoke out by stuffing rags, clothing, towels, or whatever is available in the cracks around the door. Call the fire department immediately and tell them your precise location.

Everyone has seen the signs next to an elevator. "In the event of fire take the stairwell." Unfortunately, we often see without comprehending. If your building is two or more stories tall or of you're located in an upper floor of a building, make sure they know this rule and understand its importance.

If your operation is large enough, have the applicant interviewed by a number of people. You could conduct one and the department manager could conduct the second. At the end of the process, compare notes and impressions. Sometimes an applicant has an "us versus them" attitude and will respond in one way to the boss and in an entirely different manner to an employee. If your staff isn't that large, it's still a good idea to get a second opinion from another manager or employee. See Chapter 24 for more on employee crime.

Surviving Fire

Fire is probably your most likely reason to evacuate your restaurant. Here are some fire control and fire exit guidelines that Randy uses. You can easily adapt them to fit other exit needs. It's vitally important that you have such a plan. Your people must know it and should be well-trained in how to carry it out. If the unfortunate event occurs during business hours, your customers will be looking to you and your staff for guidance and support.

Study and Practice Fire Prevention Techniques

Know how to put out a grease fire and an electrical fire. For example, never use water to douse an electrical fire.

Utilize Smoke Detectors, Fire Extinguishers, and a Sprinkler System

Install smoke detectors in every room. Check their functionality and their batteries regularly. Place fire extinguishers strategically. Make sure everyone knows those locations and how to use each type you have in place.

The use of a sprinkler system is also highly recommended.

Contact your local fire department for help and advice about ways to be prepared for a fire emergency.

Post Emergency Numbers

Post emergency telephone numbers in several places in your restaurant, certainly next to every phone. With the growing use of cellular phones, you can place the notice in break rooms without phones, on bulletin boards, hallways, and even the restrooms.

Emergency Exit Procedure for Employees and Customers

Follow these fire exit strategies:

1. Walk, don't run.
2. Don't stop for anything, certainly not your belongings. Your life is worth far more than anything left in your purse, backpack, or locker.
3. Test a door before you open it. An open door can provide the fire more oxygen and literally "add fuel to the flame." Before opening a door, kneel down or crouch. Place the back of your hand on the door, the doorknob, and the space between the door and the frame. If those spots are warm, there's a fire on the other side. Use an alternate escape route. If the door is cool, you can open it, but still be careful about what could be on the other side.
4. If you enter a smoky or smoke-filled room, crawl under the smoke to escape. The air is cleaner and easier down low because heat rises, carrying deadly gasses with it. If you find smoke in your primary escape route, try the alternate route before trying to crawl your way out.
5. Once you're out, stay out. It is extremely dangerous for untrained persons to attempt a rescue from a burning building. Meet at your appointed location, conduct a head count, and alert the fire department of any missing persons.

Practicing Exit Drills

Sometimes security can be defined as "getting the heck outta Dodge." Building evacuations can be necessary due to all types of reasons. Fires break out. Tornadoes come rolling through. Hurricanes change directions. Earthquakes arrive unannounced, and several U.S. cities are close to active volcanoes.

Sketch the Exit Plan

Sketch a simple floor plan or have one prepared for you. This shouldn't be an architectural rendering, just a basic diagram. Mark two exits for each room, the exception being rooms with only one way in and out, such as closets or storage areas.

Agree on a Meeting Point Outside the Restaurant

After an evacuation, all employees should go there immediately for a head count. If someone is missing, alert the fire department.

Practice Different Scenarios

A fire is unpredictable. Throw your people a few curves so they can learn to react without panic. For example, block one of the exits so they can practice alternate routes.

Conduct Fire Drills on a Regular Basis

Practice fire drills at least twice a year. Everyone should understand his or her role even if that role is only to "follow Fred." Monitor your drills to discover problems.

Provide Access to All Doors and Windows

Make sure that all doors and windows can be unlocked and opened easily. Too many people have suffered unnecessarily directly in front of an exit that did not function properly.

Reviewing Emergency Procedures Check Lists

There are three critical events that, handled poorly, can lead to additional problems, loss of property, or even loss of life or limb. These are robbery, fire, and a power failure. Lack of preparedness will inevitably lead to panic, which may cause much more damage and harm than the original problem. People have to know how to react, and they have to be trained to react properly and quickly. Here is a brief check list that Randy uses provide an overview of what must happen in these emergencies.

Lack of prepared-
ness will inevit-
ably lead to
panic, which may
cause much more
damage and
harm than the
original problem.

Robbery

When a robbery occurs:

- Make no sudden movements. The robber is probably more nervous than you. Sudden movements may look to him as if you're making a move for a weapon, to run for help, or to start a physical confrontation. A smart restaurateur trains his or her people in the philosophy of "you don't want to fight with anyone anytime in here."
- Do exactly as the robber says. Follow orders. If you don't, he might mistake your actions as resistance and cause you, a customer, or a coworker harm.
- Only speak when spoken to. You're not trained in hostage negotiations, so don't even think about trying. When speaking, be direct and calm and make your answers short and sweet.
- Don't panic. Try to maintain your composure. Panic spreads like wildfire. Showing your fear could cause someone else to react foolishly (running, putting up a fight, losing control, etc.), which will only worsen the situation.
- Pay attention. Try to get an accurate description of the robber. Note his or her age, race, height, weight, identifying marks, clothing, manner of speech, and any other facts you notice.

After the robber has departed:

- Ask the nearest employee to notify a manager. Do your best to help everyone else to remain calm.
- Dial 911 and report an "armed robbery." Keep your voice calm and cool and answer any questions quickly. Don't elaborate unless asked to do so by the operator.
- Do not speak with anyone other than a manager about the incident until the police arrive.

Fire

If a fire occurs, notify a manager immediately. Lots of things must happen at once, and you'll need an experienced manager to take control. Here are some guidelines, however:

- Don't panic. It is contagious and potentially as dangerous as the fire.
- The manager will call 911 if the fire is out of control. This call is a management decision. The exception to this rule follows.
- If a manager is not around or cannot be contacted and the fire is larger than something you can put your arms around, call 911 yourself immediately.
- If an evacuation is called for, the manager will make an announcement over the intercom. Evacuations are management decisions.
- Employee duties during an evacuation include:
- Assist the patrons out of the building in an orderly fashion to the assigned meeting area.
- See that all kitchen equipment is turned off.
- Kitchen personnel and people in the kitchen should exit via the kitchen door and meet with the other employees and patrons at the designated evacuation meeting place.
- Front-of-the-restaurant employees should hold the doors for customers and assist in the evacuation of the elderly and disabled.
- The kitchen supervisor collects the time cards on the way out so that he or she can take an accurate head count to ensure that all employees have evacuated the building.

- Once out of the building, do not reenter unless authorized by the fire department.

Power Failure

In the event of a power failure:

- Ask the customers not to panic. Reassure them and state that an announcement will be made momentarily. Remain calm and speak in a calming voice. Act as if the event is nothing more than a temporary inconvenience. It probably is just that.
- Stop the movement of all food and beverage in the front of the restaurant. In the dark, movement is an open invitation to accidents. Moving around can be particularly dangerous around hot food, ice, or liquids that could cause falls, or potentially dangerous items such as knives and forks.
- All food preparation should cease. Any food on the grill or in the fryers should be removed.
- The kitchen supervisor should open all kitchen exit doors to allow ventilation of the grills and fryers.
- Do not open any coolers or freezers.

Chapter 24

Reducing Employee and Supplier Theft and Other Losses

Part One

Part Two

Part Three

Part Four

Part Five

Part Six

PART SIX   RUNNING YOUR RESTAURANT DAY-TO-DAY

■ CHAPTER 22 Dealing with Unruly Customers ■ CHAPTER 23 Creating a Plan for Burglary, Fire, and Other Disasters ■ CHAPTER 24 **Reducing Employee and Supplier Theft and Other Losses** ■ CHAPTER 25 Conducting Inventory ■ CHAPTER 26 Finding Additional Sources of Revenue

Reducing Employee Theft

The real key to preventing employee theft is to have security in mind at all times. This is not to say that all employees are thieves or thugs. Quite the contrary, most are good people trying to do a good job. The problem is that the dishonest folks make a habit of looking and acting just like honest employees. Just realize it's quite likely that some of the people you hire during your career will be thieves.

Establish Consistent Kitchen Procedures

This is where the product that draws in the patrons is created. Measurement procedures are essential. Make your kitchen manager responsible for your food costs. Make it absolutely clear just how important this responsibility is to the operation and the success of the entire team. Reinforce the importance of these duties every once in a while so that he or she doesn't become lax.

Every item that is made should have a ticket. Even if a surprise birthday cake is cooked up for the owner, that item should have a properly completed ticket. Track all your giveaways through the promo keys on your register. The principle is basic—have an accurate accounting for everything. That includes your waste, too.

Maintain a close watch on your ordering level. Is your staff ordering too much or too little? If so, what is causing the problem? Is someone having to run to the store a lot because you're continually running out of a certain supply or group of supplies? How do you correct the situation so that kitchen staff stays in the kitchen and not on the road to the neighborhood grocery? Are you having problems with a lot of spoilage? If so, is that a problem over which you have some control (ordering procedures) or something out of your control (the hurricane which shut you down for a week)?

Develop Policies about Coming and Going

Develop a set of policies, explain them to everyone, and see that they are implemented properly. One of the best things you can do is to remove temptation or at least make thievery a difficult process. Have all your employees enter and exit through the front door when it is unlocked.

Restrict the types of accessories employees may bring into the building. Large purses or backpacks, for example, can carry out a lot of your goods. They are often bulky, which helps disguise what has been taken.

Create a Break Room

A break room is a great perk for your employees. It also allows management to keep a better watch on those employees because they're either at their stations or, when on a break, confined to one location.

Make Trash a Two-Person Job

It's a good idea to have your trash taken out by two people. Many managers fail to realize how incredibly easy it can be for one person to hide stolen merchandise in the trash. They then hand it over to an accomplice or just dump it for later retrieval.

Add Lighting

Sufficient lighting inside and out can also eliminate dark areas where mischief can take place. The extra few cents added to your energy bill are nothing compared to the losses they can prevent.

Limiting Comps

"Comp" refers to a complimentary drink, an appetizer, dessert, or even an entire meal. A free meal or drink is a small cost to a restaurant, but the effect of the good will gesture on a customer can be enormous. In addition to reinforcing the loyalty

Allow Employees to Express Complaints

Many crimes in business happen because the employee feels that he or she has been slighted, mistreated, or discriminated against. To guard against this, write up a specific and detailed set of policies and procedures. Distribute it to all employees and explain it in detail. Include in those policies and procedures an employee "safety valve" so they can express any complaints. Sometimes you can diffuse a tense situation by allowing a frustrated employee to let off a little steam. The procedure has to be genuine and sincere. Otherwise, the employee may feel you are just pandering to his or her concerns or that the procedure is worthless. Your lack of commitment to the policy could make a bad situation much worse.

of that customer, you'll also grab the interest of all the friends and acquaintances he or she will tell.

Take a close look at the number of comps handed out. Who is making them? Who is on the receiving end? Are loyal customers getting the freebee or are they being handed out to friends of some of your managers? A good way of tracking the situation is to have any manager offering a comp to write up a ticket. Be sure to insist that the manager include the reason for the comped item. For example, if a meal is unreasonably late, the manager in charge may comp that meal. This is completely acceptable. Just make sure there is a paper trail so that you can make sure certain "friends" aren't always the victim of late arrivals.

Discuss your comp policy with everyone. Giving away drinks to friends may seem like a good idea to some, but explain that it is nothing less than theft. Comps are useful tools, but make sure everyone follows the correct procedures, such as filling out a comp ticket for every freebee—even for the boss.

Controlling Portions

Over time, you can lose a fortune in small dribs and drabs back in the kitchen. Portion control will help you keep the food and your profits safely contained.

Conduct Employee Criminal Background Checks

You can conduct criminal background checks prior to hiring someone. This isn't nosing into someone's private affairs. It's protecting your own business. The process can be as simple as checking with your local police department or the department in the community where the applicant lives. Private investigators are also a good source, although a relatively expensive one. If nothing else, make a few calls on your own. Call the references listed, but also check in with the schools listed. If the applicant lists organizations or clubs in the "other" category on the application, give them a call, too.

Define proper proportions for all items in every recipe and put them in writing as a ready reference for your staff. Educate the staff on portions and plate presentations. If necessary, test all the members of your staff on these subjects. Make sure they get it right. The point isn't that you're just losing a fraction of a cent every time the meatloaf portions are over. If the meatloaf is over, then so are the potatoes, the carrots, the wine, and the whiskey. That's a lot of fractions, and over time it can add up to a significant loss. You can't tolerate sloppiness on the plate any more than you can in your accounting procedures, because everything is connected to the bottom line.

Provide your kitchen staff with the proper size and shape ladles and scales so they can measure accurate portions consistently. Whenever possible, make up preportioned bags for their convenience and accuracy. Consistency is important not only for your staff and patrons' enjoyment, but also to help maintain the profit part of your profit and loss (P&L) statement

Establishing Strict Bar Procedures

Coolers have locks on them for good reasons. Put out only what you need for the night each night and then lock the coolers. Why provide temptation for mischief when with a simple click of a tumbler you can avoid the problem? When the bartender needs a full bottle of liquor, he or she must have an empty bottle that needs to be replaced.

Ring Up Comps

Ring up all drinks, even if you are providing a giveaway. If you have a spill and lose a drink, have the bartender ring it up anyway. You can't track it if you don't write it down. Track all your giveaways through the promo key on your register.

Use Cameras

If you've ever been to a major casino in Las Vegas or some other major gambling mecca, you've been on television. These places are constantly barraged with some of the cleverest thieves in the world. Ongoing vigilance is a matter of profitability and security. Your restaurant may not ever deal in the high-dollar numbers of a major casino, but you face the same challenge—clever thieves.

Security cameras are so inexpensive and easy to install these days that there's no excuse for not using them. Smart managers have put them to good use for decades. You can't be everywhere at once, but you can put cameras just about anywhere.

They're excellent security devices, but they're equally effective for keeping your employees on their toes. Randy scans his various workstations to monitor the work habits of his employees. If he catches someone goofing off, he doesn't "go ballistic." Rather, he buzzes the employee on the intercom. "Hey, Janet, while you are resting would you go over to the camera and move it to the left just a bit," he says. The startled employee always complies. When he checks back later, the employee will be busy as a bee even if there are no customers at his or her station. In addition to enhancing your overall security, cameras can be a very inexpensive way to get more profitable work from your employees.

Everyone, including bartenders, will be more honest if they know they're being monitored. Look at it this way, big department stores have cameras watching their socks and underwear bins. How much more tempting is a bottle of good liquor?

> Everyone, including bartenders, will be more honest if they know they're being monitored.

Eliminate Free Pouring

Portion control is very important in your bar. Have your bartenders use a jigger. Never permit them to free pour. Make sure your bartenders know the appropriate portions for each drink you offer. Test them periodically to be sure. You should certainly test all newly hired bartenders. Again, patrons and the P&L statement respond well to consistency.

Eliminating Supplier Theft

Supplier theft can be an issue, too. During hours when the restaurant is not open to the public, see that all doors are locked at all times. If an employee must go outside, keep the door locked until that task is completed, and have someone let the worker back in. If there are no other employees, then the office should be notified of the outside work so that someone there will be available to unlock the door. Many facilities instruct the maintenance crew to not answer the door, but to notify the office so the situation can be handled by management personnel. Management should see that all maintenance calls, visitor calls, sales calls, etc. are scheduled for times when a manager (or two) is present.

Always have a trusted employee monitoring the receiving area when a supplier makes a delivery. Every order should be carefully checked. You don't have to go overboard. For example, the employee doesn't have to open a case of canned peas to count each can. He or she just needs to make sure the case is properly sealed. If any items are missing, make sure the employee has the driver document the loss on the invoice. When you bring in repair personnel, assign someone to be in the area to monitor the situation while repairs are being made.

Develop Check-In Procedures

When suppliers deliver their goods, you can't just show them where to unload, say "have a nice day," and start unpacking. A good manager will establish and stick to a formal check-in procedure. Flour is different from raw fish, which is different from bottles of liquor. You'll need to adapt your procedures to the items being delivered, but certain steps will be part of every check-in procedure.

- Check the receipt of each item.
- Circle or put a check mark by the number received of each item.
- Note any discrepancies on the bill.

Lock Your Coolers

Lock all the coolers when the kitchen closes. There's no reason to provide temptation for thievery. Keep the back doors closed at all times, except when in use. Have someone assigned to monitor the back door, too. You'd be amazed at how easy it can be for some crook to sneak in and out unnoticed.

- Make sure the person assigned to check-in signs all proof of deliveries.
- Keep a copy and give the original to accounting.
- If charged by weight, verify by weighing.
- Check all produce to make sure it is fresh.

Get Your Money's Worth

The owner and/or the management team has to take responsibility to ensure that the supplies and materials delivered are exactly what have been ordered. It's very easy to miss small matters, but small losses can add up to substantial drains on your profit picture. The problem with losses isn't always the fault of the supplier, either. Here's a perfect example of an imperfect delivery.

Randy once had problems with his expenses for soft drinks. He just couldn't get the numbers under control. He decided to remedy the situation and began monitoring the system the moment a delivery pulled up to his back door. He did a bit of research and found out how much a barrel of soft drink syrup should weigh, which is fifty-five pounds. Barrels coming into his restaurant weighed about four pounds short.

He contacted the authorities, who began investigating the apparent theft. A few months later, the deliveryman was arrested. He was siphoning off about four pounds of syrup from the barrels on his truck and storing the material in empty barrels. He then sold the stolen merchandise to a friend who owned a restaurant across town. Sometimes soda pop syrup is like liquid gold. It's worth a lot of money—your money. Keep an eye on it.

Using Your Income Statement to Pinpoint Problems

You can find out about the "how" of an income statement (commonly called a P&L statement) in Chapter 7. In this section, we take a look at the "why" of that document. This subject deserves extra treatment because it is the lifeblood of your business. You'll be a much more successful and happier businessperson if you master this measurement tool. If you've never been a numbers person, now is the time to hit the books and become one.

Identify Problem Areas

A P&L statement can tell you whether or not you're making money, but it can do so much more if you understand it. One of the best aspects of this measurement tool is that it can help you find problem areas in your operations, even hard-to-find and hidden problems. It allows you to play the percentages in your favor.

Are any funds leaking from your labor pool? Are some of your employees stealing? If stealing is going on, is it from the cash register or from the storage area? Are your bar costs in line with the norm for your type of operation and your community? Are operating costs too high? Do you need to find another, more reliable or cost-effective supplier for linen? Should you drop linen altogether and start using paper?

All or at least a significant portion of the answers to those and a hundred other questions can be answered by a solid P&L statement. It is essential that the owner knows what the cost percentages should be compared to actual costs and projected or ultimate cost percentages. That's your financial compass. It tells you where you've been, where you're going, and what course corrections need to be taken. Look to the deviations from your projected/ultimate cost figures. That's where the problem lies.

It's important that the owner understands these numbers because a time factor may be involved in the problems discovered. Let's imagine that

Study Theft

You don't study theft to become a thief. You just want to know how the thieves are stealing from your business. It is highly recommended that you invest a significant amount of time on the subject, for you will encounter the problem as long as you own a restaurant. Find a seminar, a lecture, or a public education course and sign up. Your P&L statement will help you find the areas where theft is occurring. Learning the tricks of the trade will show you who's doing it to you and how they've been getting away with it.

Get smart. The crooks are.

you suspect one of your top managers of stealing money. You don't understand your P&L statement, so you send it off to the accountant for review. By the time you get the accountant's report confirming your fears, the employee could have cleaned out the till and be headed out for parts unknown. Had you been able to read the numbers correctly, you could have spotted the source of the problem in time to do something about it. The same rule applies for inefficient suppliers, poor working habits of your staff, wasted advertising funds, and a host of other situations.

You'll need average numbers to compare with your own. In addition to your own research in your local market, log on to the Web site of the National Restaurant Association. Information there will include cost percentages for the industry.

Track Your Sales

By all means get a good POS (point of sale) register that will track your sales. This will prove to be one of your best measurement devices. Check around. Shop for value and make sure you get the best possible price. You'll find lots of suppliers, if not locally then through magazines, trade journals, or the Internet. Also, check out warranties and maintenance/replacement plans. You don't want to be caught with your registers down.

By all means get a good POS (point of sale) register that will track your sales.

Chapter 25

Conducting Inventory

Part One

Part Two

Part Three

Part Four

Part Five

Part Six

PART SIX   RUNNING YOUR RESTAURANT DAY-TO-DAY

■ CHAPTER 22 Dealing with Unruly Customers ■ CHAPTER 23 Creating a Plan for Burglary, Fire, and Other Disasters ■ CHAPTER 24 Reducing Employee and Supplier Theft and Other Losses ■ CHAPTER 25 Conducting Inventory ■ CHAPTER 26 Finding Additional Sources of Revenue

Understanding the Relationship Between Inventory and Food Costs

You have to find problems with food and inventory fast. Inventory is the building block of the fare offered your customers. Slack controls on inventory will please neither your customers nor your accountant. At least for your first few months in business, conduct inventories every week.

Inventories are costly because they're so labor intensive. Once the operation is coming under control, it's okay to schedule your inventories for every other week. Regardless of how long you've been in business, always conduct an inventory on the last day of the month so your accountant can draw up your financial statements.

Whenever possible, conduct your inventory with your kitchen manager. If the kitchen manager cannot be present, do it yourself. Be certain that you know the proper procedure.

Why Conduct Inventory?

The reason an owner or manager conducts inventory is to measure the amount of product used for a specific period of time. That information is then compared to sales for that same period. You measure how much it costs in product to produce a specific period's sales.

Inventory keeps the management in touch with usage so they can make accurate orders for ingredients, materials, and supplies. Inventory is money on the shelf, and if it's not being put to use, it's not making money for the restaurant. Inventory is therefore essential to profit. You want just enough inventory on hand to take care of the business of the day. Industrial facilities call this Just-in-Time inventory. Raw products and supplies arrive just in time for their use and aren't sitting back in the warehouse draining on the operating budget.

Inventory also keeps management up-to-date on pricing. This is why you must update your prices every week. Also, if you are aware of normal usage for your facility, you can quickly spot aberrations in trends. An unusually high usage could indicate sloppiness in the operation or even employee theft. It's also a pretty accurate measurement of how you are doing as a manager. If everything is in line, chances are you're doing a pretty good job.

> Inventory keeps the management in touch with usage so they can make accurate orders.

Understanding Inventory Formulas

Here are three formulas necessary for an accurate inventory. By the time you begin the procedure, you should know the accurate cost (*cost-out* is the term) for your menu.

Here's how you determine usage:

Beginning Inventory + Purchases – Ending Inventory = Usage (also called or Cost of Goods Sold)

Your Cost of Goods Sold percentage is figured as follows:

Usage ÷ Sales = Cost of Goods (COG) Sold %

Compare this number with the Ultimate Cost of Goods Sold for your product mix. To figure your ultimate cost of goods sold, first multiply the cost of each menu item times the number of that menu item sold. For example, if making a hamburger costs you $1.10 and you sold ten, 10 X 1.10 = $11.00 total cost. Run these figures for all menu items, then add those costs together. Use the formula as follows: Sum of Cost For All Menu Items Sold + Cost of Waste = Ultimate Cost of Goods Sold.

It's also pretty easy to determine the ultimate cost for beer and wine. Here's the formula:

Average Cost For Each Category ÷ Average Price = Ultimate Cost Of Goods Sold (for that category)

Bar Inventory

Inventory your bar weekly, at least until you get the hang of it, and then always inventory after sales on the last day of the month. Break down your bar sales into the following categories:

- Liquor
- Domestic bottle beer
- Import bottle beer
- Draft beer
- Wine sold by the bottle
- Wine sold by the glass

Your goal is to cluster menu items with similar costs. For example, all domestic bottle beer costs about the same. Prices will be within a few cents regardless of brand. Clustering your inventory this way makes things simpler and a lot easier to track.

Next, inventory liquor, domestic bottle beer, import bottle beer, draft beer, bottle wine, wine sold by the glass, and bar consumables. Consumables are nonliquor items consumed in a drink, such as soft drinks, juices, mixes, and so on. Total the cost for each category. Inventory items at the smallest unit. For example, bottle beer is purchased by the case, but it is consumed by the bottle. That's the smallest unit, so inventory beer by the bottle. Liquor is inventoried by its smallest unit, the tenth of a bottle.

The best means of operation is the use of two people in the inventory process. The count should be done by the bar manager, with someone from the office doing the recording. Optimum times are very early in the morning or the previous night. Office personnel can then key in the information while the manager prepares the restaurant for opening. Your office person should be familiar enough with your operations to immediately check out anything that appears out of line. Ideally, that person will do this prior to opening.

The office person should be knowledgeable enough to conduct the inventory if for some reason the manager cannot. The bar manager must be kept informed about the "big picture," such as inventory, costs, and prices. This shouldn't take up too much of anyone's time. Another good factor about a two-party process is that you institute a system of checks and balances.

Bar Inventory Worksheets

Inventories are set up as one large worksheet and then broken down by using the view manager.

Count Sheet: The first two blank columns are for recording purchases (number of units and price). The order column at the end is handy because the checker can make sure all invoices are in. The other blank columns are the areas where the inventory is kept. This makes it easy to double-check inventory items when there is a problem. After totaling each inventory item, everything can be keyed into the computer off this single sheet. The invoices are then stapled to the back of the count sheet so it can be checked if you want.

Weekly Inventory View: Ending inventory is copied to beginning inventory. Purchases and new prices are keyed in off the count sheet first. Ending inventory is keyed in off the count sheet, noting any negative usage numbers. Recount as necessary. The total page is completed automatically (separate sheet in Excel). All the numbers and the date are linked to the totals on the actual inventory.

Monthly View: This view just hides the columns to show inventory on hand figures instead of usage figures.

Tracking Liquor Sales

Tracking your liquor sales can be a lot trickier because there are so many variables that can come into play. For example, a shot of bar brand whiskey is easy to estimate—one jigger at a flat rate. The same is true for a premium brand. But rum 'n Coke with a twist of lime adds other variables: the Coke and the twist. Don't forget to factor in the cost of ice and that swizzle stick. If you've had the swizzle stick imprinted with your logo, that's another added expense.

Break down the sales on your register into drink categories:

- Well
- Call
- Premium
- Top shelf
- Frozen

You want to get an idea of your product mix sold. Your vendors can provide a lot of help here. They can, and should be willing, to provide you with what your liquor costs should be given your product mix and pricing structure. If you track

Track Everything

Track and ring up everything at your bar. Leave nothing out, including spillages, mistakes, drinks on the house (bought) for good customers or in an effort to mollify an upset patron, and everything else.

Track your costs by net and by gross. Net is what you sell; in other words, what you have paid for. Gross includes everything—complimentary drinks, spills, errors, etc. When you set your prices, you expect everything to be sold, right? That's the idea. Your gross costs should stay pretty parallel to the bottom of the page. Your net costs will vary slightly depending on complimentary drinks, happy hour discounts, and so on.

Monitoring your costs precisely helps you maintain accurate cost controls. Additionally, when your employees know that you're tracking your beer, wine, and liquor sales this closely, there's very little incentive to steal.

promotions and giveaways, as you should, your cost percentage should be a straight line. Liquor costs will vary a little depending on the product sold, but beer and wine should be straighter.

Food Inventory

The primary difference between bar and food inventory is that a column on your inventory sheet is set up for case prices (or whatever price is listed on the invoices) and a column for the number of units in a case. Price per unit is then calculated automatically. This permits an easy check on price on invoice against price on inventory without doing any calculations.

Consider using one of the two following methods. The one that's best for you depends on the number of inventory items and how often you order. Quantity or volume isn't really a consideration. The method chosen also depends on whether you have sufficient office staff, which is preferable to loading down your kitchen manager with clerical duties. If you can't post purchases to each individual item, you might want to try a combination of the two methods or use very small departments for the other method.

Post Purchases to Each Individual Item

With this method, you have usage per item, and it is easy for someone else to take over the responsibility for kitchen ordering. It is also easier to see fluctuations, which may indicate problem areas.

Add Up Purchase Per Department and Post the Total Only

Examples of departments are meat, dairy, produce, and so on. When using this method, you don't have the advantage of seeing the usage per item, so you won't be able to see a trend that you can monitor with any degree of accuracy. This method is, however, a faster method.

Another consideration is price updating. This is especially true if the office will be doing a lot of the keypunching. You might want to give the department manager a price fluctuation report. After conducting each inventory, copy the price column (with the date at the top) to a database and print the list with the current and previous week's prices.

Spot Checking Your Checkers

If you don't conduct your own inventory, at least go behind the person who does and conduct some spot checking. Don't allow any mixed feelings into the process. "Are you saying you don't trust me, boss?" You're just following sound business procedures. Treat it that way and expect your employees to understand.

Randy once had a manager who seemed to be on top of things and was always able to hit his target on food costs. A 100 percent success rate on anything is highly unusual. Randy did a little inventory control of his own. His manager was just picking his target numbers to make sure he always looked good. In other words, he padded his inventory to make sure he hit his target cost. It's easy to look like you're in control when you cook the books.

This is your inventory. Stay on top of it at all times. Also, remember to monitor your prices and update them accordingly.

Reviewing Ways to Control Your Inventory

Unlike money in the bank, inventory doesn't draw interest. It can't make you money until it's put to use. It is important that you have enough on hand to serve your customers, but not so much that you are unnecessarily tying up capital. This section provides a plethora of ways to improve your inventory control and, therefore, the bottom line.

Ordering

- Keep inventory low.
- General manager checks order.
- When ordering, have count ready to verify against computer.

Keep Invoices Handy

Because different people check in orders, and they normally do not have access to the office, hang invoices on a clipboard. At the end of the week, the manager of that department is responsible for making sure the office gets the original and that a copy goes with the inventory. That way only one person has control.

To keep your computer files straight, add a directory called inventories and save all inventories in that directory. Back up all weekly inventories to a disk using the date the inventory was taken. The inventory on the hard drive is overwritten weekly, so the inventory on the hard drive is the most current one.

- Order dark meat cases when possible.
- Proper rotation maintained.
- Date all incoming inventory.
- Receive credits for spoiled product or incorrect product.
- Use approved vendors only. Do not buy products from the grocery store.

Receiving Product

- Always use two-person check-in so proper inspection can occur.
- Check all frozen products for damage.
- Always store frozen products in freezer immediately. Do not let them sit out.
- Check for dented cans.
- Check kill dates on chicken cases.
- Inspect chicken product for ice coverage.
- Check chicken temperature.
- Weigh chicken for short weights.
- Check random individual birds for correct weight.
- Check egg cases for damage.
- Check for freshness of all products.
- Make milk vendor aware of out-of-date milk products.
- Buy bulk produce when possible.
- Check all orders at the back door.

Product Storage

- Maintain all gaskets so they are in proper condition.
- Check freezer temperature regularly.
- Keep freezer doors shut to prevent thawing.
- Check first in, first out.
- Check for ice build-up on coils.
- Periodically check defrost cycle.
- Do not overstack. It can cause crushed product on the bottom.
- Check walk-in temperature regularly.
- Do not place cooked foods under raw foods.

- Do not over-prep salads.
- Check for proper air circulation in walk-in.
- Make sure all containers have lids.
- Keep shelves clean to avoid contamination.
- Keep food frozen as long as possible.
- Be sure cooling unit remains unobstructed.
- Keep walk-in doors shut.
- Keep walls, ceiling, and floors clean to prevent bacteria growth.
- Make sure air curtains are in working order and in place.
- Keep all products off floor.
- Keep dry foods dry.
- Keep all shelves neat and straight for accurate inventories.
- Rotate roast chicken in display correctly.
- Check heat lamps daily.

Food Preparation

- Prepare yields each week.
- Taste salt/sugar before preparing recipes.
- Proper marination run by managers.
- Proper measuring utensils or equipment.
- Manager designates how much to prep. Do not over-prep. Stick to guidelines.
- Follow recipes.
- Keep perishables out of temperature danger zone as much as possible.
- Make sure all containers (cans, bottles, and bags) are completely emptied.
- Make sure prepped product is properly rotated.
- Pull only one tub of chicken to cut, not several.
- Utilize day-dot system.
- Check for cull on lettuce and cabbage.
- Maintain proper roll water temperature.
- Prep salads in line with demand.
- Grease roll pans.
- Use correct salt weight.

- Ensure proper cuts.
- Thaw liquid eggs before use.
- Sixteen cut 20 X 20 cinnamon loaf.
- Measure nuts, raisins, and cinnamon sugar.
- Do weekly yeast test.
- Count biscuits (fifty per batch).
- Check number of tea bags.
- Use spatula to get all product out of cans.

Production Calling

- One person calls production.
- Open all segments with small amounts. Good quality means not replacing food.
- Consult projections and yields. Adjust hourly according to sales.
- Cook less, but more often (don't overdo precooking).
- During slow periods, cook slow-moving products to order.
- Monitor portioning by employees (veggies, rolls, nuggets, etc.). Check scoop and spoon sizes.
- Stay visible on front to discourage giving away food and short ringing. Train proper register procedures.
- Maintain waste bucket to track waste.
- Control closing waste.
- Regularly check food temperature to prevent waste.
- Regularly check thickness of gravy.
- Regularly check water levels in steamwells to prevent scorching. Check temperature.
- Make sure that employees are filling cups completely with ice.
- Make sure fryer checks are being done.
- Make sure the dining room person is picking up unused butter, etc.
- Make sure employees are not giving out condiments automatically.
- Ensure correct orders (training).
- Monitor employee meals, drinks, and post in register.
- Monitor daily inventories for usage.
- Use a spatula to change pans.
- Check condiment bar for two-ounce cups for honey and ketchup.

- Turn chicken on skin side up.
- Pull chicken from correct side of slide in peak periods.
- In peak periods, cook right amount.
- Utilize production chart.

Training

- Proper receiving and storage techniques.
- Proper platter presentation, including portioning and packaging.
- Proper recipes.
- Suggestive selling.
- Heating liquid shortening when making rolls.
- Making sure employees are familiar with timers to avoid burning.
- Proper use of filter powder.
- Retrieving condiments from tables in dining area.
- Taking orders correctly.
- Checking orders going out in drive-through.
- Have weekly food cost meetings.
- Utilize training films.
- Train managers to understand food cost controls.
- Report quality control problems to the purchasing department.

Equipment

- Check freezer and walk-in temperatures.
- Check gaskets and door closures for proper maintenance.
- Label all containers (such as salt, pepper, etc.).
- Check timers for labeling and proper working order.
- Regularly brix drink machines.

Cooking

- Use timers.
- Check fryer temperatures.
- Rotate shortening correctly.
- Sift every use.

- Stir batter before using.
- Store batter in cooler.
- Use proper shortening levels.
- Make batter by recipe.
- Fully proof rolls and cinnamon rolls.
- Check grill temperatures.
- Use filter powder.
- Use the right scrambled egg ladle—twenty-four ounce.
- Measure six ounces of cheese correctly.
- Post cooking time/temperature charts in kitchen.

Security

- Ensure back doors are locked and manager is present.
- Ensure proper cash procedures.
- Ensure proper system shutdown procedures.
- Make sure only manager has keys.
- Check trash cans for theft.
- Check personal belongings/no purses or coats in kitchen.
- Use drawer audits.
- Do not allow employees to loiter.

Accounting

- Compare inventory prices to actual invoice prices.
- Track all waste.
- Update yields on regular basis.
- Make accurate inventories.
- Keep boilout chart up to date.
- Make sure all transfers are being recorded.
- Do a line-by-line check on preliminary ledger to make sure all information matches.
- Make sure all invoices are processed in a timely manner.
- Make sure cash tickets are processed in a timely manner.
- Make sure E.O.M. (end of month) procedures are correct.
- Do daily inventories and audits.

- Make sure no food goes home at night.
- Audit coupons with drawers.
- Check ticker file.

Staying on an Inventory Schedule

This schedule is an efficient, day-by-day method of conducting an inventory.

Tuesday

___ Conduct inventory count.

___ Key in purchases and count to computer from the count sheet.

___ Recount any items that come up negative usage—check purchases.

___ Print final inventory.

___ Staple purchases to count sheet.

___ Paperclip count sheet to final inventory and give to (name) by Wednesday 8 A.M.

Wednesday

___ Print count sheet and hang on clipboard.

___ Order inventory.

___ Write order on count sheet.

Thursday

___ Check items delivered against invoice.

Friday

___ Post purchases to count sheet, checking off as you post.

___ Refigure price per unit and post new price to count sheet.

___ Check purchases against order to verify that you have all the invoices for that week.

Chapter 26

Finding Additional Sources of Revenue

Part One

Part Two

Part Three

Part Four

Part Five

Part Six

PART SIX   RUNNING YOUR RESTAURANT DAY-TO-DAY

■ CHAPTER 22 Dealing with Unruly Customers ■ CHAPTER 23 Creating a Plan for Burglary, Fire, and Other Disasters ■ CHAPTER 24 Reducing Employee and Supplier Theft and Other Losses ■ CHAPTER 25 Conducting Inventory ■ CHAPTER 26 Finding Additional Sources of Revenue

Looking for Extra Income

The income streams from your restaurant don't have to be limited to the dollars and cents forked over by walk-in and sit-down customers. There are a number of other revenue-generating activities open to the visionary-yet-pragmatic restaurateur, and this chapter discusses several.

Getting into Catering

The industry rule of thumb says that the profit margin for a restaurant will be about 6 percent. That's a pretty slim margin, albeit one that thousands of owners and operators make work every day. The profit margin for catering can reach a whopping 38 percent. If you think about it, it's easy to see why. The caterer gets to charge for everything. You can charge good money for ice! A restaurant struggling to make it on local and walk-in traffic can still be a phenomenal success just on its catering business. It's definitely a source of considerable revenue, but there are a number of important factors to be evaluated.

Catering is closely related to the restaurant business, *but it is not the restaurant business.* Catering has its unique set of challenges and opportunities, and it's not an area to enter lightly or without due consideration. You can't just shout, "I have a kitchen, a staff, and a bunch of foodstuffs, I'll cater something!" That kind of cavalier attitude might have you catering your own economic funeral. Even if operated out of the same restaurant, catering is a very different, very separate business.

Four options are open to you:

- Social events, such as weddings or parties
- Business catering, such as corporate dining events or cafeterias
- Food preparation for other businesses, even other restaurants
- Institutional food service, for hospitals or schools, for example

Not only is catering very different from the standard restaurant business, each of these four categories has significant differences. An institution may allow, encourage, or even insist upon a regular menu with items rotated on a regular and predictable basis. Monday is meatloaf, Tuesday is

> Catering is closely related to the restaurant business, *but it is not the restaurant business.*

fish, Wednesday is lasagna, and so on. Your profit margin may be built on reduced prices on bulk orders from reliable suppliers. Social catering may require you to create an entirely different set of courses for each event. Here your profit margin may be based on creativity, flexibility, and connections for unusual or rare food items.

Speaking of contacts, a caterer often has to have connections for all kinds of rentals, such as tables and chairs, tents and tarps, music and entertainment, and perhaps swans and peacocks. Your client may very well expect you to handle an entire range of services only remotely related to food and beverage.

Before entering this arena, decide whether your activities will be full-time, part-time, or just whenever the opportunity knocks. If you want to go into catering full-time, consider really going full-time and forgoing your efforts to build a restaurant at the same time. The pulls of two different businesses, even related ones, may be too much to handle, at least early in your career.

Inform Your Bosses

Do not assume that anyone who hires a caterer has the slightest idea of the complexity of the business. You will have to take responsibility to protect yourself, your staff, and your business from misconceptions and misunderstandings. Expecting your clients to understand all that is involved, to handle the details, or even to care is to walk on shifting sands. Each job or series of jobs will be different, but here are a number of key items and considerations.

- **Menu.** Be very specific on even the most basic items. Does "ice" mean ice cubes, crushed ice, Hawaiian shave ice, or ice flown in from the pristine slopes of Mount Shasta?
- **Price.** Set a price per person or a flat rate. Build in some flexibility should more or less than the expected number show up for the event.
- **Date/time/place.** Find out how early you can get in for set-up and preparation. Find out the exact time you must be cleaned up and cleared out.

- **Responsibilities.** Develop a line-item list of who does what, and don't change it unless those changes are in writing.
- **Payment.** As a rule of thumb, you can expect to charge 40 percent up front. Set a specific date for final payment, including any conditions that could affect that payment.
- **Refund policy.** Should you or your suppliers drop the ball, your client will obviously and rightly so want to recover some of his or her loss.
- **Insurance.** Who's policy covers what? You are heavily insured, aren't you?
- **Staffing.** Who provides people for what tasks? Is there an existing staff you will work with, or do you bring some or all of your own people?
- **Entertainment.** Sometimes the caterer is expected to provide the classical trio, the piano player, or the clown with the kazoo.
- **Rentals.** Are you expected to provide the tables and chairs, etc?
- **Clean-up.** Is your service responsible for any or all of the clean-up? What happens to leftover food and beverage? Are you responsible for just your immediate work area, or are you expected to provide a pooper-scooper for the peacock?
- **Contracts.** Make sure you have one for each event and that all responsibilities, costs, items, etc. are clearly defined.
- **Staff training.** Staff duties can be as simple as pouring coffee and handing out doughnuts, or you might be required to provide professionals capable of serving the king and queen of Moldavia or Bert and Sugar Neulyrich, who think they're the king and queen of Moldavia.
- **Secrecy agreements.** Don't laugh. Many catered events involve high-powered business and government people. Some of these events may be scheduled in or around important negotiations and meetings. You may be required to agree to certain secrecy conditions. Staff personnel may not always appreciate the importance of such arrangements. Make sure they do, especially if the crowd includes anyone with the title ambassador, special envoy, or the nickname Ice Pick Vinnie.

Staff Up or Shut Down

The quality of the staff will make or break a catering operation. Needless to say, but we're saying it anyway, the staff should be the best possible for each event. "Best possible" can vary with the needs of the job. Sugar Neulyrich might be delighted with someone who's neat and clean, flirts politely, and who keeps her mai tai glass filled. The real queen of Moldavia will probably expect a higher caliber of professionalism, and you might even have to find waitpersons who speak Moldavian. Guys and gals who look good in Tarzan and Jane outfits, who can carve meat and pour "jungle juice" from a barrel, and who can handle good-natured drunks at the XYZ Co. Summer Jungle Blast may require less formal training.

When hiring staff for any event, spell out the necessary skill set for that job. Make sure everyone knows exactly what is expected by you, the client, and the client's guests. Be very specific about your standards of dress and hygiene. Barefoot might be fine for the jungle blast, but no queen of Moldavia should be forced to look at ingrown toenails over her pâté and champagne. Schedule the entire event, assigning specific tasks to specific individuals or groups, and make sure that everyone knows his or her tasks well in advance. Most smart caterers interview their clients after each event to get feedback, spot troublesome areas, and to see what he or she is doing well. Interview your staff, too. Sometimes the owner is too close to the situation to make an honest, unemotional evaluation of his or her operation. The staff can often provide the same type of valuable information from an important perspective—from the inside.

Discovering the Keys to Successful Takeout

Takeout food at one time consisted of little more than a burger and fries or a wax paper-covered plate stuck in a

Promote Your New Service as if It Were a New Restaurant

Define your niche. Let potential customers know the reasons to select your company for its catering. Clearly the quality of your food and menu can be a major draw, but there could be any number of other very good reasons to hire your services: quality of food prep and service staff; connections with related suppliers such as performing artists or an ice sculptor; proximity to the client's operations; menu flexibility; speed of service in emergency situations; pricing and other issues.

Place your advertisements where they will reach the largest number of catering customers, not necessarily the largest number of individuals.

Feed the prospect. When making your business presentation, take lots of samples of your wares and make a food and beverage presentation. Cast your net into your network. Never pass up an opportunity to earn a referral from a satisfied customer.

paper sack and driven home in the family flivver. Today takeout is a rapidly expanding sector of the restaurant market. According to the National Restaurant Association's "Takeout Foods: A Consumer Study of Carryout and Delivery," 78 percent of the nation's households made one or more takeout or delivery food purchases during a typical month. Perhaps because many of the patrons are "unseen" or only briefly seen, many restaurateurs are probably missing a rather substantial boat here. This is a major opportunity. The NRA reported that on any given day in 1998, 21 percent of American households took advantage of some type of takeout or delivery.

Key ingredients of a successful takeout operation are as follows.

Good Food

The convenience of takeout and delivery is a real bonus, but nobody buys takeout to toss out. Your food has to meet or exceed expectations, if for no other reasons than the environment in which it is eaten. With takeout you don't have the benefits of your restaurant's pleasant atmosphere, the friendly wait staff, or the solace of a nearby fully stocked bar. Also, the food will naturally be less than hot off the grill by the time the customer reaches the home or office. Quality in takeout is no less important than when the patron is dining in. Pleasing your takeout customers with good food is good business. Even if the prices for takeout versus dine-in are the same, takeout orders tend to bring in more revenue because many people order for the entire family.

Accuracy

Accuracy in delivering the order is essential. You can blow a lot of good will and even lose some customers by sloppy order handling. Customers expect and deserve to get all that they've ordered. Frustration over an incomplete or inaccurate order is enhanced by distance. Often the customer is many miles away at the home or office and a return trip to rectify the order is impractical or impossible. Staff must be trained to check and verify every order for every item before it's handed to a customer. That includes such "minor" details as little packages of condiments. When people order "extra hot" sauce they don't want "mild." And they'll remember the discrepancy the next time they want takeout.

Correcting a problem is often easy within a restaurant. An apology, a free dessert, or in extreme cases a complimentary meal can smooth over many a ruffled feather. Customer frustration at home has no such pressure valve to be released and can build until you have lost a customer. Worse, the offended former customer may decide to spread the word to his or her friends and neighbors. Some restaurants will even unpack a sack in front of the customer and double-check the items to make sure that the food ordered is the food delivered.

Freshness

Freshness is a major consumer issue. America is health-conscious, and, despite the popularity of fast foods, people expect that food to look and taste as if the raw materials were delivered the morning of the order and prepared no sooner than the moment the order was given. Salads and French fries should be crisp. Ice cream should be cold and not approaching the consistency of soup. And bread shouldn't have hues of blue or green or be able to double as penicillin. If you plan to offer takeout, make sure you give the food and service the same priority as you do your dine-in service. Your customers should neither see nor experience any difference. You may want to serve a limited menu or a full menu. Whatever is right for your restaurant is right for your customers, but remember that some foods continue to cook long after being taken off the grill or out of the oven. Make sure you eliminate any item that will not travel well. If it won't make the ride home, the customers will remember with a vengeance and probably won't make the ride back to your takeout window.

> If you plan to offer takeout, make sure you give the food and service the same priority as you do your dine-in service.

Speed

Takeout and delivery service should be fast. People expect it, and as many restaurants and chains begin to promise delivery within a specified time, you will have to become and remain competitive. If someone wants takeout, that by definition means he or she has somewhere else to go. Your restaurant should be perceived as a welcome convenience along the way, not as a roadblock.

Are You Losing Customers?

A 1999 national survey by the National Restaurant Association revealed that 42 percent of those surveyed would be likely to take advantage of a drive-through window at their favorite restaurant if it were available. That figure is even higher (55 percent) for those 18 to 34 years old. Such information should give any restaurateur pause for contemplation. Can you afford the risk of not putting in a takeout procedure? Do you risk losing business to the competitor who does?

The bottom line in takeout is that more and more individuals and families are enjoying the benefits of takeout. The takeout option provides them with a quality meal, yet one that can be enjoyed in the pleasant environment of the home. Provide that excellent service, and you could easily find yourself a welcome and regular member of the family.

Convenience

Consider setting up an independent takeout section if at all practical. Have a separate counter and separate cash register to facilitate rapid order-taking, food preparation, and delivery. Separate operations aren't essential, and many don't practice the division of labor, but it can be a significant plus, especially for smaller operations. Drive-through pickup windows are becoming normal extensions of even the smallest, single-unit, mom-and-pop restaurants. Drive-through has become a norm in American society, so why not let the phenomenon drive up your profits?

Adding Merchandising to Your Mix

Think Hard Rock Café. Where in public can you go without encountering a T-shirt imprinted with this familiar logo? Yes, restaurants can earn money from T-shirts. And baseball caps, coffee mugs, drinking glasses, shot glasses, rulers, key chains, notepads, pens, pencils, and just about anything else that can hold the ink of a logo. Merchandising isn't limited to large, national chain operations, either. Many a family-owned restaurant or small café adds to the bottom line with a shelf or two of imprinted items for sale. This can be a particularly lucrative sideline for restaurants in areas drawing a lot of tourists.

Marketing Your Business

In addition to producing immediate income, merchandising advertises your restaurant, which may lead to more eat-in sales. Every time someone wears your T-shirt or drinks from your imprinted mug, he or she is reminded of your business. Anyone within eyesight of that person also is exposed to your message. And the benefit is even better than that. The individual using your merchandise takes a bit of your dining experience home and becomes a living testimonial. Use of your product is an endorsement. After all, who's going to wear a T-shirt from a restaurant they didn't enjoy?

Merchandising is a terrific way to increase your word of mouth in the community. It's great visual advertising that keeps on advertising until the article wears out. In the case of something as substantial as a coffee mug, that could be for many years. More important, the profits from merchandising head straight for your bottom line because there's no extra labor involved. There's no food prep, cooking, serving, or cleaning up afterward. You just hand over the item and take back the customer's money with a friendly "Thank you. Come again."

Also consider the considerable value of periodically or even regularly giving away some of your merchandising items. In the case of inexpensive items, such as pencils, the cost is negligible compared to the good will created. "Freebees" are great marketing tools.

Finding Merchandising Items

Finding, pricing, and ordering merchandising items is the easiest part of the job. Wherever you are, there is an advertising specialty salesperson nearby. He or she may own a specialty store, operate a division of another firm such as an advertising agency, or may just offer specialties as a way to earn extra income. You can also find direct sources for many, many items advertised in the food and beverage trade journals. Prices can vary considerably from source to source and from salesperson to salesperson. Be sure to get at least three quotes on any item you want to order.

Matching Retail Items to Your Image

There's a lot more to successful merchandising than applying your logo or trade character to a bunch of retail

Increased Demand for Takeout Increases Take-Home Profits

The demand for takeout is increasing, and that trend is expected to continue. National chain restaurants have taken notice of the trend, with Chili's and Outback currently taking the lead.

According to a November 2001 article in *Restaurant Business*, Chili's now has takeout sections in about 75 percent of its 683 U.S. units. Outback operates 640 restaurants across the nation and reported takeout revenues of almost $121 million for 2000. That's a jump of more than 70 percent over figures for the preceding year. Outback-owned Carrabba's Italian Grill reported takeout sales of more than $10.8 million for 2000, a 219 percent increase in sales over 1999. Applebee's 1,300-plus units reported about $131 million in takeout sales for about 5 percent of its total revenue. Red Lobster's 660 restaurants brought in takeout revenues topping $62 million, or about 3 percent of revenues.

items for sale. Remember, you're a restaurateur, not a retail department store. Make sure your merchandising items complement your image. Hard Rock Café has done a masterful job of merchandising. Do you realize people have been seeing that round logo on T-shirts for more than thirty years? So successful has the retail end of their business been that it now accounts for 48 percent of annual sales.

Cracker Barrel has done an excellent job. Their old country store look and feel complements the wide variety of retail products offered and actually enhances the atmosphere of the restaurant section. Taco Bell recently had a hit by selling plush toy models of the frisky Chihuahua puppy used in a very successful advertising campaign. Many coffee shops offer a line of coffee related retail items, such as cups, mugs, ground coffee, and even coffee beans. Starbucks gets about 6 percent of sales from retail merchandising.

Keep the Restaurant Your Number-One Business

Retail sales can be a very profitable addition to your food and beverage business, but always keep in mind that it's a separate and quite different business. That end should never be allowed to create problems for your bread and butter business. For example, how will your customers feel about a rack of T-shirts and ball caps in their favorite dining establishment? Will the retail end impede the easy flow of customers and servers? Can you afford to stock a sufficient inventory?

Appendix A

Resources

Appendix A

Appendix B

Appendix C

■ Organizations

Here are a number of valuable sources. Some will be helpful in limited areas, while others can provide information on a variety of subjects. The addresses include an e-mail address wherever possible.

Bureau of the Census
U.S. Department of Commerce
✆ 301-457-4608
✎ *www.census.gov*

National Restaurant Association
1200 17th St., NW
Washington, DC 20036
✎ *www.restaurant.org*

Small Business Administration
1441 L Street, NW
Washington, DC 20416
✆ 202-205-7064
✎ *www.sba.gov/financing*

National Business Association
✆ 1-800-456-0440

National Federation of Independent Business
✆ 1-800-634-2669

SCORE
✆ 1-800-634-0245

The American Franchise Association
✆ 312-431-0545
✎ *www.infonews.com/afa*

Franchise Info Mall
✆ 1-800-INFO-MALL
✎ *www.franchiseinfomall.com*

■ Recommended Reading

We recommend the following books and guides:

The Restaurant Planning Guide, Peter Rainsford and David H. Bangs, Jr., available from Dearborn Trade

Uniform System of Accounts for Restaurants from the National Restaurant Association.

Restaurant Industry Operations Report from the National Restaurant Association and Deloitte & Touche

Food For Fifty by Grace Shugart, available from Prentice Hall

The Essentials of Good Table Service pamphlet from Cornell Hotel and Restaurant Administration Quarterly of Ithaca, New York

Applied Food Service Sanitation from The Educational Foundation of the National Restaurant Association and available from Wiley Publishing, Inc.

Management of Food and Beverage Operations by Jack D. Ninemeier, from the American Hotel and Motel Association

Fundamentals of Menu Planning by Paul J. McVety and Bradley J. Ware, from Van Nostrand Reinhold

■ National Restaurant Association

The National Restaurant Association (see contact information in the "Organizations" section of this appendix) will prove to be one of your most valuable resources and deserves special mention in these pages. Their Web page is full of industry and related news, important data, how-to columns, opinions, and information on all aspects of the restaurant business. Your state will have an affiliate, and you'll find membership plaques posted in virtually every community large enough for a restaurant or café. Whether you are just starting to plan your restaurant dream or you're an owner/operator with enormous experience, you'll find the association a treasure trove of information.

■ Magazines and Newsletters

There are too many good magazines covering too many subjects to even consider listing them all. Here are a few national publications to get you started on a reading program. You can contact them easily on the Internet.

Restaurants USA is the official publication of the National Restaurant Association.

Restaurant Hospitality is a resource for managers and can be reached via *☞ www.food servicesearch.com.*

FoodService Director is one of a number of related publications, which includes *FoodService Today* and *Restaurant Business.* You can link to all of them through *☞ www.foodservicetoday.com.*

If you can think of a restaurant-related subject, there is probably a magazine, newsletter, and Web site devoted to it. For example, you can reach *Nightclub & Bar* magazine through *☞ www.nightclub&bar.com.* When you want information on a particular topic, just type it in on your favorite search engine, and the Internet will probably take you to a number of relevant sources.

■ Competitive Analysis Form

Use this form to make notes on your competition for later study and evaluation.

Date_____

RESTAURANT (Name) _____

LOCATION_____

Comments _____

_____

_____

TYPE (Café, franchise, etc.)_____

ESTIMATED SQUARE FEET_____

NUMBER OF TABLES _____

BANQUET FACILITIES ____Yes   ____No

LIQUOR SERVED ____Yes   ____No

LOUNGE/BAR ____Yes   ____No

STAFF SIZE _____

MEALS SERVED ____Breakfast   ____Lunch   ____Dinner

SIGNIFICANT FEATURES_____

_____

_____

OWNERSHIP _____

ESTIMATED AVERAGE CHECK _____

AVERAGE AGE OF CUSTOMER _____

PROMOTIONS/EVENTS _____

_____

_____

IMPRESSIONS/COMMENTS_____

_____

_____

_____

_____

_____

■ Food Safety Check List

Health and safety is an important concern to the public and to governmental agencies. You must make this matter a priority. Be sure that everyone on your staff adopts the same attitude. This Food Safety Check List was adapted from a form provided by the Texas Department of Health/Retail Food Division. It covers the basics. Feel free to adapt it to your own needs.

Check "Yes" for items in compliance.
Check "No" for items not in compliance. Correct the situation immediately.
The letters PHF stand for Potentially Hazardous Food.

A. FOOD TEMPERATURE/TIME CONTROL

Yes   No   1. Cold holding area: Refrigerators, display cases, salad bars, dessert machines, etc. hold cold PHFs at 45 degrees F or below.

Yes   No   2. Cooking: PHFs cooked to the proper internal temperatures:
        a. Poultry, meat stuffings, & stuffed meats at 165 degrees F or above.
        b. Ground/shredded beef & hamburgers at minimum 155 degrees F for eight seconds.
        c. Pork & pork products at 150 degrees F or above
        d. Most other PHFs at 140 degrees F or above.

Yes   No   3. Hot holding area: Steam tables, warmers, crock pots, etc. holding PHFs at 140 degrees F or above.

Yes   No   4. Cooling: Cooked PHFs cooled to 45 degrees F or below within four hours.

Yes   No   5. Reheating: Foods reheated rapidly to 165 degrees F or above before use/sale.

Yes   No   6. Facilities: Adequate equipment/facilities to maintain PHF temperatures.

B. HYGIENIC PRACTICES/HAND WASHING

Yes   No   1. Food handlers free from: exposed cuts, sores, or boils that could contaminate food or equipment; free from respiratory and infectious illnesses.

Yes   No   2. Eating, drinking, and tobacco use restricted to approved break areas.

Yes   No   3. Fingernails on food handlers clean and cut short.

Yes   No   4. Hand washing sink available & convenient to food prep areas.

Yes   No   5. Hand washing sinks accessible; working; all with hot & cold water.

Yes   No   6. Hand washing sinks used strictly for hand washing; nothing stored in basins.

Yes   No   7. Hands washed: before work; after breaks; after handling raw foods; before handling ready-to-eat foods; after coughing, sneezing, touching the head/face or any other time hands may become contaminated.

Yes   No   8. Hands properly dried; aprons & wiping cloths not used.

Yes   No   9. Hands washed in hand sinks, not utensil or prep sinks.

C. SOURCE & CONDITION OF FOODS

Yes   No   1. Food, iced & water source safe.

Yes   No   2. Severely dented, swollen, expired, & other potentially unwholesome foods restricted from use or sale.

Yes   No   3. Raw milk not purchased or used.

Yes   No   4. Shellfish from approved sources as demonstrated by presence of shell stock tags.

Yes   No   5. No home or prepared food used or sold.

Yes   No   6. Meat & meat products obtained from approved State/USDA sources.

D. CLEANING & SANITIZING

Yes   No   1. Proper wash, rinse, and sanitize steps followed.

Yes   No   2. Sanitizer mixed to the correct strength (50 PPM for chlorine, which equals one tablespoon standard bleach per one gallon of water).

Yes   No   3. Sufficient supply of hot water available for cleaning & sanitizing.

Yes   No   4. Rinse water clean.

Yes   No   5. Sanitizing solution kept at 75 degrees F or above.

Yes   No   6. Mechanical cleaning & sanitizing equipment properly functioning (e.g. water temperatures; pump pressure; wash times; & rinse times).

E. FOOD PROTECTION/CROSS-CONTAMINATION

Yes   No   1. Contamination of cooked or ready-to-eat foods with raw foods prevented.

Yes   No   2. Food service gloves and serving utensils used properly to prevent cross-contamination.

Yes   No   3. Back-flow preventer, vacuum breaker, or atmospheric break installed at each faucet where a hose remains attached.

Yes   No   4. Sewage, mop water, and other waster properly disposed.

Yes   No   5. Hot and cold water under pressure provided in food preparation areas.

F. CHEMICAL USAGE

Yes   No   1. Chemicals properly stored (below food, food equipment, utensils, and single service items) in designated areas.

Yes   No   2. Approved general-use pesticides stored separate from cleaning and sanitizing materials in a designated area.

Yes   No   3. Spray bottles/buckets used for detergents and sanitizers properly labeled; correct chemical in the spray bottle/bucket.

G. PEST CONTROL

Yes   No   1. Door, pipes, and other openings to the outside sealed/maintained to prevent pest entry.

Yes   No   2. Establishment free of rodents, roaches, flies, birds, and other pests.

Yes   No   3. Pest control equipment properly installed and maintained.

■ Clean-Up Check List

Cleanliness and sanitation isn't just of good management or common sense. It's a matter of law and government regulation. This form was used at a two-story club/restaurant. Adapt its provisions to your specific needs. This is a pretty good idea starter. Add any additional items as required.

Date: _____

DAILY CHECK LIST	S	M	T	W	TH	F	S
Sweep floors; vacuum all carpeted floors	☐	☐	☐	☐	☐	☐	☐
Sweep & mop all wood floors (be sure to sweep next to edge of bars)	☐	☐	☐	☐	☐	☐	☐
Remove gum from floors	☐	☐	☐	☐	☐	☐	☐
Mop dance floor if needed (at least weekly)	☐	☐	☐	☐	☐	☐	☐
Mop upper dance floor	☐	☐	☐	☐	☐	☐	☐
Mop frill floor	☐	☐	☐	☐	☐	☐	☐
Mop entrance floor	☐	☐	☐	☐	☐	☐	☐
Wash bathroom walls & stalls	☐	☐	☐	☐	☐	☐	☐
Clean club & grill bathroom sinks	☐	☐	☐	☐	☐	☐	☐
Clean club & grill urinals & toilets	☐	☐	☐	☐	☐	☐	☐
Clean club & grill bathroom mirrors	☐	☐	☐	☐	☐	☐	☐
Make sure all toilets flush	☐	☐	☐	☐	☐	☐	☐
Check toilet paper fill box for night supply	☐	☐	☐	☐	☐	☐	☐
Check paper towels in bathroom, kitchen, and bathrooms in break room	☐	☐	☐	☐	☐	☐	☐
Check ice machines & keep ice pushed over	☐	☐	☐	☐	☐	☐	☐
Polish brass handrails	☐	☐	☐	☐	☐	☐	☐
Clean parking lot of trash & rocks	☐	☐	☐	☐	☐	☐	☐
Clean trash along fence line	☐	☐	☐	☐	☐	☐	☐
Clean & sweep around dumpster	☐	☐	☐	☐	☐	☐	☐

WEEKLY CHECK LIST   **CHECK OFF AS COMPLETED**

Tables—mop all bottoms   ❏

Move all tables & sweep under each   ❏

Sweep & scrub between footrail & bar   ❏

Mop all wood stairs   ❏

Mop kitchen & back area—use broom to loosen dirt   ❏
  & clean around edges

Sweep pool tables & wipe down ledge   ❏

Shine pinball machine   ❏

Vacuum offices   ❏

Dust shelves in pit   ❏

Clean all glasses   ❏

Clean all mirrors   ❏

Polish footrails   ❏

Wipe down fan blades & check for loose blades   ❏

Clean bathrooms in break room   ❏

Mop floors in break room bathrooms   ❏

Clean sink & toilet in break room bathrooms   ❏

Report all defective or broken items to the office   ❏

Thurs/Fri. only—pull weeds in flower bed & sweep patio area ❏

MONTHLY CHECK LIST   **CHECK OFF AS COMPLETED**

Week One

Deep clean exterior & check all equipment   ❑

Wash all exterior doors   ❑

Clean grill windows   ❑

Check exhaust fans—clean   ❑

Clean evaporator coils   ❑

Clean A/C return air grilles   ❑

Week Two

Deep clean floors—look down to see what needs cleaning   ❑

Wash all bar fronts & scrub behind footrails   ❑

Scrub between rails on the dance floor   ❑

Scrub molding around dance floor   ❑

Scrub all molding, especially in front of the pit and VIP room   ❑

Scrub all wooden stairs   ❑

Week Three

Deep clean all walls—check to see if anything needs painting   ❑

Wash all dirty walls   ❑

Week Four

Look up to see what needs dusting   ❑

Clean light bulbs in ladies restroom   ❑

Clean all bar lights over the pool tables   ❑

Clean all lights over tables in the grill   ❑

Dust pictures & items on the walls   ❑

SPECIAL INSTRUCTIONS

_____

_____

_____

_____

■ Offenses That Could Result in Termination

Here's a form that very clearly and specifically details the various reasons a restaurant owner or manager should fire an employee. Most of these have security implications. This is one of those documents each employee should read and sign prior to beginning work.

- Theft—including payroll theft.
- Eating in the kitchen.
- No call/no show. This is self-termination.
- Reporting under the influence or consumption of alcohol or narcotics while on duty.
- Smoking in unauthorized areas.
- Profanity towards peers, management, or guests.
- Falsifying any information pertaining to the well-being of this restaurant.
- Improper guest check additions.
- Absence from mandatory staff meetings.
- Possessing any weapon on restaurant property.
- Excessive tardiness.
- Variance in approved recipes.
- Fighting or attempting bodily injury to another.

- Deliberate damage or misuse of restaurant property.
- Gambling on restaurant property.
- Soliciting gratuities from guest or commenting in any way about the amount of gratuity given by a customer.
- Sleeping while on duty.
- Insubordination, willful disregard or disrespect toward a supervisor or representative of management.
- Failure to report accidents, breakage, or damage to equipment, or giving false testimony regarding accidents.
- Sexual harassment of ANY kind.
- Using cell phone while on duty, especially in view of customers.

VIOLATIONS OF THESE POLICIES MAY INVOLVE REPRIMAND, SUSPENSION, AND/OR DISMISSAL FROM EMPLOYMENT.

I _____ (PRINT NAME) HAVE READ AND I UNDERSTAND ALL OF THE POLICIES PRESENTED TO ME AND FUTHER ACKNOWLEDGE THAT THE VIOLATION OF THESE POLICIES AND PROCEDURES MAY RESULT IN IMMEDIATE TERMINATION.

_____   _____

SIGNATURE   DATE

_____   _____

WITNESS/MANAGER   DATE

Sexual Harassment

Sexual harassment is a growing problem in all parts of the country, in all types of industries and environments, and the restaurant industry is not exempt. The following form can be used to inform each employee that your restaurant takes this matter very seriously, that it will not be tolerated, and violations of policy can have severe consequences.

Sexual Harassment Policy

Sexual Harassment is a violation of Title VII of the Civil Rights Act of 1964. (Restaurant) complies with Equal Employment Laws. The definition of sexual harassment includes:

Unwelcome sexual advances, requests for sexual favors and other verbal or physical conduct of a sexual nature when such codex is made explicitly or implicitly as a term or condition of employment, is used as a basis for employment decisions, or has the purpose or effect of interfering with performance or creating an otherwise hostile or offensive environment.

Any harassment of employees, whether by a manager, supervisor, employee or non-employee will not be tolerated.

Management employees of (Restaurant) have the responsibility for maintaining a work environment free of any form of sexual harassment. Responsibility includes discussing the policy with all employees and assuring them that they are not required to endure insulting, degrading, or exploitative sexual treatment.

Any employee who is found to have engaged in sexual harassment of another employee or non-employee will be subject to appropriate disciplinary action, up to and including termination.

I have read the above Sexual Harassment Policy. The policy has been explained to me fully, and I will conform to the Standard of Operations set forth by (Restaurant). Additionally, I realize that an infraction of any kind to this policy can result in a written reprimand up to and including termination.

_____   _____
Signature   Print Name

_____   _____
Date   Position

■ Sample Promotion Proposal

Marketing promotions are key to the success of many clubs and restaurants. They often involve cross-promotion with other businesses. Careful planning and thorough preparation are essential to success. Here's a form illustrating how to make an effective presentation to one of those businesses. It can be adapted to just about any situation.

ABC RESTAURANT PROMOTION PROPOSAL

Happy Hour Party Proposal for XYZ Travel Agency

Goal: Increased awareness for XYZ Travel Agency through additional advertising and marketing exposure via ABC Restaurant promotion.

Goal: Increased traffic, exposure, and good will for ABC Restaurant.

Method: Co-op advertising venture between ABC Restaurant and XYZ Travel Agency.

Target Audience: Young professionals ages 25 to 45.

Secondary Audience: Single adults ages 18 to 34.

Date: Wednesday, July 15, 5:30 to 7:30 P.M.

Project Summary: ABC Restaurant Premiere Customer mailing list will be invited to attend a special Hawaiian Party at which guests will be eligible to register for a four-day, three-night vacation on the island of Maui in Hawaii, airfare included. A winner's name will be drawn at the conclusion of the event.

XYZ Travel Agency Receives:

Radio tags during seven days leading up to the event.

Name and logo printed on all promotion mailed to 2,500 premier customers.

Minimum of ten in-house promotional announcements.

Hawaiian Party at ABC Restaurant.

Leads for addition to XYZ Travel Agency mailing list collected at the event.

A promotional area inside ABC Restaurant for banners, demonstration table, etc.

Estimated Value: $5,000.

ABC Restaurant Receives:

A four-day, three-night trip to Maui, including airfare.

A copy of the XYZ Travel Agency mailing list.

XYZ Travel Agency Responsibilities:

Providing the trip/airfare to Maui.

ABC Restaurant Responsibilities:

Successfully host the Hawaiian Party.
Cost on all radio advertising and production.
Cost on all artwork and printed materials.
Cost of postage for invitations.
Ensure in-house exposure for XYZ Travel Agency.

Agreed _____

       XYZ Travel Agency (authorized signature)   Date

    _____

       ABC Restaurant (authorized signature)   Date

■ Promotion Development Outline and Check List

Once you have developed your promotion, you'll need to organize it and carry it out. As you will discover, even a simple promotion becomes a complex process. This form will help you organize your promotion, track its progress, and even evaluate it after the fact.

Location: _____ **Date:** _____

1. Name of Promotion: _____

Day(s) _____ Date: _____
Theme/brief description: _____
_____
_____

2. Objective/Brief Description (How does the promotion...)

a. Build traffic _____
_____

b. Provide increased sales _____
_____

c. Enhance product positioning _____
_____

d. Create publicity_____
_____

e. Increase market awareness _____
_____

f. What specific market is addressed? _____
_____

3. Sales Goals/Projections—Ongoing or One-Night Event

Week One: $_____ Week Two: $_____
Week Three: $_____ Week Four: $_____
Total $_____
Divided by four = $_____ for average weekly sales goal
Sales goal for one-night event $_____

4. Decorations: Yes: _____ No: _____ Amount budgeted: $ _____

Responsible person: _____

Brief description: _____

_____

Decorating committee: _____

Personnel/meeting dates & notes: _____

_____

5. Special Costumes: Yes: _____ No: _____ Amount budgeted: $_____

Person responsible: _____

Date employees to be given notice: _____

Restaurant staff: _____

Bar staff: _____

Wait staff: _____

Door staff: _____

DJ/booth staff: _____

Management: _____

6. Drink specials: Yes: _____ No: _____

Drink name: _____ Description: _____ Price: _____

Drink name: _____ Description: _____ Price: _____

Drink name: _____ Description: _____ Price: _____

7. Buffet/Food: Yes: _____ No: _____

Person responsible: _____ (notify kitchen) Date: _____

Special food items and decorations for buffet: _____

_____

_____

8. Music, Lights, Entertainment: Yes: _____ No: _____

Person responsible: _____ Amount budgeted: $ _____
Special music: _____
Special lights: _____
Special entertainment: _____

9. Contests/Promotions: Yes: _____ No: _____ Date(s) of event: _____

Person responsible: _____
Name of event: _____
Brief description/Objective: _____
_____
Rules: _____
Sponsors: _____
Prizes: 1st _____ 2nd _____
3rd _____
Judges: _____
Start time: _____ End time: _____
Event MC: _____
Music/light selection: _____
Prizes secured by: _____
Special entertainment: _____
Equipment rental: $ _____
Amount budgeted $_____ Hotel/Airfare $_____
Persons responsible: _____

10. Rehearsal/Walk-Throughs: Yes: _____ No: _____

Rehearsal Dates: _____
Staff: _____
Rehearsal coordinator: _____
Event MC: _____
Persons who should attend: _____
Date to be notified of the rehearsal: _____
Labor costs (if applicable): $ _____

11. Corporate or Agency Marketing Support/Unit Print:

Print budget: $ _____ Unit print budget: $ _____

Poster(s): Date needed: _____ # Needed: _____

Invitations: Date needed: _____ # Needed: _____

Fliers:_____ Date needed: _____ # Needed: _____

Entry forms: Date needed: _____ # Needed: _____

Other (t-shirts, buttons, etc.): _____

Date needed: _____ # Needed: _____

Invitations mailed to: _____ Date: _____

Person responsible: _____

In-House distribution by: _____ Date: _____

Outside distribution by: _____ Date: _____

Where: _____

Date entry forms available: _____ Person responsible: _____

12. Advertising: Yes: _____ No: _____

Person responsible: _____

Radio station(s): _____ Budget: $ _____

Radio party: Yes: _____ No: _____ Date: _____ Hours: _____

Talent fee: $_____ Talent booked: _____

Radio copy approved by:_____

Artwork approved by: _____ Date:_____

Special instructions: _____

13. Recap Promotion Budget Estimates:

a. Decorations $ _____

b. Special costumes: _____

c. Contest prizes, entertainment fees, hotel/airfare, equipment rentals: _____

d. Labor costs: _____

e. Corporate/agency print costs $ _____

f. Unit print costs $ _____

g. Radio schedule, talent fees, production costs: $ _____

h. Newspaper/magazine: $_____ Placement/production: $ _____

i. Other: _____

TOTAL: $ _____

■ Takeout Procedures

- All takeout orders are to be routed through the bar. (Your facility may vary.)
- Each takeout order is to be checked by the expediter and then double checked by the bartender (or whomever you have assigned).
- Fifteen minutes after the order has been picked up, the bartender will call the customer to verify his or her satisfaction.
- Takeout orders are not to be taken thirty minutes prior to closing. Any customer making orders the last hour before closing should be informed of the time the doors will be locked.
- A 10 percent off card will be issued to each takeout order for the use on the next dine-in visit.
- When the customer is waiting in the restaurant, use the "waiting" prep key.
- One bartender will be assigned to takeout orders, server check-out, and phone messages.
- After completion of the takeout order form, it will be the bartender's responsibility to watch for the car to pull up. At the time of arrival, the bartender is to deliver the order to the customer.

■ Takeout Order Form

Customer's Name   Time Order Was Taken

Customer's Phone Number   Time Order Is to Be Picked Up

Customer's Color/Model/Make of Car Method of Payment

Order Taken By   Amount of Takeout Order
ORDER: _____

SPECIAL INSTRUCTIONS: _____

Appendix C

FAQs

■ Raising the Rent

Q: My landlord says he needs to raise my rent. I can't afford it. What should I do?

A: Experience has shown Randy that sometimes a once-ideal location might no longer be a premier area of town. Traffic drops off, but your lease is like that little pink bunny in the battery commercials. The payments keep going and going.

In this situation, Randy approached the landlord and told him his concerns about how the area was not as attractive as it once was and how customer counts were down, which meant sales were off. He voiced his need plainly. "I need to adjust my rent." The landlord wanted to keep the restaurant from closing or moving and was willing to renegotiate the lease. Randy's lease was reduced from $4,250 per month to $3,000 per month. Open communication, a willingness to negotiate, and a view to the long term was a good move for both.

Another restaurant having difficulties also approached the landlord about rent reduction. This landlord was not willing to negotiate any reduction of monthly rent or to shorten the term of the lease. Sometimes people have their eyes only on the short term. Still, you may as well be direct, honest, and friendly. The worst that could come of the discussion is that you remain in the same financial position.

There are times when landlords know they have a hot location and become greedy. At the first sign of trouble, or if you have a temporary default in your lease, they will use it to evict you or raise your rent. Be careful if you know you have a great location. You don't want to lose it. Keep yourself current while you negotiate. For if it is really good, the landlord knows he can rent it quickly. He has very little to lose.

It is important to negotiate your lease as well as possible. Sometimes you can negotiate a lease that will take a smaller base rent and add a percentage of sales for part of the rent. This is a good policy, because when your sales are down, the rent expense drops, too. When sales are up, your rent goes up accordingly, and that's when you can afford to pay more.

■ Deciding Between New or Used Equipment

Q: Should I purchase used restaurant equipment?

A: Used equipment can be a real bargain, saving you thousands of dollars. Examine all equipment carefully to make sure it is in good shape and functions properly. You want equipment with a lot of useful life left in it. If something is on its last legs, the purchase will probably lead only to financial grief. Get a history of any major equipment and contact the previous owner for an opinion. Consider the following tips to help you assess buying used equipment:

- What's the price of it new?
- How old is it, and how many moving parts does it have?

- Can you still find/buy parts for it?
- Was the equipment serviced on a regular basis?
- Does the piece of equipment still have a warranty?

- If it needs repair, how much will it cost?

Double-check any used equipment before you make the purchase.

■ Costs of Running a Restaurant

Q: How am I most likely to be spending my money in my restaurant?

A: Every operation is different, but according to a 1997 Restaurant Industry Operations Report, this is how typical restaurants break down their expenses per dollar (numbers in percentages).

	Full Service*	Full Service**	Fast Food	Cafeteria
Cost of food sold	29.0	26.8	31.1	31.2
Cost of beverage sold	3.5	6.3	0.7	0.5
Salaries and wages	29.6	28.1	26.3	28.2
Employee benefits	4.8	4.6	2.5	5.3
Direct operating expenses	6.3	7.1	5.4	2.8
Music and entertainment	0.3	0.7	0.1	0.0
Marketing	2.8	2.8	4.9	4.3
Utility service	3.1	2.7	2.8	4.6
Restaurant occupancy costs	5.7	5.7	6.6	5.2
Repairs and maintenance	1.8	2.1	1.6	1.9
Depreciation	2.5	2.1	2.0	1.2
Other operating expense (income)	(0.4)	(0.1)	0.0	0.4
General and administrative	3.3	4.3	3.8	5.5
Corporate overhead	2.1	2.0	2.2	1.0
Interest	0.6	0.6	0.6	1.0
Other	0.3	0.5	0.4	0.0
Income before taxes	4.7	3.7	9.0	7.2
Food and beverage income percentages:				
Food sales	86.2	77.2	97.5	98.7
Beverage sales	13.8	22.8	2.5	1.3

Average per person check under $10

**Average per person check over $10*

■ Rising Food Costs

Q: My food cost has gone through the roof. Where should I look to bring things under control?

A: Start with your vendors. Check to see if their prices have gone up or if they're fluctuating. Are you or is someone in receiving checking your orders for accuracy? Is the math right? Weigh what is sold to you by weight and count what is sold by the unit. Are you offering too many types of food on your menu? This adds to waste and increases your food costs. If all of that checks out, then double-check your menu pricing. Have you underpriced some high-moving items? Next take a look in the kitchen. Are the cooks and prep staff properly trained? Are you serving the right-sized portions for your menu price? Maybe the day crew (or prep cooks) are prepping too much and are not able to use it before it goes bad. This happens a lot. You should track your sales by item and compare it to what is being prepped. This cuts waste drastically. Try portion control. If you are selling a twelve-ounce rib-eye, weigh it and make sure they haven't cut it to weigh fourteen ounces. You can preweigh or premeasure a lot of items on your menu. Portion control is probably the main culprit in your high food costs, with employee theft a close second. Look at your policies and try to close any areas that can be an easy target. Keep doors locked along with seafood and steaks or anything else that is expensive and good to eat at home. Randy keeps his steaks in a locked cage and issues out the amount they expect to sell on the upcoming shift.

Look for theft. Is the kitchen feeding the employees and not recording it? Is an employee selling inventory out the back door? Is a bartender giving away drinks? Has a waitperson come up with a scheme allowing him or her to not ring up food items but collecting the money? Theft happens often in the restaurant business and most often it is that otherwise "perfect" employee who does it. Think proactive. How can a dishonest person steal from me? Then put into place measures that will stop it. You need to be smarter than the thieves to survive. This may sound harsh, but theft is out there and very prevalent.

■ Cash Register Ideas

Q: What sort of cash register/point-of-sale system should I purchase?

A: The POS or cash registers of today can get about as sophisticated as you can imagine. They can calculate your payroll up to the second, can track each department for payroll budgeting, inventory usage and costs, average ticket times, average ticket sales, how many times a table turned, and the list goes on. They can be linked to the bar and to the kitchen with remote printers to get that all-important order started faster.

If you want to compete with the big guys, buy a sophisticated register. Knowing what you sell and when you sell it is very important when making business decisions. "Which menu item should I delete on the new menu?"

"When should I schedule the wait staff?" With a good register system, it is usually easier to control theft. The system can be linked to the kitchen, so it can even help control kitchen flow. On the other hand, small mom-and-pop operations can sometimes get by with a simple electronic cash register and a good calculator. It is highly recommended to attend as many restaurant trade shows as possible to see firsthand and side by side the new POS systems that are available. Ask the salespeople as many questions as possible to see exactly what may be right for your budget and operation. Remember, you don't need to buy a Ferrari to race on a dirt track. So don't buy more than you plan on using.

■ Statistics on Dining Out

Q: What is the most popular day for people to dine out?

A: Saturday. The most popular month for eating out is August. The most popular dining out meal is dinner, which represented 52 percent of the national restaurant traffic in 1999. Lunch followed with 37 percent, with breakfast accounting for just 11 percent of the traffic.

■ Future Projections for Restaurants

Q: What does the future hold for the restaurant industry?

A: *Restaurant USA* made a number of predictions for the year 2010 in its September 1999 issue such as the following.

- Success will depend on providing food and food service of the highest quality.
- Competition will be intense.
- Monitoring profit and loss will be faster and easier as new technologies emerge.
- More equipment will be fitted with wheels so that it can be easily moved.
- Equipment will be built with quick-disconnect systems to facilitate cleaning and repair.
- Treating patrons as *people* will continue to be the focus of successful operations.
- Cost controls and management efficiency will be enhanced by increased use of technological breakthroughs.
- Vendors will be under increasing pressure to improve food quality and safety.
- POS systems will be tied to a restaurant's ordering system.
- POS systems will continue to improve, becoming faster, more accurate, and simpler to use.
- The demand for higher-quality takeout will continue.
- The percentage of a family or individual's food dollar allocated to dining out will increase.

■ Federal Tip Credit

Q: Am I allowed under federal law to take a tip credit?

A: Yes, provided certain conditions are met.

An employer can take a tip credit equal to the difference between the minimum wage and the cash wage of $2.13 per hour. For example, the current minimum wage is $5.15 an hour. That means the owner can deduct $3.02 an hour from the minimum wage, providing the following conditions are met.

The tip credit can only be taken from employees who customarily and regularly receive $30 or more in tips per month. The credit can't exceed the amount the employee actually received in tips or more than the prescribed percentage of the applicable minimum wage. If the tips earned by an employee are less than the allowable tip credit, the owner has to make up the difference between the reported tips and the minimum wage. Employees must be notified of the amount of tip credit taken. Employees have the right to keep all their tips. Pooling of tip money by employees is permitted. The owner has to be able to prove that the employees received tips equal to the amount of the tip credit taken.

■ Calculating Overtime

Q: Which of my employees are due overtime pay, and which ones are exempt?

A: According to the Fair Labor Standards Act, executive, professional, or administrative employees are exempt from overtime pay. All others may earn overtime, which is based on an employee's "regular rate of pay." Multiply that figure by 1.5 to compute the employee's overtime.

Be careful. Overtime is figured a little different when a tip credit is applicable. Get with your state's labor office to determine how it is figured in your state. Also, for most states (California is an exception), overtime is based on hours worked over forty hours in a pay week—not on hours worked over eight hours per day. Your pay week must be predetermined. For example, Randy sets his pay week as Monday through Sunday.

This regular rate of pay does not include reimbursement for expenses, optional bonuses, payments made as gifts (Christmas, birthday, etc.), or payments for periods when no work is performed (vacation pay or due to an illness).

■ Employee Pay

Q: How much should I pay my hourly employees?

A: There are a lot of factors involved. For example, economic conditions in areas where quality employees are in short supply will probably require owners to pay more to attract and hold good employees. The following numbers are estimates of average wages paid nationally. They were derived by a 2001 nationwide survey of restaurateurs conducted by the U.S. Department of Labor, Bureau of Labor Statistics.

JOB DESCRIPTION	2001 WAGE ESTIMATES
Chefs	$14.58
Cook	8.88
Assistant cook	8.04
Short order cook	7.98
Baker	9.02
Food/salad prep	8.07
Food checker/expeditor	8.07
Crew person (fast food)	6.99
Crew supervisor (fast food)	7.13
Cafeteria server	7.50
Waiter/waitress	3.68
Host/hostess	7.25
Banquet server	7.13
Bartender	7.03
Cashier	7.10
Busser	5.75
Dishwasher	6.98
Janitor/porter	7.10
Delivery driver	5.78

The wages paid in your area may vary. You should get online and get an up-to-date report on average wages paid in our industry either on the National Restaurant Association's Web site, the NRA organization in your state, or the Bureau of Labor Statistics at *www.bls.gov.*

■ Employee Dress Code

Q: What is the proper dress code for my employees?

A: That depends on the theme of your restaurant, the expectations of your customers, and your local codes. Here is a dress and personal hygiene code used in one of Randy's club/restaurants.

Standard: All dining room personnel must wear required uniforms and adhere to appearance and hygiene requirements.

Appearance: Must be neat in appearance with combed or brushed hair, clean and pressed uniform, nails must be clean and trimmed, and must have a smile on.

Name tags: Must be worn on left side of uniform at all times on duty. Wear the name tag designed for the restaurant.

Uniforms: Must be clean, wrinkle free, and in full repair.

Jewelry: Limited to a watch, wedding/ engagement ring, graduation rings, and earrings that do not fall below the earlobe. All other jewelry must be approved by management.

Shoes: Must be closed heel and toe, low heel, and polished. Sneakers, sandals, and boots are not permitted.

Women's undergarments: Seamless nylons or pantyhose of natural color no darker than "coffee." Brassiere and slip are recommended.

Eyeglasses: Are perfectly acceptable, but sunglasses or highly ornamental frames are not permitted.

Combs or brushes: May not be exposed in pockets while working.

Hygiene:

Hair: Cannot fall forward over your face or touch trays when carrying food. Facial hair must be well trimmed.

Nails: Must be clean and trimmed to no more than one-half inch beyond your finger tips. Polish is subject to management approval.

Make up: Conservatively applied, natural color.

Body: Wash and use deodorant daily, no strong perfume or cologne.

Mouth: Brush daily, keep breath freshener available if you smoke.

■ Employee Alcohol Awareness Program

Q: Should I go to the trouble of establishing an employee alcohol awareness program?

A: Yes. More than forty states have laws for which restaurant and bar owners, bartenders, waiters, and waitresses can be found legally and financially liable for serving alcohol to minors, habitual drunkards, or intoxicated persons. This has become very serious business.

If a third party is injured in person, property, means of support, or otherwise by an intoxicated person, the third party has a right to sue the persons responsible for dispensing the alcohol. Never serve alcohol to an obviously intoxicated or underage person. Don't allow people who are intoxicated into your restaurant or lounge in the first place. Create an atmosphere in your facility that encourages responsible drinking. When dealing with an intoxicated person, always make a reasonable attempt to prevent that person from driving. Try to enlist the aid of the inebriated person's family or friends if they're available.

Third-party injuries aren't limited to automobile accidents, and the principle can apply to any type of injury caused by someone who is inebriated with alcohol. Liability cases are rarely settled out of court for less than $100,000, and jury awards have been settled in the millions of dollars.

It's no "trouble" to prepare a thorough alcohol-awareness program. That program and the awareness it creates will most likely help keep you out of trouble.

■ Complaints about Employees

Q: I've had complaints about the service my employees deliver. Where do I start correcting the situation?

A: Investigate. Be sure you are correcting the right problem. A slow kitchen will sometimes initiate complaints about bad service. This may at first appear in the form of complaints about the wait staff. Look for the real source of the problem.

Stay on the floor. Walk around. Talk to your employees and your customers. Get information from the source and don't rely on "he said-she said" reports. You can also hire a mystery shopper (or ask a friend or associate) to check out the situation from a customer's perspective. Be sure to get their reports in writing. Written documentation can be used for training purposes. It's also helpful when you have to terminate an employee.

If the problem is with the wait staff, your chances of fixing the problem are quite good. Communicate with all the parties involved. Get all sides of the story. Is this a training problem? Is it an attitude problem? Should you work with the individual, or is discharge the best route for all involved?

Whatever the problem, whoever is involved, always act quickly and appropriately. Putting off resolution to a problem only makes it worse.

■ General Complaints and Complainers

Q: What is the best way to handle complaints and complainers?

A: Carefully. A complainer represents much more than just a single dissatisfied customer. Statistics show that the average complainer will share that complaint to nine or ten people. Thirteen percent of complainers will tell twenty people. But handled properly, these people can become loyal customers. Statistics indicate that when the complaint is resolved, the complainer will tell five people about getting good service. If their complaints are resolved, half to nearly three-quarters of complaining customers will return. If the situation is resolved promptly, that figure rises to 95 percent.

Here are a few proven tips on handling complaints. 1. Never argue with someone making a complaint. Don't get defensive or try to explain your way out of the situation. All this does increase the level of your customer's dissatisfaction. 2. Listen to the nature of the complaint and to the needs of the customer. Show that you're listening by nodding your head and occasionally saying something along the lines of "I see." 3. Take notes. This shows that you are really interested. The notes may also be helpful at a later time. Be sure to ask for permission before you start writing. 4. Restate what has been said. This is a technique that's proven very useful in sales. Be specific. Don't elaborate and don't try to explain your way out of the situation. 5. Get confirmation that you have correctly under-stood the problem. Make sure you really understand the nature of the complaint. 6. Ask "How can I make this right?" or use some similar question. Statistics show that most often the customer will ask for less than what the owner is willing to offer. Besides, asking the customer for suggestions shows that you are really concerned with solving the problem and retaining a good customer. 7. Follow their suggestion. Few customers will ask for anything outrageous, but if you run across one, do exactly what he or she asks of you, including a full refund. In the long run, it's a very minor expense.

Bibliography

"Economic Landscape Rocky," Restaurants USA, December, 2001 from ✍ *www.restaurants.org.*

"Restaurant Financing: How Easy Is It to Get Money Today?" Restaurants USA, Jan./Feb., 2001 from ✍ *www.restaurant.org,* accessed 17 February 2002.

Restaurant Hospitality, 9/98

Restaurant Business, Nov. 1, 2001 "Carried Away"

Restaurant Business, July 15, 2001

Restaurant Spending, February 17, 2002, ✍ *www.restaurant.org*

Index

About the Authors

John R. "Randy" James has built a twenty-nine-year career in creating, owning, and operating successful restaurants and clubs in Louisiana, Arkansas, Oklahoma, and Florida. While serving as vice president and later senior director of operations of A&M Food Services during the 1970s, he helped create the largest and most successful Pizza Hut franchise of all time. His experience encompasses virtually all facets of the hospitality industry. He is the owner of several highly successful clubs and restaurants. His Entertainment Systems of America, Inc., is a management and consulting firm booking acts and shows and developing and operating food and beverage services for other organizations.

Dan M. Baldwin is a freelance writer based in Arizona. His writing has earned numerous national awards. He has written or cowritten several books, including: *Tom Hopkins' Sales Prospecting for Dummies: Sell It Today, Sell It Now,* by Tom Hopkins and Pat Lieby; *Be "Money Smart"* by Bob Davis; *Upgrade,* by Mark Sanborn; *Energy in the Organization,* by Dr. Robert Rausch; *Heading for a Crash: How Pro Sports Rip You Off,* by Robert J. Tanterri; *Frequently Asked Questions About Alcohol & Drug Abuse* by Dan Baldwin and George Sewell; *Value-Match: Sales, Sales Management, & Human Relations,* by William Nowell; *High-Impact Leadership,* by Mark Sanborn; and *Streetwise® Landlording & Property Management,* by Mark Weiss and Dan Baldwin.

STREETWISE® BOOKS

New for Spring 2003!

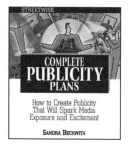

Complete Publicity Plans
$19.95 (CAN $29.95)
ISBN 1-58062-771-4

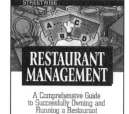

Restaurant Management
$19.95 (CAN $29.95)
ISBN 1-58062-781-1

Also Available in the *Streetwise* Series:

24 Hour MBA
$19.95 (CAN $29.95)
ISBN 1-58062-256-9

Achieving Wealth Through Franchising
$19.95 (CAN $29.95)
ISBN 1-58062-503-7

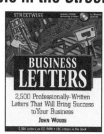

Business Letters with CD-ROM
$24.95 (CAN $37.95)
ISBN 1-58062-133-3

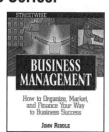

Business Management
$19.95 (CAN $29.95)
ISBN 1-58062-540-1

Complete Business Plan
$19.95 (CAN $29.95)
ISBN 1-55850-845-7

Complete Business Plan with Software
$29.95 (CAN $47.95)
ISBN 1-58062-798-6

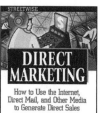

Customer-Focused Selling
$19.95 (CAN $29.95)
ISBN 1-55850-725-6

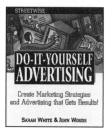

Direct Marketing
$19.95 (CAN $29.95)
ISBN 1-58062-439-1

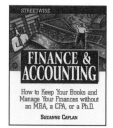

Do-It-Yourself Advertising
$19.95 (CAN $29.95)
ISBN 1-55850-727-2

Finance & Accounting
$17.95 (CAN $27.95)
ISBN 1-58062-196-1

Financing the Small Business
$19.95 (CAN $29.95)
ISBN 1-58062-765-X

Get Your Business Online
$19.95 (CAN $28.95)
ISBN 1-58062-368-9

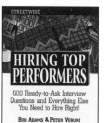

Hiring Top Performers
$17.95 (CAN $27.95)
ISBN 1-55850-684-5

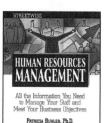

Human Resources Management
$19.95 (CAN $29.95)
ISBN 1-58062-699-8

Independent Consulting
$19.95 (CAN $29.95)
ISBN 1-55850-728-0

Adams's *Streetwise*® books for growing your business

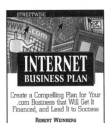
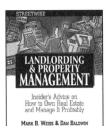

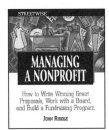

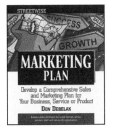

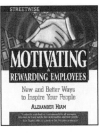
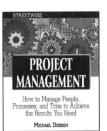

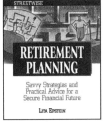

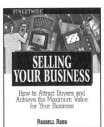